CULTURAL STUDIES AND THE WORKING CLASS

Cultural Studies and the Working Class

Subject to Change

Edited by

Sally R. Munt

CASSELL
London and New York

Cassell
Wellington House, 125 Strand, London WC2R 0BB
370 Lexington Avenue, New York, NY 10017–6550

First published 2000

British Library Cataloguing-in-Publication Data
A catalogue record for this book is available from the British Library.

ISBN 0–304–70548–9 (hardback)
    0–304–70549–7 (paperback)

Library of Congress Cataloging-in-Publication Data
Cultural studies and the working class/edited by Sally R. Munt.
    p. cm.
    Includes bibliographical references and index.
    ISBN 0–304–70548–9 (hardcover). — ISBN 0–304–70549–7 (pbk.)
    1. Working class — Great Britain — History — 20th century.   2. Industries —
Great Britain — History — 20th century.   3. Sex role — Great Britain — History
 — 20th century.   4. Great Britain — Social conditions — 20th century.
I. Munt, Sally.
HD8391.C85 1999
305.5'62'0941—dc21   99-22404
                                                                          CIP

Typeset by York House Typographic Ltd
Printed and bound in Great Britain by [to follow]

Contents

Contributors

Anita Biressi is a lecturer in Media Studies at Buckingham University College. She is completing a doctoral thesis in British true crime narratives at the Department of Cultural Studies, University of East London.

Sandy Brewer is the Subject Area Co-ordinator for the Communication Studies programme at the University of East London. She is currently completing a doctoral thesis, *The Hope of the World*, which investigates the relationship between popular representations of Jesus Christ and the formation of identity in working-class girls. She is also an active trade unionist.

Roger Bromley is Director of the School of Graduate Studies and Research in the Faculty of Humanities at Nottingham Trent University. Other recent publications are *Narratives of New Belonging* (1999), *Borderlines: The Films of Wim Wenders* (1999) and a co-edited collection, *The Hybridity Reader* (1999).

Jon Cook is Dean of the School of English and American Studies, University of East Anglia. He is currently working on a book on poetry and modernity. He has previously published in the areas of cultural and critical theory, Romanticism and contemporary fiction.

Glen Creeber is a research fellow in the Department of Journalism, Media and Cultural Studies at Cardiff University. His publications include *Dennis Potter: Between Two Worlds, a Critical Reassessment* (1998). He is currently compiling a reader on television drama and researching the rise and development of the television serial.

Chris Haylett is a lecturer in the Geography Department of Birmingham University. Her research on class, discourse and social policy has developed from her PhD thesis on 'The Making of a British "Underclass" in the 1990s: A Geography of Power/Knowledge', written at Edinburgh University.

Joanne Lacey is a lecturer in Cultural Studies at the University of Sussex. She has recently completed her PhD thesis entitled 'Seeing through happiness. Class, gender and popular film: Liverpool women remember the fifties film musical'. Her current work is a collaboration on the visual culture of First Holy Communion.

Steph Lawler is a lecturer in the Department of Sociology and Social Policy at the University of Durham. Her publications include *Mothering the Self: Mothers, Daughters, Subjectivities* (1999).

Andy Medhurst teaches Media Studies at the University of Sussex. He is the author of *A National Joke: Popular Comedy and English Cultural Identities* (1999), co-editor with Sally Munt of *Lesbian and Gay Studies: A Critical Introduction* (1997), and has published widely on questions of identity, representation and popular culture. Alongside his academic writing, he works as a critic and commentator for many newspapers, magazines, radio and television programmes.

Leslie J. Moran is a Reader in Law at Birkbeck College, University of London. His current work is on homophobic violence. His previous works include *The Homosexuality of Law* (1996), *Legal Perversions* (1997), a special edition of the journal *Social and Legal Studies*, and a co-edited collection, *Legal Queeries* (1998).

Sally R. Munt is a Reader in Media and Communication Studies at the University of Brighton. She is the author of *Murder by the Book: Feminism and the Crime Novel* (1994) and *Heroic Desire: Lesbian Identity and Cultural Space* (1998). She is the editor of *Butch/Femme: Inside Lesbian Gender* (1998), co-editor with Andy Medhurst of *Lesbian and Gay Studies: A Critical Introduction* (1997), and editor of *New Lesbian Criticism* (1992). She is currently co-editing a volume on new technologies and spatial practices.

Diane Reay is a research fellow, currently working at King's College, University of London. She has written extensively in the areas of social class, race, gender and social justice, and is still struggling to make sense of the influence of her working-class background on her contemporary subjectivity as an academic researcher.

Tracey Reynolds is a research fellow at South Bank University, London. She has recently completed her PhD, which explores African-Caribbean mothering and black family structures in Britain. Her publications include work on representations of black mothers in the media and black women in research.

Garry Robson is a research fellow in the Department of Sociology and Anthropology at the University of East London. He received his PhD in sociology from Goldsmiths College, University of London, in 1998. A book based on his research there, *No One Likes Us, We Don't Care: Millwall Football Club, Community and Identity*, is forthcoming. He is currently working on a project on middle-class gentrification and the future of London.

Beverley Skeggs has recently stepped down as Director of Women's Studies at Lancaster University. She is now co-directing a research project on 'Violence, Sexuality and Space'. Previous publications include *Formations of Class and Gender: Becoming Respectable* (1997), *Feminist Cultural Theory: Process and Production* (1995), and *The Media* (with John Mundy, 1992). She has written widely on issues of ethnography, popular culture, feminist theory and methodology.

Dedicated to my dad, Herbert Munt

Introduction

Sally R. Munt

Cultural Studies was a field formed by social class. Changes in post-Second World War Britain, forced by the turmoil of modern industrialized nations, had meant that the social stratifications still operable in the 1930s were perceived as permanently disrupted. Radical change was anticipated, so that citizenship for the working classes could now include a new sense of entitlement to welfare, health, employment and education, raising a sense of social identity for working-class people that promised to destroy the Victorian imaginary of the lumpen, threatening masses who lurked on the edges of British society like a savage breed. After 1945, when the new Labour government had been elected, the working classes who had fought against Nazism entered the national political imagination in unprecedented forms. Ordinary people embraced an anticipatory consciousness, and acted with faith that, with popular co-operation, this new body politic would facilitate their dreams of an opportunity to belong to a social fabric which until then had sought to define and exclude them. In the 1945 election, what had formerly existed as a disparate opposition became a coherent government with a huge Labour victory which was ideologically merged to the Allied victory over fascism. When Winston Churchill stood on the steps of Bradford Town Hall in 1942, boasting that 'All are united like one great family; all are standing together ... ',[1] his speech was intended to mobilize national unity for the war, but his rhetoric produced unanticipated results. In order to win the war, the powerful rhetoric of inclusivity mobilized people, but these promises anticipated fulfilment. The Conservative Churchillian government won the war, but lost the peace – ordinary Britons looked to the Labour Party to deliver social inclusion. In terms of a national identity which refigured class relations, it was a powerful paradigm shift.

It is difficult now to grasp the experience and significance of that shift, as Alan Sinfield writes:

To win the war, people were encouraged to believe that there would not be a return to widespread injustice and poverty. The war exemplified (though not without contest) a pattern of state intervention and popular co-operation to organize production for a common purpose. And its successful conclusion afforded a rare opportunity to recast British society. Full employment and the welfare state created, for a while, the sense of a society moving toward fairness, in which remaining 'pockets of poverty' would soon be eliminated.[2]

My short, schematic interpretation of what Sinfield called 'this shocking social experiment' certainly could be labelled as selective and utopian, in that we know that the Left in Britain had been consolidating a political and cultural movement which by the 1930s had become a well-established force; we also have the benefit of hindsight in order to evaluate the vaunted political entitlement as so much electoral puff. Despite this, the principle that working-class identity emerged into a new self-consciousness after the war is pivotal to comprehending the eventual consolidation of working-class cultural studies. These postwar historical economic and political changes – the material conditions – were active in cementing changes in meaning, in the ideological realm, in the way that we can think.

Sinfield, writing in 1989, remarked upon how 'the failure of the postwar settlement has allowed the initiative to pass to the New Right, and [so we have] experience[d] a return to the conditions that the settlement was designed originally to avoid: unemployment, poverty, social rupture and authoritarian government'.[3] Ten years later, in the Britain of 1999, we have been seemingly blessed with New Labour for two years, apparently long enough for the trauma of Thatcherism to have ebbed. The election of 1997 also seemed historic to those of us who participated, but once again, optimism seems to have outrun reality. Class differences are seen by many as irrelevant to Blair's Cool Britannia; since the Death of Di, we are New Britain, cobbled together in a new national truce of participatory politics. However, perhaps Bourgeois Britannia is a more apposite epithet, given that in December 1998 the Office for National Statistics spelled out the eight new categories for measuring social class by occupation, which for the first time made the majority of those designations middle class/ professional. (This was despite the fact that in a recent national newspaper poll 55 per cent defined *themselves* as working class.)[4] Why, given the historical intransigence of social stratification, is the rhetoric of inclusion and equability so successful? The seductive promise of belonging seems to supersede the experience of estrangement, evidently a truism for political analysts of all persuasions. Yet we recognize that material deprivation is organized, it is not merely incidental – whether explained through nature or nurture, failing schools will fail their pupils, even right- and left-wing analysts concur. But against all the evidence, common-sense approaches to class amongst the contemporary intelligentsia insist that it is irrelevant, to both the public and the private spheres. Talking about class is unpopular; many conversations about this book have provoked curiosity, disapproval and unease, as though it is an ill-conceived project of marginal merit – as one journalist recently put it, 'the very phrase "working class" tends to stick in the throat like a large chunk of stale Hovis'.[5] Class, it appears, is a dead issue; regurgitating it tortures us with the misplaced belief in heroic struggle, reminding us of the failure of 'collective dreams and noble intentions'.[6]

Despite its objective existence as an empirical category, and its enduring subjective existence as lived experience, the effects of relative deprivation not only affect life-chances (quantifiably), but also lifestyles, in the way that we measure and differentiate our social status (qualifiably). The gradations of such social status inform and prescribe our mobility through social space; they affect our bodily practices, circumscribe our ideational reality, our sense of self. In social interaction the identifying characteristics for deploying classed designations tend to be *aesthetic*, to do with way of life, appearance or language. Sociologists have been the most fond of studying social class, traditionally deploying it as their first order of interpretation. In social surveys, class in Britain is usually measured by occupation, whereas in the USA the academic or governmental signifiers are income or education. Nowadays, most class theorists have become Weberians, who rather ignore discussions of capital and labour, so even in this sphere Marxist models have declined. Occupation, however, is not the same as class; as Beverley Skeggs has noted,[7] designating by occupation evacuates structural inequality and exploitation from perceptions of lived experience. There is a tendency to depoliticize class analysis so that it naturalizes social divisions, to take the engine of protest and replace it with a resigned, imperceptible social organicism.

Critical consensus on 'culture' prior to the war has been epitomized by the tradition of Matthew Arnold, that culture must morally and aesthetically constitute the 'best' of human creativity. It was an unashamedly elitist conception which retrenched romantic, individualistic nineteenth-century values in its approach to popular or 'mass' culture. But the concept of culture has changed: attacks on Oxbridge/Bloomsbury elitism initiated by F. R. and Q. D. Leavis in their journal *Scrutiny* led to the idea that the working classes could be educated to appreciate Great Art, previously the unique preserve of the aristocracy. Coupled with this was the emergence of a discrete working-class literary heritage out of the cultural politics of worker–writer organizations and worker-education movements of the 1920s and 1930s, which began to publish more assuredly and to create a left-wing 'literary formation'.[8] After the influential 1934 Writers' Congress in the Soviet Union, which coined the new aesthetic of 'socialist realism', the concept of a working-class culture had consolidated and became more visible in postwar discourse. 'Culture' had become a focus for disputation. The development of left-culturalism,[9] together with a conjunction of changing national imagery, social mobility, disciplinary expansion and critical ingenuity, brought into being the concept of inquiry – maybe even the epistemological break – that was Cultural Studies.

In a classic poetics of transgression and emergence, by the late 1950s and 1960s, those previously deemed beyond critical appreciation began to bite back on their own behalf – the working-class academic began to speak for himself. Two scholarship boys begat Cultural Studies: Richard Hoggart, from Leeds, and Raymond Williams, from Wales. It is conventional to credit the field's emergence with a third figure, the social historian E. P. Thompson, whose *The Making of the English Working Class* (1963) was roughly contemporary with Hoggart's *The Uses of Literacy* (1957) and Williams's *Culture and Society* (1958), *The Long Revolution* (1965) and *Communications* (1962).[10] Thompson's 900-page epic sustained the heartfelt historical gravitas necessary to validate the new subject.[11] Their collective work was concerned with working-class cultures 'from within', and in that sense it focused on working-class culture as a *point of origin* for the first time in British intellectual life. Thus, Cultural Studies had from its inception an ethical practice to recentre the experiences of those traditionally excluded from the analytical gaze. The prick of experience was to inform this critical labour, this avowedly invested knowledge. Thus, British working-class culture became the text, as well as the theory, for the new discipline.

Richard Hoggart established the Birmingham Centre for Contemporary Cultural Studies in 1964, and was its first director. He was succeeded in 1969 by Stuart Hall, who presided over an intellectual shift which saw the qualified adoption of Gramscian Marxism. Hall and others have

described the contested origins of Cultural Studies as 'theoretical noise . . .
It was accompanied by a great deal of bad feeling, argument, unstable
anxieties and angry silences.'[12] In part this struggle was engaged with
Marxism, but unstraightforwardly: the political allegiances with the Left
were ambivalent, the interaction with Marxist theory problematic. But in
Hall's view, the Centre did concur with Gramsci's vision of the organic
intellectual, seeing the importance of an intellectual practice which was
ethically embedded in politics. This continued to be its principal, though
not uncontested, theoretical approach in the 1970s, when the CCCS
moved away from working-class (primarily youth) subjects and subcultures, to critique other social structures such as sexuality, gender and race.
More general political transformations were influencing its subject matter:
the British Left in the early 1970s was dominated by male trade unionism,
but popular liberation movements fronted by black, feminist and/or lesbian and gay organic intellectuals further problematized both Marxist
analyses and collective notions of a unitary Left. These debates and
affiliations caused much struggle over the direction of Cultural Studies in
the early years, lines of inquiry diversified to reflect the interests of the
identity politics which were the landscape of oppositional ferment in
Western societies. Infamously, Hall describes how feminism (and later
'race') 'interrupted' the work of the Centre in the mid-1970s: 'As the thief
in the night, it broke in; interrupted, made an unseemly noise, seized the
time, crapped on the table of cultural studies'.[13] He describes it as 'rup-
tural' (the painful language is telling); feminism reorganized the field,
so much so that gender, sexuality and, later, 'race' came to dominate
approaches into the next decade and after. Perhaps these were the appropriate concerns for the times, certainly the analytical shift into the
representation of major social formations has brought methodological
benefits. To see this as a battle over *positions* though is to restrict one's
perception of what Cultural Studies must become, i.e. one homogenizing
discourse.

American Cultural Studies in the 1980s and 1990s has concentrated
even more on identitarianism, becoming fascinated by the effect of
popular (mass) culture on identity formation, deploying new developments in European theory strategically (such as Barthes and Bourdieu)
but in ways that have often detracted from working-class subjects themselves. This movement has been depicted as 'the linguistic turn' (the
discovery of language and textuality) and, more negatively, the 'decon-
structive deluge'.[14] American Cultural Studies can be accused of a kind of

liberal-pluralist approach to pleasure, in that historically its interest has been in a certain 'can-do' approach to culture, i.e. it is more attuned to resistance than repression and (paradoxically) to consumption rather than production – a criticism that can, more latterly, also be levelled at contemporary British work too. Within this accusation is a parody, that Marxism has sunk into postmodernism, which is itself caricatured as a kind of undifferentiated and unlicensed polyvocality. Social Science has ridiculed Cultural Studies, bemoaning the reduction of Marxism to the 'merely cultural',[15] and it seems that we are awash with an unfair amount of hyperbole as to Cultural Studies' institutional and discursive supremacy. But still, its institutional growth in the USA seems not disassociated from at times a questionable glorification of popular culture which seems to see power as purely semiotic, and theory as professionally profitable.[16]

I am crudely generalizing, but it is important to recognize the principle of the relationship between political materialities and academic reflections. 'Class', in Britain and in the USA, carries different meanings and creates different superstructural effects. In British university life, Marxism still has a small, credible and necessary place in the humanities curriculum (despite that, stereotypically it is anticipated to emanate from an 'unreconstructed', putatively masculine bully). Not so in the USA, where the voices of opposition are firmly located within ethnic groups *other than* the white working class, or white trash, as they can be evocatively called.[17] American academics still seem to look to Britain for a working-class intelligentsia, whereas in Britain, within Cultural Studies, we have been busily incorporating the American model into our syllabi. To demonstrate, in 1998 I designed a course on representation for my first-year Media Studies undergraduates. Following the rubric of the past twenty years I designed units on race, gender and sexuality, which were perhaps over-supported with glossy books from academic publishers. The seminar reading bred multitudinous references. Many of these treatises actually disseminated analysis that did depend upon Marxist paradigms, mixed with judicious doses of Structuralism, Semiotics, Feminism, Postcolonialism, Postmodernism, Poststructuralism, Queer Theory and so on. But for the session on class, I only had a handful of contemporary sources, so reluctantly I had to return to the CCCS work of the 1970s, the classic research by Paul Willis, Angela McRobbie and Dick Hebdige. Good though it admittedly is, this body of work is: (1) historically pertinent but not very interesting to today's student ('this is about my *parents*!'); (2) early CCCS research which therefore has not benefited from later theoretical insights; and (3) typically concerned with the young, reproducing the anthropological and stereotyped exotic of working-class culture – is this something to grow out of? I do not wish to demean this consequential effort from the 1970s, but it was incipient work, part of the evolution of Cultural Studies. Despite the fact that Cultural Studies in Britain has been deeply informed by the legacies of historical materialism, which has enabled people to understand the present through the penetrating lens of the past, and despite the irrefutable quality of recent historical work, Cultural Studies continues to have as one of its chief objectives a concern to illuminate the *present*. Where is the work on contemporary working-class cultures?

It is hardly useful to reinvest the victim position at this point, and complain that within the hierarchies of oppression, class has sunk to the bottom because it is not sexy enough for the intelligentsia (unlike feminism, 'race' studies, and lesbian and gay studies, all of which have attracted at times the intellectual eroticism of studying 'the Other'). The anticipated retort that 'poverty isn't sexy' has been deployed to explain away the paucity of critical attention paid to working-class studies.[18] What is being expressed in these envious attacks? What they do reveal, besides the successful fragmentation of sympathetic discourses, is the tenuous installation of working-class academics within universities who are encouraged to see 'others', but not themselves. This reflects a poverty of representation, attached to the vaunted death of Marxism, the Thatcherite/Blairite project to assert that Britain is now a classless society, and the bourgeoisification of a profession which demands that upward mobility, connected to dreams of escape, entails a personal rewriting of one's own biographical habitus.

I want to return to a neglected concept here – alienation. Originally, Marx described this disposition as being caused by the working man's inability to claim the value of his own agency – he worked, but the product of his labour was taken from him. This 'wage slave' 'becomes an append-age of the machine',[19] he becomes commodified, degraded, dehumanized. Of course, this process of proletarianization includes Marx's radicalization-revolution thesis that once the workers recognize their alienation they will organize a collective resistance to their oppression and, through mutuality, reclaim their subjectivity. Thus we can see how Cultural Studies is still implicating Marxist models of autonomy, looking for instances of how dominant narratives can be reinscripted through the appropriation of texts-for-needs.[20] It is the bread-and-butter work of Cultural Studies to refuse the victim position, to refuse the search for authentic selves in communities of consumption. In a sense, the desire to talk up all those heroic tales of resistant readings rests upon a profound alienation, a feeling that we must escape the place ascribed to us, as passive, mindless, indiscriminate consumers of pap. These are still the 'hidden injuries of class'.[21] Whereas there has been public debate for the last twenty years on positive images of women, people of colour, and gays and lesbians, there has been no such equivalent clamour for working-class representation. Instead, the primary interest has been in finding audiences who read against the grain. The approach has been to place the locus of responsibility onto readers, rather than producers. Isn't there a kind of shame existing here? Aspiration, in class terms, is largely concerned with escape, rather than the reconstruction of available icons. We must be careful, though, that our methodologies do not seek to impose dignity where there is none, to impose working-class pride where there is just as much shame, to insist that the only good worker is a revolutionary one.

Many working-class academics have left the Left behind because it is associated with a dichotomous imaginary which has its roots in the Victorian notion of the 'deserving poor', as opposed to the 'working-class-gone-wrong' – the underclass, which deserves nothing.[22] So, there are the good poor, who are industrious and know their place, rendered in such archetypes as the honest factory hand or 'our Mam', symbol of hearth and home. On the other hand there are the bad poor, who make childish, dangerous and unrealistic demands – archetypically the offensive *Sun*-reader, beyond the efforts of educational patronage, too stupid and self-interested to join a union. Gender roles are seen as extremely differentiated: there are lads and tarts, yobs and slags. With the destruction of Britain's industrial economy the working classes have become feminized and, like the female body, working-class people have come to be discursively associated with 'waste', typified by the profligate spender and the feminized couch-potato. What shall we do with all those unemployed industrial workers? Their lost labour was seen as their only social contribution, now their reproduction is to be discouraged; they're useless in the home, all they can produce is feckless children, cultural malaise and dissolution, and make insuperable demands on the Welfare State ... The threat here seems to emerge from boundaries being threatened, from a feminine excess which needs restraint, of fat, cigarette-smoking, beer-drinking men who have become a drain on the social body (they leak, they weep, they rage: excrescent and grotesque).

Race, too, occludes the view of the working-class; the factory hand nowadays is more likely to be seen as an Asian female too illiterate to vote.

The damage of deploying such stereotypes is evident not just in the harm it does to these ascribed groups, but also in the internalized disgust it evokes in the rhetorician. I have lost count of the times I have been interpellated by these typologies in academic environments, and concurred that they are the common sense of university life. After the fact, I get angry. And still, with colleagues, there are quiet conversations about origins, shifty discussions about our discomfiture, and a kind of general hopelessness that we don't belong, can't belong, are just pretending, fearful of exposure. The parallels with being gay are glaring: many working-class academics are in the closet, waiting for our liberation moment. Symbolically, my coming-out moment occurred in the USA, at a Queer Studies conference in Iowa. Someone had organized a workshop for working-class academics; a room full of us sat there, some cried. I hadn't really articulated until then the intensity of shame I had brought with me. Silent, not speaking, I began to realize how my career as a lesbian academic had been prefaced on a professionalization which demanded that certain other identities had to be forsaken. Thus, I was caught between two forms of silence: that of the American identity politics context, in which having a 'voice' seems so troublesome, and that of the British bourgeoisification of my perversity, which resulted in my feeling that in Huddersfield, where I grew up, I am ashamed of being gay, whereas in Brighton, I am ashamed of coming from the northern working class.

Likewise, intellectual classifications demand exceptions; perhaps because of this, I'm interested in the things that don't fit together. After a decade in Lesbian and Gay Studies, I begin to question what it elides. My work has necessarily privileged sexuality; as with most critical/campaigning approaches, its existence is to redress an omission. I lived in Brighton through the years of lesbian feminism, when class became a wound, when to articulate its concerns was to be labelled a spoiler, a guilt-tripper, a Manichean thinker, a fifth columnist. For a predominantly middle-class movement, 'class' (a metonym for 'working class') seemed to denude the privilege of victimhood. My identities didn't fit – I would be angrily told that I had no 'right' to a working-class identity, that from a financial and educational perspective it was pretentious. I knew hardly any working-class lesbians, I'd ended up as a middle-class lesbian with a working-class past; these strata were seemingly independent. As a butch lesbian, my sexual status was visible; it was my (classed) history that feared exposure. Let me express the ways: in eating, talking, domestic rituals, professional practices, money, shopping, clothes, in my subtle daily being, in my 'structure of feeling' there existed an anxious anticipation that my carefully wrought emplacement would at any time produce ejection, that I'd be found out as the cuckoo in the nest. It is this precariousness which produces defensiveness. The task is then to make this awareness work, to put it to use, to ask what meaning can be gained. It's just not enough to get angry, to create another injurious subjectivity, to react without analytical redirection.

Is trying to intellectualize 'working classness' any use any more? There is plenty of empirical data to support the view that inequalities in society are structural; the fact that this view is not recent may support the idea that class studies are not popular because these 'realities' are ostensibly intransigent, i.e. there is nothing new to be said. Within Social Science generally, although working-class studies formed the backbone of many disciplines, there has been a diversification of the stratification model using gender, race, disability, regionalism, sexuality, age and similarly conceived 'other' positions. Still, the either/or approach to structural inequality (choose one only) has been rightly problematized as cognitive reduction-ism. Presumably, an ethical and integral method is required; as the chapters in this book will demonstrate, there is no distinct working class to be operationalized in academic research, there are only many working classes, each to be investigated whilst avoiding the unitary anthropological gaze. If you take out 'class' from an exploration of gender and so on, you ignore a crucial determining factor of the experience of being a woman, man or transgendered person; to qualify our classifications has become a tiring critical mantra, as though it dilutes specificity, instead of enhancing it.

Cultural Studies is above all the stories/study of everyday life, and it is axiomatic to claim that everyday life is saturated with class relations. The fact that not everybody believes this doesn't make it untrue, it merely alludes to the success of entrenched beliefs in liberal pluralism. It is the aim of Cultural Studies to introduce *ostranenie* – defamiliarization – to disturb the unspoken suppositions which determine our daily entities, to make us look again at the natural, the normal, the taken-for-grantedness of life. Cultural Studies is a peculiarly personal discipline in this respect: it is critically performative in the sense that it asks us to place our selves in focus, while our experience is being contested as both a product of discourse and generating that discourse, producing interpretation and in need of interpretation. So, as long as class – and, in this volume, specifically working-class – experience exists, it determines the meanings we can make; for middle-class and working-class academic subjects alike, identity comes through identification and differentiation. There is no evidence that class differentiation has withered away in contemporary Britain;[23] there is no convincing argument that class analysis can be consigned to the Apple wastebasket, or that the 'excess baggage' of working-class origins should be stashed outside the seminar door. The argument is not to reify 'class' and deselect other paradigms, but to return to sites of class experience and theorize out of them, as situated knowledges. This is only a partial attempt, concerned specifically with a slice of contemporary British working-class cultures. Middle-class cultures are there too, but only as a backdrop, an indistinct counterposition. This book is not an attempt to proselytize working-class culture as an authentic folk culture, but it does contain a premise: that cultural participation is delineated and characterized by powerful relations of production. Therefore, to be part of the working class or underclass will influence that participation in distinguishing ways.

So, what resources are available to those who wish to approach class from a Cultural Studies perspective? It would probably be wise to avoid the sort of social science research that tables 'Consumption of red wine and brown sauce by housing area', or quantifies class by counting households with 'motorcycle kept in living room; any pictures depicting cowboys; any items relating to Tutankhamun'.[24] More useful theoretical approaches are widely disseminated, taken from the writing of various European Marxists such as the Frankfurt School, Althusser, Gramsci, Bourdieu and Barthes. The critical work of Raymond Williams and Richard Hoggart is still essential, but tellingly both figures chose autobiographical novels to explore the sentient disjunction between their latent cultures of origin and their later careers. Some more of the classic works linked to CCCS remain pertinent to contemporary critical investigation, particularly Carolyn Steedman's *Landscape for a Good Woman* (1986), and Stuart Laing's *Representations of Working-Class Life, 1959–64* (1986). For more recent explorations, Roger Silverstone's *Visions of Suburbia* (1997) and Barbara Ehrenreich's *Fear of Falling: The Inner Life of the Middle Class* (1990) are the most cogent and distinctive explorations to date of middle-class cultural experience.[25] British working-class studies are exemplified by the stubborn longevity of socialist feminism in the British academy; recent publications include Valerie Walkerdine's *Schoolgirl Fictions* (1991) and *Daddy's Girl* (1997), Beverley Skeggs's *Formations of Class and Gender*, and Pat Mahony and Christine Zmroczek's collection, *Class Matters: 'Working-Class' Women's Perspective on Social Class* (1997). In the USA there are a few recent studies, including Matt Wray and Annalee Newitz's *White Trash* (1997), Kathleen Stewart's *A Space on the Side of the Street* (1996), Steven J. Ross's *Working Class Hollywood* (1998), and David E. James and Rick Berg's *The Hidden Foundation: Cinema and the Question of Class* (1996). Reading Pamela Fox's *Class Shame: Shame and Resistance in the British Working-Class Novel, 1890–1945* (1994), in conjunction with Steedman, Skeggs and Walkerdine, it is evident that this synchronous research on class and gender provides a new methodological impetus for refusing the mandatory celebratory progressivism of resistance theorists, asking us to look more tangentially for evidence of survival, of 'getting by', to temper the appetite for heroic potency. Importantly, they don't reinscribe the idea that incorporation and loss are to be derided or ignored, not do they imply that analysis at the structural level precludes examination of the psychic affects of cultural (non)participation. Simply, understanding work-class culture should avoid imposing a condescending glamour.

The writings in this collection fall into three parts. Part One, 'Issues in Working-Class Identity and Methodology' takes up directly the legacy of Cultural Studies in the way it approaches class formations, illustrating how the experience of lived identities so central to critical performativity needs to be rethought in the light of contemporary conditions. The chapters focus upon autobiography, academic identity, the underclass, race and nation, in order to reframe cultural debates on class and academic assumptions with more analytical precision. The chapters in Part Two, 'Class, Taste and Space', directly address the intrinsicality of class with aesthetic judgements, showing how Cultural Studies has often replicated ingrained values, rather than challenged them, revealing the persistent injurious subtext of class analysis when it approaches that pernicious social arbiter – taste. The aesthetics of class identity are lived through spatial practices: subjects exist within spaces that are marked by circumscription and symbolic violence – these chapters read class through spatial metaphor in order to illuminate how the movement of working-class people is framed, fraught and fought. Part Three, 'Gender, Fictions and Working-Class Subjectivities', reads class through the critical lens of gender, reminding us that social identities are narrated through composite structures which simultaneously question co-implicated levels of discourse and their material existence. These chapters synthesize a nuanced critical process which reinscribes class into Cultural Studies both as text and as methodology, and are instances of the potential which can be reached when the intellectual concerns of the 1980s with gender and race can be reinscribed with the return of class as an analytical category. All of the writings in this collection are concerned to evaluate how working-class cultures can reinvest Cultural Studies with method, form and content, with political relevance to contemporary social relationships, and with a more inclusive (and therefore more astute), critical agenda. The heart of the discipline is its affective scrutiny of material existence, and class, as a meaningful location for us all, is elemental to that effort.

Notes

1. This reference is taken from Sinfield (1989), p. 10.
2. *Ibid.*
3. *Ibid.*, p. 3.
4. Quoted in Andrew Anthony, 'What about the workers?', *Observer*, Review Section, 13 December 1998, pp. 2–3.
5. *Ibid.*
6. *Ibid.*
7. Skeggs (1997). See Chapter 5, pp. 76–97, for a full discussion.
8. See Janet Batsleer, Tony Davies, Rebecca O'Rourke and Chris Weedon, *Rewriting English: Cultural Politics of Gender and Class* (London: Methuen, 1985).
9. See Sinfield (1989), pp. 241–5, on the formation of postwar left-culturalism, which basically believed that 'good' (i.e. high) culture should be democratically made available to the masses, for their general edification.
10. See Graeme Turner, *British Cultural Studies: An Introduction* (London: Unwin Hyman, 1990) and John Storey, *Cultural Theory and Popular Theory* (Hemel Hempstead: Harvester Wheatsheaf, 1993) for two useful introductory overviews of these works.
11. Over the summer of 1999, I read Thompson's book whilst on a trip back to Huddersfield to see my father. Most of the West Riding weaving villages Thompson discusses are familiar to my family, and for the first time in my academic life I had the pleasure of sharing my intellectual labour (900 pages, remember) with them. I learned an important thing then: that Cultural Studies may not always mean a bourgeois practice. My family's pride in hearing about the weavers' revolts, their fascination with their own local history, their relief that I was finally doing something they could participate in (since I'd let them), their input and engagement with the material, and my dad's request to borrow my annotated copy when I'd finished with it, this all felt like a rapprochement I wished I'd risked before. This oscillation is

something that Raymond Williams wrote about in his novels, and I think it's a common, and painful, experience to judge.

12. Stuart Hall, 'Cultural studies and its theoretical legacies', in David Morley and Kuan-Hsing Chen (eds), *Stuart Hall: Critical Dialogues in Cultural Studies* (London: Routledge, 1996), pp. 262–75, 263.

13. *Ibid*, p. 269. Evidently, these arguments were experienced as traumatic for various contenders – Charlotte Brunsdon takes up this one in particular in her response to Stuart Hall's essay: see 'A thief in the night' in Morley and Chen (1996), pp. 276–86.

14. Hall, *op. cit.*, p. 274.

15. See Morley (1998) and Butler (1997).

16. I am reminded of one MLA panel I sat through in 1996 eulogizing the resurgence of Gucci through its corporate resignification. I waited for the critique in vain.

17. There is a nascent area of White Trash studies, however; see the brilliant collection by Wray and Newitz (1997).

18. There are exceptions, of course, such as George Orwell's homoerotic writing on miners, indicative of a long-standing gay male tradition of eroticizing 'a bit of rough'. The heterosexual parallel is George Bernard Shaw's Pygmalion syndrome.

19. Marx and Engels (n.d.), p. 60. First published in 1848.

20. Explained as: 'I read this/view this, because it gives me that . . . '

21. See the wonderful and painful classic by Richard Sennett and Jonathan Cobb, *The Hidden Injuries of Class* (Cambridge: Cambridge University Press, 1972).

22. And as Beverley Skeggs pointed out to me, many middle-class academics left the Left behind because their middle-class projections didn't work either – the 'workers' just didn't seem to revolt when they were told.

23. See Reid (1998).

24. Taken from Michael Argyle's rather weak *The Psychology of Social Class* (London: Routledge, 1994), which seems to endorse as many stereotypes as it seeks to illuminate.

25. See also Savage, Barlow, Dickens and Fielding (1992) and Lury (1998).

Bibliography

Butler, J. (1997) 'Merely cultural'. *Social Text* 52–3, 15(3–4), pp. 265–77.

Ehrenreich, B. (1990) *Fear of Falling: The Inner Life of the Middle Class*. New York: Harper Perennial.

Fox, P. (1994) *Class Fictions: Shame and Resistance in the British Working-Class Novel, 1890–1945*. Durham, NC: Duke University Press.

Hebdige, D. (1979) *Subculture: The Meaning of Style*. London: Methuen.

Hoggart, R. (1957) *The Uses of Literacy*. Harmondsworth: Penguin.

James, D. E. and Berg, R. (eds) (1996) *The Hidden Foundation: Cinema and the Question of Class*. Minneapolis: University of Minnesota Press.

Laing, S. (1986) *Representations of Working-Class Life, 1959–64*. London: Macmillan.

Mahony, P. and Zmroczek, C. (eds) (1997) *Class Matters: 'Working-Class' Women's Perspectives on Social Class*. London: Taylor & Francis.

Marx, K. and Engels, F. (n.d., first published 1848) *Manifesto of the Communist Party*. Moscow: Foreign Languages Publishing House.

McRobbie, A. and Garber, J. (1975) 'Girls and subcultures'. In S. Hall and T. Jefferson, (eds) *Resistance Through Rituals*. London: Routledge.

Morley, D. (1998) 'So-called cultural studies: dead ends and reinvented wheels'. *Cultural Studies* 12(4), pp. 476–97.

Morley, D. and Chen, K. H. (eds) (1996) *Stuart Hall: Critical Dialogues in Cultural Studies*. London: Routledge.

Reid, I. (1998) *Class in Britain*. Cambridge: Polity Press.

Ross, S. J. (1998) *Working Class Hollywood: Silent Films and the Shaping of Class in America*. Princeton: Princeton University Press.

Savage, M., Barlow, J., Dickens, P. and Fielding, T. (1992) *Property, Bureaucracy and Culture: Middle-Class Formation in Contemporary Britain*. London, Routledge.

Silverstone, R. (1997) *Visions of Suburbia*. London: Routledge.

Sinfield, A. (1989) *Literature, Politics and Culture in Postwar Britain*. Oxford: Basil Blackwell.

Skeggs, B. (1997) *Formations of Class and Gender: Becoming Respectable*. London: Sage.

Steedman, C. (1986) *Landscape for a Good Woman*. London: Virago Press.

Stewart, K. (1996) *A Space on the Side of the Street: Cultural Poetics in an 'Other' America*. Princeton: Princeton University Press.

Thompson, E. P. (1963) *The Making of the English Working Class*. Harmondsworth: Penguin.

Walkerdine, V. (1991) *Schoolgirl Fictions*. London: Verso.

Walkerdine, V. (1997) *Daddy's Girl*. London: Macmillan.

Williams, R. (1958) *Culture and Society*. London: Chatto & Windus.

Williams, R. (1965) *The Long Revolution*. Harmondsworth: Penguin.

Williams, R. (1962) *Communications*. Harmondsworth: Penguin.

Willis, P. (1977) *Learning to Labour: How Working Class Kids Get Working Class Jobs*. London: Saxon House.

Wray, M. and Newitz, A. (eds) (1997) *White Trash: Race and Class in America*. New York: Routledge.

Acknowledgement

Thank you to Andy Medhurst and Beverley Skeggs, who kindly read and commented upon an earlier draft of this introduction. I would like to thank all the contributors for seeing this book through to completion, and for their grace under pressure.

Part 1

Issues in Working-Class Identity and Methodology

1

If Anywhere: Class Identifications and Cultural Studies Academics

Andy Medhurst

> As two women from working-class backgrounds, the experience of going through university as students and then working in the academy as teachers and researchers left us confused about our own class positioning ... While we believed that it was insulting to other working-class people to pretend that our lives were the same as theirs ... neither did we feel that we inhabited the world of the university in the same ways as the majority of our colleagues ... As we began talking about these issues ... we discovered that we shared a massive sense of confusion about where we fitted in (if anywhere). (Mahony and Zmroczek, 1997, p. 1)

I come from a working-class family. My mother's parents met because they worked in the same factory, my father's because they were employed as a maid and a gardener by the same moneyed household. My parents themselves did clerical jobs, which in other circumstances might have enabled them, and by extension me, to clutch at that especially anxious label, lower-middle-class, but where we lived, whom we socialized with, our sense of selves and our available cultural capital meant that this never happened. We only had to mix with indisputably middle-class people to know that we belonged elsewhere. Other relatives over various generations have been gravediggers, seamstresses, typists, postmen, chauffeurs, carpenters, policemen, road-sweepers, mechanics, upholsterers, print-workers, coalmen, shuttlecock-makers and ketchup-bottle-fillers. It is undoubtedly a working-class family, but many of them now own their own houses, some run small businesses, and I myself occupy the paradigmatically bourgeois roles of academic, writer and broadcaster. There have been changes, but these are only recent developments, and class is never simply a category of the present tense. It is a matter of history, a relationship with tradition, a discourse of roots.

So although I am paid a middle-class salary to do middle-class things, I never think of myself as an entirely middle-class person. I simply do not feel middle-class, an important point to stress since one of the main arguments of this chapter is that class is not just an objective entity, but also (and mostly?) a question of identifications, perceptions, feelings. Yet equally I cannot pretend to be working-class any more, whatever the temptations of striking that pose – temptations I can't always resist, if only to relish the contortions of guilt it can engender in unequivocally middle-class colleagues. Any academic who claims an uncomplicatedly working-class identity is at best self-deluding, at worst grossly appropriative. Beverley Skeggs' acidic words, 'Who would want to be seen as working-class? (Perhaps only academics are left.)' (1997, p. 95), are a timely warning against masquerades of underprivilege. But where does that leave me, both an avid consumer of middle-class lifestyle magazines and a devotee of brashly downmarket television? I suppose I live, if anywhere, in a space between, but I don't want to make that sound like the latest tiresomely fashionable trope of postmodern indeterminacy. Those triumphalist celebrations of fluidity always overlook the fact that being unfixed, mobile, in-between, can distress as much as it liberates. So my sense of class identity is uncertain, torn and oscillating – caught on a cultural cusp.

That location, and the sense of *dis*-location it generates, is nothing new: 'Almost every working-class boy who goes through the process of further education finds himself chafing against his environment during adolescence. He is at the friction point of two cultures . . . ' (Hoggart, 1957, p. 239). So wrote Richard Hoggart in the 1950s, and indeed the whole of *The Uses of Literacy*, that flawed, maligned and unavoidable book which helped to give birth to Cultural Studies, stems from the class cusp, the friction point, on which Hoggart anxiously stood, a boy from the sooty terraces who made it to the ivy-covered quad. Similarly, the early work of Raymond Williams strove to negotiate the cusp between working-class rural Wales and the high citadels of British literature and history, though as a more chilly and reserved writer than Hoggart he kept his emotions about where he found himself more tightly under wraps. Not always, however: here is Williams's reminiscence of accompanying a fellow student to a lecture at Cambridge in the 1940s, a lecture given by one influential academic and attended by another:

> Mankowitz and I went to hear L. C. Knights give a talk on the meaning of 'neighbour' in Shakespeare. Leavis was leaning up against the wall at the back of the room. When Knights said that nobody now can understand Shakespeare's meaning of neighbour, for in a corrupt mechanical civilisation there are no neighbours, I got up and said I thought this was only differentially true; there were obviously successive kinds of community, and I knew perfectly well, from Wales, what neighbour meant. Mankowitz ... then attacked me bitterly for sentimental nonsense. Leavis was nodding approvingly while he was doing so. (Williams, 1979, p. 67)

It strikes me as highly significant that Williams chooses to make this anecdote emblematic of his intellectual disagreement with the approach to literary criticism embodied by Leavis and Knights. Crudely summarized, this was a dispute about the value of first-hand experience, more precisely the first-hand experience of working-class life. Tellingly, the word which slapped Williams down, exposing and chastising his upstart breach of intellectual protocol, is the word sentimental.

Anyone who speaks about a working-class upbringing, certainly in a British context, is liable to find themselves accused of sentimentality. This is hardly surprising, since class is an emotional business. Class privilege and class prejudice are not reducible to dispassionate debate or the algebras of abstraction. Class is felt, class wounds, class hurts, and those of us on a cusp between classes bruise particularly easily. If those bruises are to recede, we need a fuller understanding of the relationships between class, autobiography and cultural analysis. This chapter is offered as a preliminary gesture in that direction.

Autobiography or apparatus?

I began this chapter autobiographically, since for me there is no other way in. My own class history is central to my understandings of how culture works, and it would be disingenuous to pretend otherwise. More broadly, I think a consideration of the role of autobiography and personal history might offer a counterweight to what I see as dangerously pervasive emphases in the field of Cultural Studies, emphases which have seen that field turned into a globalized, corporatized, depoliticized commodity. It is now an internationally recognized brand, tasting the same wherever you go, McCultural McStudies. One way of resisting that decline into homogenized mulch, I propose, is to re-examine the issues of class, belonging and culture with which the Cultural Studies project began.

Class, after all, was what ignited Cultural Studies, the primary social problematic it set out to address, but its importance has been diminishing in recent years, to the point where, according to Martin Barker and Anne Beezer, 'At best, it has become one "variable" among many . . . at worst it has dissolved away altogether' (1992, p. 16). Barker and Beezer offer a number of reasons for this shift, which they see as primarily centred in the rise in poststructuralist arguments which see all social struggles as merely discursive and thereby facilitate a retreat from concrete political engagement, but I want to focus the issue a little differently. The loss I most regret in recent Cultural Studies is that intersection between class and autobiography, that fraught business of trying to understand the ways in which questions of cultural involvement intersect with lived material circumstances. Without it, all that's left are texts like the self-professed Manifesto for Cultural Studies published in 1991 by the American academic Cary Nelson as the field began to boom in the USA. It contains sixteen lengthy, densely argued points, it even insists on the importance of Marxism, but it does not mention the word 'class' once (Nelson, 1996, pp. 281–3). I am not advocating the imposition of class as a master paradigm to which all other, equally important, identities must be subjugated, but I cannot suppress a gnawing feeling that there were autobiographically driven insights about class in those early Cultural Studies texts which have been too peremptorily discarded and to which we could profitably return.

This is a risky proposition. For one thing, any talk of a 'return' needs to acknowledge the dangers of assuming there is a commonly agreed starting point for the Cultural Studies project. There has been increasing and wholly appropriate concern (Schwarz, 1994; Jones, 1994; Geraghty, 1996) that the prevailing historiography of Cultural Studies, as it is being shaped and sculpted in textbooks and anthologies, presents far too neat and linear a narrative, taming 'the profane history of real ruptures, of excitement and despair, of furious polemics and bewildering uncertainties' into a 'polite . . . myth of origins which eases the journey of cultural studies into the academy' (Schwarz, 1994, p. 381). Nonetheless that myth now exists, and like any text is there to be challenged. The most troubling aspect of it is the trope that portrays early British forays into the field as an endearingly naive cruise along nostalgic backwaters before the tidal wave of Proper Theory arrived to tighten and toughen things up. In this story, it is now taken as axiomatic that Hoggart was given to 'romanticization' (Stratton and Ang, 1996, p. 374), that Williams's early work was marred by 'nostalgic organicism' (Turner, 1990, p. 57), that both writers were guilty of 'humanist ... moralising' to the extent where – the horror! the horror! – 'there is simply no attempt at theory' (Easthope, 1997, p. 9).

In this paradigm, cosy old pipe-and-slippers British writing is suddenly driven into obsolescence by the cavalry charge of structuralism, which was 'systematic, rationalist ... and theoretically explicit' (Easthope, 1997, p. 19). Now it is perhaps unfair to expect nuanced accounts of intellectual history in the cramped confines of textbooks, but acknowledging that simplifications have to be made should not blind us to the ideological assumptions behind choosing what gets left out and kept in. The 'nostalgic sentimentalizing dethroned by demanding theory' story does indeed tell part of what happened in the growth and institutionalization of Cultural Studies, but it also implies that this was a purely positive shift: all gains, no losses.

So when Simon During concisely and unemotively describes that story as a process in which 'culture was thought about less as an expression of local communal lives linked to class identity and more as an apparatus within a large system of dominance' (1993, p. 5), it sounds like a useful expansion of an intellectual project, a broadening out that requires no regrets. But look more closely at what sits on the debit side: expressivity, locality, communality, class. These have been the real casualties in the hyper-theorizing which have marked the recent trajectory of Cultural Studies, and perhaps it is time to reassert their importance against the colder, purer terminologies (note During's use of 'apparatus' and 'system') that have for too long held sway. This means, in the terms of the binary influentially mapped out by Stuart Hall (1980), a reappraisal of 'Culturalism', although it is crucial to note, as Michael Pickering has shrewdly pointed out, that Culturalism was never a term used by those writers and thinkers to whom the label was applied, but rather 'an externally imposed term of condescension ... a means of inferiorising it as an antecedent to structuralism' (Pickering, 1997, p. 164). Culturalism, in fact, was never an 'ism' at all, it was a loosely aligned collection of tendencies with no pretensions to rigid parameters; the fact that Hall, writing at the high-water mark of British academics' besottedness with abstract theorizing, felt the need to 'ism-ise' the early work of Hoggart and Williams, says far more about the fetish for systemization characterizing that particular intellectual moment than it does about the texts stuffed and buckled into the Culturalist holdall. Getting those texts out from under that stigmatizing Culturalist label might be a way of rediscovering their riches.

Above all this means a revaluation of *The Uses of Literacy*, since whereas Raymond Williams can be forgiven his Culturalist sins and deemed recuperable through his later role in absorbing and disseminating the work of European Marxist theory, Richard Hoggart stuck to his under-theorized and indeed anti-theory guns. Thus Paul Jones's attempt to redress the lazy lumping together of Hoggart and Williams that has become commonplace in the historiographical myth of Cultural Studies starts out by even-handedly insisting on the important differences between the two writers, but soon makes its sympathies clear: Williams is the theorist, the Good Father of the discipline, but Hoggart was culpable of 'defensive populist nostalgism' (Jones, 1994, p. 408). That's a phrase very reminiscent of those broader attacks on the whole Culturalist tradition, but it now seems that a tighter focus is suggested, heaping all the blame onto Hoggart alone.

Here and there, if you search long and hard enough, you can find academics prepared to defend aspects of Hoggart. Richard Dyer (1981), outlining the thematic connections between *The Uses of Literacy* and the soap opera *Coronation Street*, has argued that Hoggart's account of working-class culture is, for all its limitations, much more nuanced and complex than its attackers allow. Stuart Laing (like Dyer, and not insignificantly, a former research student at the Birmingham Centre for Contemporary Cultural Studies which Hoggart founded) goes further, and is prepared to state that the 'move to theory' which displaced and denounced Hoggart had negative as well as positive aspects: 'In ... the business of creating more sophisticated analyses ... that sense of the immediate pressure to connect cultural analysis to the whole life experience and situation of working-class people ... had been lost' (Laing, 1986, p. 217). More recently, and an encouraging indication that it is not only a particular generation of British scholars who feel this way, Mark Gibson has made a tentative defence of the Hoggartian approach, commending its 'sensitivity of observation and respect for the cultural specificity of "ordinariness"' (1998, p. 40).

I cite these not to absolve Hoggart's book from its limitations. Its version of working-class culture is, as his detractors never tire of insisting, frequently backward-looking, apolitical, insular, sexist and slushy, and its swipes at the emerging Americanized youth culture of Britain are wrongheaded and mean-spirited. At the same time, however, it is a book which still moves me, prompting intense jolts of recognition that few other texts can match. The reason is simple: Hoggart's account of the cultural cusp still resonates, and it is precisely his deployment of emotionality and autobiography (those softest of targets for theorists committed to system-building and apparatus-chasing) which ensure that this resonance persists. He writes from his feelings, he writes about himself and he writes about class – those are the interwoven approaches that fuel *The Uses of Literacy*. They don't constitute anything like a rigorous methodology (though what are rigorous methodologies other than laughably vain attempts to glue a sense of order on to the emotional complexities that cultural experiences summon up?), but they do give the book its power and its commitment.

If *The Uses of Literacy* is a pained and contradictory book, this is not because Hoggart, as later caricatures imply, was working without the appropriate theoretical frameworks; it stems from his attempt to confront and understand the painful contradictions of his own cultural position. Such contradictions are still evident in British culture. The feminist academics with working-class backgrounds who contributed to the collection *Class Matters* (Mahony and Zmroczek, 1997) write movingly about the difficulties of being between classes, pulled in different directions by personal histories and current circumstances. Diane Reay, addressing these dilemmas of uncertainty and ambivalence, uses words like complicity, treachery, tokenism, collusion, rage, disloyalty, guilt (1997, pp. 23–4) – stronger, less guarded, more urgent words than academics usually let loose, and words worth comparing to those Hoggart litters through the 'Scholarship Boy' section of *The Uses of Literacy*: insecurity, unease, fear, shame, vertigo (1957, pp. 238–49). Beverley Skeggs, similarly, has reflected on the contradictions and difficulties faced by once-working-class academics trying to think about class from that unsettled, unsettling position. The chapter on class in her book was, she admits, 'excruciating to write' (1997, p. 15), disclosing through the force of the adjective how wrenching such thinking can be.

Evidently, the cusp still chafes, Hoggart's friction point still pertains, although it should be noted that, in a direct and overdue refutation of Hoggart's sexual politics, today it seems to be women who write most affectingly about these issues. Is this, as Carolyn Steedman (1986) has suggested, because academic men from working-class backgrounds, since Hoggart and indeed often *using* Hoggart as a weapon in such a campaign, find it relatively easy to transmute the raw material of their upbringing into intellectually respected currency? Perhaps – there's always a market in some academic quarters for a bit of rough – but I have to say it's never felt like that to me. Even on those occasions when I have resorted to an assertion of working-class roots in order to win arguments or respect, that tactic is little more than an evasive swerve away from the perplexities of reflecting on the difficult identity location of *having been* working class.

The fact that *The Uses of Literacy* comes out of those same perplexities – they are the veins that pump blood through the body of the text – ensures that I cannot consign it to some dustbin of theoretical inadequacy. The form of the book, its attempt to juxtapose autobiography and analysis, is also crucial. It's not entirely successful, but that very awkwardness both mirrors the awkwardness of Hoggart's class location and testifies to the newness of what he was trying to do. As a recent interview with Hoggart makes clear (Gibson and Hartley, 1998), the book's shape was motivated by a wish to insist on the usefulness of the experiential dimension in studying popular culture:

> 'When I started *The Uses of Literacy* I was heavily under the influence of F. R. and Q. D. Leavis ... but the more I wrote ... the more uneasy I felt, particularly about Q. D. Leavis' *Fiction and the Reading Public*. She talked brilliantly about popular fiction, but it was always distant from her as if she had a peg on her nose ... Then I started writing ... a description of the context of working-class people, working-class culture, as I had known it.' (p. 14)

This is the same debate Raymond Williams recalled from that Cambridge lecture, although here Queenie Leavis replaces her husband Frank. (I have often wondered how differently the Leavises might have struck future generations had they used their homely first names rather than those prickly initials.) It is a debate about distance, about whether first-hand experience of a lived culture is a valid tool in cultural analysis. Cultural Studies is a discipline fundamentally predicated on yanking that peg off Queenie's nose, demanding that the experiential is respected – except, of course, that one view of the 'move to theory' would be that its downplaying of experience put the peg right back, albeit a peg newly carved from French wood.

What Hoggart realized through his dissatisfaction with Leavisian distance was that there were just no academic vocabularies available which contained the words he needed for conveying his experiential understandings of working-class culture. Hence his recourse to autobio-graphical modes. It is a somewhat displaced form of autobiography, tending to generalize out from first-hand experiences rather than risking the naked 'I', but it is autobiography nonetheless, and as such inaugurated and authorized the usage within Cultural Studies of the non-distanced voice. One of the most important books in the tradition that followed, a book that rebukes Hoggart's ideological assumptions while deploying the form he developed, is Carolyn Steedman's *Landscape for a Good Woman* (1986). Running through Steedman's account of her own and her mother's child-hood is an anxiety about how best to tell the story, about what should be the properly complex, properly sensitive voice to use. In his review of the book, Raymond Williams recognized the difficulties Steedman faced in her quest to preserve the dignity and vividness of working-class experience while still interrogating it through theoretical frameworks, difficulties which face any Cultural Studies bid to hold together autobiographical and analytical perspectives on class. Steedman's book, said Williams, exemplified 'the formal problems of that hybrid of autobiography and argument which is now so clear a consequence of the shifting class relations of our time and within these, shaping the mode, of the specific situation of the intellectual from a working-class family' (1989, p. 35).

In other words, it is the need to convey this specific ambivalence of class location – a need felt by Steedman, by Williams himself, by Hoggart, by many of the writers quoted in this chapter and by the person writing it – which demands a particular kind of writing, a tone and approach that cannot be comfortably reconciled with the depersonalized conventions of many academic theories. If this approach is accused of lacking rigour, of being theoretically naive, of constructing a rest-home for indulgently sentimentalizing nostalgists, then that is a risk we have to take. Hoggart and Williams knew this back in the 1950s (Hoggart, 1958; Hoggart and Williams, 1960), with Hoggart acknowledging that experiential writing on class was prone to 'sentimental over-valuing' but that such a 'danger has to be met if we are to get away from the ... attitude which thinks of working-class people as almost blank slates, with none of the rich and elaborate manners of the middle and upper classes' (1958, p. 132).

In the classroom

One of the trickiest places to identify and confront that attitude is in our own everyday working environments. What can we do when ignorance of or indifference to working-class lives and cultures surfaces in the groups we teach, the texts we read or the colleagues with whom we work? What is the best response to those unthinking assumptions of class coherence that middle-class people display so often? How can I negotiate the anger I feel when fellow lecturers tell me, in everyday chatter, they couldn't move to a certain area because it is too near to a council estate?

If I was given to hideously reckless generalizations, I would say that there is a certain correlation between the degree to which Cultural Studies academics happily subscribe to abstract theoretical systems and their class backgrounds. I could only produce flimsily anecdotal evidence to back this up, such as the occasion when a former colleague, who espoused theoretical rigour with all the self-assurance his family had bought for him at a prestigious public school and Oxford University, listened to a lecture in which I championed the validity of experiential approaches to popular culture and then told his students that he couldn't have disagreed more with every single word. Such a comment indicates that while he saw studying popular culture as having a certain intellectual and political usefulness, the actual lives of those who most often consumed and participated in that culture were, at best, a side issue. That's a view which tackles popular culture only with the brain, but never with the heart or the guts (let alone even more carnivalesque organs), a perspective memorably characterized by Gillian Skirrow as that of the 'snooping health visitor, sniffing out whether someone's environment is fit to live in' (1990, p. 321).

My antipathy towards such snoopers should be clear by now, but in saying this I'm not suggesting that only academics with working-class backgrounds should be teaching about popular culture. My background gives me certain insights, but it does not constitute the only plausible standpoint from which to speak. The key issue here is not where you're from, but that you do acknowledge you're from somewhere. Too many academics speak from a position not exactly of classlessness, since there is no such thing, but of class blindness. There's a further twist, perhaps the most pernicious of all, in which class as an abstract social factor, a system of dominance, is recognized and often vigorously critiqued, but there is no self-reflection regarding the class location of the individual concerned.

For example, I teach mostly middle-class, white students, and where they have political affiliations, these are usually radical. That radicalism is selective, however, being most often centred on sexual politics, sometimes with a Green tinge, usually sensitive to questions of ethnicity. If class figures, they know the right general noises to make about the evils of elitism, but they never look inwardly at their own class identities. When I teach seminars about soap operas, I can guarantee that these students will simultaneously defend the genre against high-cultural snobberies, point to the usefulness of feminist readings, cluck like good white liberals about the paucity of black characters, but yet also make fun of the working-class accents, lifestyles and even names found in those serials. I have even had otherwise impeccably progressive students distribute handouts to groups which give characters' names not as they are really spelled, but jokingly re-spelled in a mocking approximation of how these students hear the characters talk. So Bianca, a leading working-class character in the BBC soap *EastEnders*, appeared on one such handout as 'Beeang-urgh', a middle-class deciphering of the actors' cockney accents. These students would be outraged if they saw an Asian or West Indian accent reproduced in such parodic terms by white people, but evidently class is fair game for the ideological exercise of linguistic condescension.

The problem many middle-class students have in reflecting on class issues is due in part, I think, to the ways in which the political agendas of Cultural Studies have cohered around a selective agenda of identity politics. Female students, lesbian and gay students, black students can all find in Cultural Studies academic empowerments for their own senses of identity, and this is an excellent development. Class, however, is in so many ways the 'lost identity' of identity politics that it almost never figures on the intellectual maps many politically motivated students draw for themselves. If it did, some uncomfortable complications would emerge. Middle-class feminists, for example, would be obliged to consider the privileges of their class position, thus upsetting the cosy assumptions of victimhood through which some versions of feminism are articulated. Nobody in a Cultural Studies setting wants to be thought of as privileged, so issues of class tend to be devalued or disavowed.

In preparing teaching materials for a course on lesbian and gay perspectives on popular culture, I found a fascinating article which talked of how *Out*, the pioneering lesbian and gay magazine series produced for Britain's Channel 4, was rescheduled when shown on S4C, the Welsh-language equivalent of Channel 4 which broadcasts in Wales. A lengthy quotation is necessary:

While Channel 4 is screening *Out* . . . S4C is showing *Rasus*, 'a series about trotting', that is, horse races . . . True, *Out* may be shown later on S4C, but much, much later: after midnight, to be precise . . . S4C tends to target a middle-aged audience with distinctly low-brow tastes and strong agricultural interests, politically incorrect and culturally undiscriminating. *Noson Lawen*, for instance, is a typical light-entertainment programme which ... thrives on humour of sexual innuendo and the most unregenerate sexism ... Often, programmes of this nature are broadcast when popular feminist programmes featuring Germaine Greer and her like are being seen on Channel 4. The assumption ... seems to be that Welsh women are not interested in feminism ... One might also suspect that this timing is a veiled censorship: consigning potentially 'corrupting' sexual material to a very safe time-slot, when all the good, Welsh-speaking *werin* (folk) will certainly be tucked up with their hot-water bottles, if not with their Bibles. (Gramich, 1997, pp. 106–7)

Reading this as a queer academic, I am ruefully outraged; it seems like just the kind of regrettable, if predictable, marginalization of minority voices that I spend much of my life attacking, and from that angle I share Gramich's dismay. Yet there are other discourses operating here, and to read the extract through a class lens is to reveal a text that positively suppurates with antagonism towards popular culture and the lived experience of working-class people. Gramich merely replaces one set of mistaken cultural linkages (Welsh-speaking people are heterosexuals uninterested in sexual politics) with one of her own (lesbians, gays and feminists are young cosmopolitan sophisticates with educated bourgeois tastes). Through sheer class blindness she fails to see that her assumptions are no less hegemonic than the ones she criticizes. Where would she place a Welsh-speaking, middle-aged, working-class lesbian who liked both horse racing and vulgar comedy, and set her video recorder so she could watch *Out* whenever she liked?

I would suggest that one of the most useful tasks that intellectuals committed to the importance of class can undertake is the identification and exposure of class blindness in academic texts, especially where such texts are ones that in other respects we would applaud and endorse. Valerie Walkerdine (1996), for example, in a rich and striking chapter that once again pulls together autobiographical and experiential strands, hints at an unspoken class dynamic in psychoanalytic film theory, while Jane Shattuc (1994) has looked at how feminist theory wrote about Hollywood melodramas in ways that secured them for middle-class intellectualized rationality through minimizing their gut-level emotional impact on working-class audiences.

A last point that needs mentioning here is the relationship between academics on the class cusp and working-class students. The latter, after all, might be rightfully suspicious if their tutor tried to ignore the differences between them and initiate some dubious sort of class bond. For one thing, as Rosalind Brunt (1992) has noted, many working-class students have become students precisely because they want to acquire some of the valuable cultural capital dispensed by universities, and under such circumstances the last thing they want or need is a guilt-ridden tutor exhorting them to glory in their roots. I was such a student once myself, so keen to absorb status through studying that I became a kind of insufferable teenage Adorno, denouncing TV game shows and tabloid newspapers to anyone foolish enough to listen, and I would have been highly displeased to be turned into some sort of trophy of authenticity. Once-working-class academics need, I think, to remember their own pasts, and let their working-class students reach their own accommodation with discourses of belonging, identity and power.

Process and access

Attentive readers of this chapter will have noted that my picture of class has been painted with very broad strokes. It is only fair to give some space, in this last section, to recent work on class which complicates my crude distinctions between class identities. John Frow (1995), in particular, approaches the issue of class with enormous delicacy and dexterity. He argues that in a world where the changes characteristic of postmodernity have rendered older categorizations of class as outmoded, class can no longer be seen as some sort of economically determined essence, into which one is born and imprisoned. This does not mean that material privilege has ceased to exist or become irrelevant, but that in the contemporary climate it is more productive to think of 'processes of class formation ... played out through particular institutional forms and balances of power ... through desires, and fears, and fantasies' (1995, p. 111). Class, for Frow, is not a pre-existing slot to which we are assigned, but a set of contestable relations; it is not a given, but a process.

As an academic, Frow is particularly concerned with what he calls the knowledge class, intellectuals characterized by working in the education and communication sectors, a group not reducible to an economic category but linked by their shared involvement in the creation and circulation of ideas. This is a useful formulation, not least because it offers people like me a way of sidestepping that clumsy binary of working/middle class, offering a more fluid label that more accurately encapsulates what I see as my role. The problem with the notion of the knowledge class, however, is that it can only describe where I am now. Since it offers an identity based primarily on occupations, it overlooks where its putative members started out, before they were ever employed as anything. Putting it bluntly, I may have ended up in the knowledge class, giving me some community of interest and shared ground with that public school and Oxford colleague I mentioned earlier, but the differences between us which go back generations and generations (for all I know, his grandparents might have owned the factory mine worked in) have not been erased just because we have attended the same committee meetings. If Cultural Studies in its old-style, class-focused, Hoggart–Williams mode taught us anything, it's that the present is meaningless without a political grasp of the past.

So when Frow criticizes Cultural Studies academics who claim an unproblematic inwardness with popular culture, as if their years of specialized intellectual training and membership of the knowledge class were irrelevant, he makes a telling point. Yet he neglects the nuance on which my chapter hangs – the position of once-working-class academics, who although they should not purport to enjoy popular texts as if they were part of 'the people', do relate to those texts in ways not open to always-middle-class colleagues. When I teach about vulgar comedy, for example, I have at my disposal both a recent knowledge-class training and a longer-standing personal history of working-class experiential consumption. This particular double perspective is unavailable to always-middle-class academics, who, thanks to an upbringing where cultural consumption adhered to more conventionally bourgeois patterns, might only have their first sustained encounter with certain kinds of popular text when tackling them as an object of study.

There are parallels here with what Jostein Gripsrud (1989, p. 199) has called the 'double access' afforded to once-working-class academics. Jumping through the hoops of academia means that they are able to consume both 'high' and 'low' culture, even if their involvement with the latter is no longer a straightforward one. Prefiguring Frow, Gripsrud has no time for academics who trumpet their membership of 'the people', arguing persuasively that having double access is a class privilege. Yet he is also fully aware that academics in this ambivalent space can never feel entirely at home in high culture either. They know too much about those lives and worlds which high culture excludes to ever feel at ease with its arrogant presumptions of universality. According to Gripsrud, those on the class cusp are forever placed in 'a sort of cultural limbo, not properly integrated in the lower-class culture they left, nor in the upper-class culture they have formally entered' (p. 196).

This is the same impasse that faced Hoggart, an impasse that has been at the core of Cultural Studies for forty years, and even the elegant invention of a bolt-hole called the knowledge class cannot erase the dilemmas it generates. Gripsrud's recommendation is this: since academics on the cultural cusp cannot find a stable class identity, their only responsible course of action is to 'acknowledge their marginal position ... and start investigating the possibilities ... from there' (p. 197). This chapter has been an attempt to follow that path, a path which means maintaining a commitment to the value of autobiography in understanding how class and culture coalesce, and which means insisting on the uses of experiential literacy as well as drawing on the insights of conceptual thought.

Bibliography

Barker, M. and Beezer, A. (eds) (1992) *Reading into Cultural Studies*. London: Routledge.

Brunt, R. (1992) 'Engaging with the popular: audiences for mass culture and what to say about them'. In L. Grossberg *et al.* (eds), *Cultural Studies*. London: Routledge.

During, S. (ed.) (1993) *The Cultural Studies Reader*. London: Routledge.

Dyer, R. (1981) 'Introduction'. In R. Dyer (ed.), *Coronation Street*. London: BFI.

Easthope, A. (1997) 'But what *is* Cultural Studies?'. In S. Bassnett (ed.), *Studying British Cultures*. London: Routledge.

Frow, J. (1995) *Cultural Studies and Cultural Value*. Oxford: Clarendon Press.

Geraghty, C. (1996) 'Reflections on history in teaching Cultural Studies'. *Cultural Studies* 10(2), pp. 345–53.

Gibson, M. (1998) 'Richard Hoggart's grandmother's ironing: some questions about "power" in international Cultural Studies'. *International Journal of Cultural Studies* 1(1), pp. 25–44.

Gibson, M. and Hartley, J. (1998) 'Forty years of Cultural Studies: an interview with Richard Hoggart, October 1997'. *International Journal of Cultural Studies* 1(1), pp. 11–24.

Gramich, K. (1997) 'Cymru or Wales? Explorations in a divided sensibility'. In S. Bassnett (ed.), *Studying British Cultures*. London: Routledge.

Gripsrud, J. (1989) ' "High Culture" revisited'. *Cultural Studies* 3(2), pp. 194–207.

Hall, S. (1980) 'Cultural Studies: two paradigms'. *Media, Culture and Society* 2, pp. 57–72.

Hoggart, R. (1957) *The Uses of Literacy*. London: Chatto & Windus.

Hoggart, R. (1958) 'Speaking to each other'. In N. Mackenzie (ed.), *Conviction*. London: MacGibbon and Kee.

Hoggart, R. and Williams, R. (1960) 'Working class attitudes'. *New Left Review* 1 (January–February), pp. 26–30.

Jones, P. (1994) 'The myth of "Raymond Hoggart": on "founding fathers" and cultural policy'. *Cultural Studies* 8(3), pp. 394–416.

Laing, S. (1986) *Representations of Working-Class Life 1957–1964*. Basingstoke: Macmillan.

Mahony, P. and Zmroczek, C. (1997) 'Why class matters'. In P. Mahony and C. Zmroczek (eds), *Class Matters: 'Working-Class' Women's Perspectives on Social Class*. London: Taylor & Francis.

Nelson, C. (1996) 'Always already Cultural Studies: academic conferences and a manifesto'. In J. Storey (ed.), *What Is Cultural Studies?* London: Arnold.

Pickering, M. (1997) *History, Experience and Cultural Studies*. Basingstoke: Macmillan.

Reay, D. (1997) 'The double-bind of the "working-class" feminist academic: the success of failure or the failure of success?'. In P. Mahony and C. Zmroczek (eds), *Class Matters: 'Working-Class' Women's Perspectives on Social Class*. London: Taylor & Francis.

Schwarz, B. (1994) 'Where is Cultural Studies?' *Cultural Studies* 8(3), pp. 377–93.

Shattuc, J. (1994) 'Having a good cry over *The Color Purple*: the problem of affect and imperialism in feminist theory'. In J. Bratton *et al.* (eds), *Melodrama: Stage, Picture, Screen*. London: BFI.

Skeggs, B. (1997) *Formations of Class and Gender: Becoming Respectable*. London: Sage.

Skirrow, G. (1990) 'Hellivision'. In M. Alvarado *et al.* (eds), *The Media Reader*. London: BFI.

Steedman, C. (1986) *Landscape for a Good Woman*. London: Virago.

Stratton, J. and Ang, I. (1996) 'On the impossibility of a global Cultural Studies: "British" Cultural Studies in an "international" frame'. In D. Morley and K.-H. Chen (eds), *Stuart Hall: Critical Dialogues in Cultural Studies*. London: Routledge.

Turner, G. (1990) *British Cultural Studies: An Introduction*. London: Unwin Hyman.

Walkerdine, V. (1996) 'Subject to change without notice: psychology, post-modernity and the popular'. In J. Curran *et al.* (eds), *Cultural Studies and Communications*. London: Arnold.

Williams, R. (1979) *Politics and Letters*. London: New Left Books.

Williams, R. (1989) *What I Came to Say*. London: Hutchinson Radius.

2

Discursive Mothers and Academic Fandom: Class, Generation and the Production of Theory

Joanne Lacey

This chapter will explore the use of the personal by feminist working-class academics as a means of bringing class back into question. It will also discuss my experiences of finding a voice in the wake of this influential writing. Ellen Seiter argues that 'everyone complains about class definition but a method for doing things differently has remained elusive' (1995, p. 141). I would argue that a 'method for doing things differently' has emerged quite clearly in the recent feminist writings around social class, and it is very firmly rooted in the personal, in the experiential as both an ontological and an epistemological project. What I will argue is that the influential work of feminist theorists such as Valerie Walkerdine, Carolyn Steedman, Beverley Skeggs and Annette Kuhn, together with the autobiographical foundations laid through the work of Richard Hoggart and Raymond Williams, have come to form a theoretical framework, accepted and deployed as a legitimate mode of interpretation on social class by scholars working under the influence of these writings.

A new generation of feminist theorists and working-class academics understand that the personal can be a critically acceptable way to talk about class. What should also be included as a significant influence on the personal work of feminist theorists on class is the writing of black feminist critics. Walkerdine herself acknowledges the debt of her writing to those interventions:

It was black women who first began to raise within feminism differences between women, and they did so in a way, which was not like that of most current ways of talking about class. They were angry, emotional, not dry and rationalist like many male academics raising class as an issue as though it had nothing to do with our subjectivities. (1990, p. 157)[1]

Although social class has gone out of theoretical fashion, it *is* still being talked about (how else would a collection like this have come together?). Because of the silences that surround the speaking of class, the work that does exist becomes even more important. What I want to explore in this chapter is the difficult relationship that I have built up with some of the work referenced above, not in terms of the writer's theoretical positions, but in terms of academic fandom. Also I want to problematize my differential location to the theorists in question in terms of age, education, institutional privilege and perceptions of ability and achievement. Out of this I hope to offer some tentative analysis of the educated working-class academic, rather than the middle-class achiever, as the object of desire and aspirational fantasy. This in turn may bring to light issues relating to class, gender, generation and the process of being 'educated out' (*ibid.*, p. 67) that might develop the conceptualization of the historical specificity of the movement from one set of classed experiences into another, and the mechanisms through which this is enacted.

I worshipped *Landscape for a Good Woman* and *Schoolgirl Fictions*. I constructed Carolyn Steedman and Valerie Walkerdine as powerful mentors. Although I only 'knew' them through their writing, I built up images of the 'real' woman behind the text, and these images were worked out through problematic, yet powerful maternal metaphors. Walkerdine and Steedman (as authors of books and my fantasy figures) cared for me, empowered me, encouraged me to go on when I have felt and been made to feel 'like a working-class thicko' (Stanley, 1995, p. 172). The best way that I can understand this relationship is to see the texts operating as discursive mothers.[2] At the time that I 'discovered' Steedman and Walkerdine, I was also rediscovering the writings of New French Feminism. I had found much of the work on the maternal body and the relationship to language gloriously seductive, if somewhat problematic. Kristeva's discursive production of the pre-Oedipal space as a utopic vessel (1980) was somehow soothing. Mary Anne Doane's interpretation of this image of a child wrapped in the 'sonorous envelope' (1980, pp. 33–50) of the maternal voice was evocative of processes of speaking and listening that could be played out in a critical exchange in which the relationships of power and knowledge were more evenly distributed. I found myself retreating into this fantasy and writing poetic accounts of the possibilities of 'écriture féminine'. Having since rediscovered the materiality of everyday life, 'the something dirty down below' that Hall urged Cultural Studies to take account of (1992, p. 278), the possibilities of 'écriture féminine' have somewhat diminished. However, it is possible to extend Doane's image of the 'sonorous envelope' beyond this pre-Oedipal maternal scene to a consideration of the maternal as a nostalgic metaphor in wider terms for fantasies of belonging, wholeness and safety which can be played out in particular networks of academic power relations.

In the process of being 'educated out' I had been separated from my real mother, and felt abandoned in a social space to which I did not quite belong. I called home for security, but my mother saw me (because she needed to) as the clever class warrior; I could not talk to her about my feelings of fraudulence, my vulnerability. I could share those feelings, and gain an understanding of them from reading the work of theorists such as Steedman and Walkerdine. And so, their writing became like the 'sonorous envelope', constructing a shared critical exchange in which I could enfold myself, be protected, and out of which I could work. At the same time, along with the fantasies of comfort and safety, there were (and are) feelings of envy that these academics had arrived at a place that I wanted to get to; they had achieved. They were good enough. I constructed a complex set of successful scenarios around them that defended against the fear that I would never ever be that good, that clever myself. The anxieties around cleverness are significant to the formation of an educated working-class identity, when our cleverness may well have been constructed in childhood as our ticket out, and worn through adulthood as a masquerade. Some of us live with a fear of the mask slipping.

I often see my life through a process of disassociation, in which I live in patterns resembling the struggle and survival narrative format of 'made-for-TV' movies.[3] In one scene I am an old woman, recounting, through camera gauze and flashback the story of my life. It's an egotistical fantasy really, in which I play out desires to be interesting and extraordinary enough to have a story to tell, not just any story, but a story of struggle and success. It's an image that grasps onto a particular fantasy of emerging out of a life that has been about struggle, deprivation and loss; not necessarily my life, but a working-class life that is given dignity, strength and drama in retrospect. It is the narration of escape, fantastically created in the imagination of someone who escaped her class through education. Lurking alongside this fantasy is another, less heroic one. What motivates the 'made-for-TV' scene is a fear that having been offered choices through education, choices that my parents and grandparents never had, I don't succeed because when I get 'there' I'm not good enough. I do not triumph and overcome. My parents think that I am enacting a class war in the university on a daily basis, a class terrorist scaling the dizzy heights of the ivory tower shouting 'sod you I'm here' from the top. I never feel like that, and so I am not filmed through the softening pink gauze but sit, in a darkly lit cramped space, vulnerable and afraid, beneath my family's perceptions of my achievements. I 'see' what they are not able to see, that in this world of academia I am ten-a-penny, not quite making the grade.

Because of the presence and achievements of the 'scholarship boys and girls',[4] we working-class academics as a generation have role models, have fantasy figures. We do not, like Walkerdine (1992), have to turn to popular films in order to see the professor at work. We can go to conferences and lecture halls (particularly in 'new' universities and community colleges) and see the educated working class in action and in positions of authority. For academics like Walkerdine and Steedman, fantasies of success and cleverness were worked out in relation to 'them' – the middle classes, wanting and needing to be as clever as 'them'. For me, potent fantasies of academic success and achievement were worked out (in part) through these others, the educated working-class academic.

What the contrasting images of my own biography highlight are the painful contradictions embedded in the development of myself as a classed subject, and the transition from working-class background to middle-class academic practice. I lived through a working-class childhood in Liverpool. Many of the material difficulties that my parents experienced were hidden from me. I knew that we didn't have much money, but neither did anyone else I grew up with. What defined my 'working classness', I have since come to see, was a sense of living with people who had been given little opportunity to be anything different. What was given to me by my parents was a belief that through education I could be something else. My dad had a stock phrase: 'Get your O levels, get your A levels and the world is your lobster.' (The change in aspirational noun was a family joke. It has always been my dad's ambition to go to a posh restaurant and eat a whole lobster Thermidor.) So I got educated, and I got out. The groundbreaking collection *Class Matters*, edited by Pat Mahony and Christine Zmroczek (1997), deals extensively with the emotional politics of class embedded in this shift.[5] Diane Reay, addressing the unfashionability of speaking about social class in the academy now, relates the silence to the outmoding of the Marxist paradigm, with its focus on the economic determinations of material reality. Reay argues that 'there have to be better ways of writing about class in academia' (1997, p. 26). Better than what? In Reay's terms, better than the determinations of the economic, rather than the emotional politics of class. To borrow Elspeth Probyn's phrase, 'the figuration of something better' (1993b, p. 3) in class terms must, according to Reay, take account of the 'psychological complexities of social class' (1997, p. 26). The quandary for Cultural Studies in a post-industrial context has been 'without Marxism how do we do class?'

Cultural Studies' relationship to Marxism is complicated and contradictory. Colin Sparks argues:

> There need be no apology for selecting the relationship between Marxism and Cultural Studies for special attention: for many years it was generally believed that Marxism and Cultural Studies were, if not identical, at least locked into an extremely close relationship. (1996, p. 71)

Yet Stuart Hall urges us to consider that:

> There never was a prior moment when Cultural Studies and Marxism represented a perfect theoretical fit. From the beginning (to use this way of speaking for a moment) there was always/already the question of the great inadequacies theoretically and politically, the resounding silences, the great evasions of Marxism, the things that Marx did not talk about or seem to understand which were our privileged object of study; culture, ideology, language, the symbolic. (1992, p. 279)

The foundation of Cultural Studies lay in a move away from, and critique of, the established Marxist tradition of cultural theory embodied in the writing of authors who were members of the British Communist Party and its international affiliates. In 1960 Williams and Hoggart set up a significant, and as yet unresolved, tension between the lived difference of class and the critical systems in place for understanding it. In a conversation with Hoggart, Williams identified this tension as 'the most difficult bit of theory':

> The most difficult bit of theory that I think both of us have been trying to get at, is what relation there is between kinds of community, that we

call working class and the high working class tradition, leading to democracy, solidarity in the unions and Socialism. To what extent can we establish a relation between given kinds of working class community, and what we call working class consciousness in the sense of the labour movement. (Hoggart and Williams, 1960, p. 28)

This conversation was reprinted in the first number of *New Left Review*, a document which Hall (1992) cites as being extremely influential in the founding philosophies and politics of Cultural Studies. Thus, Cultural Studies locates explanations of social class through its contradictory relationship to Marxism, and the experiential differences of class that Marxism was unable to handle. The current crisis around the place of class in Cultural Studies then can be located within this tradition. This 'most difficult bit of theory' is being re-enacted within the contexts of post-structuralism and post-Marxism as part of a wider reinvention. It is a re-enactment that serves to reflect on Cultural Studies as a discipline that 'is not infrequently caught in the act of reinventing itself . . . being forced to re-examine and (perhaps) to reinvent what kind of explanation of cultural and social processes [it] is able to offer' (Ferguson and Golding, 1997, p. xxiii). Peter Dahlgren (1997) identifies the tensions between Cultural Studies and the analysis of the structures of political and economic power in which cultural practices are cited as ongoing.[6] It is important to address the implications of these tensions for the study of class: why when Cultural Studies shifted away from class as the economically determined axial principle of social difference did class become *so* difficult to talk about? In part because the contradictions embedded in 'the most difficult bit of theory' remain unresolved. Interestingly Hoggart and Williams made use of the personal in order to negotiate these contradictions between accepted conceptual frameworks and lived difference, in order, as Hoggart says, to bring theory 'into relation with my own experience' (Hoggart and Williams, 1960, p. 26). Personal experience is not constructed as a reified category allowing access to the 'truth' of working-class life, but as an ontological and epistemological category that can bring to light inadequacies within available systems of explanation for those lives. Thus, when Reay yearns for 'better ways of talking about class' than an economically determined analysis, the framework is already in place within Cultural Studies to work out 'the figuration of something better' through the personal, through the emotional politics of class. Marxism never was a fixed and defined theoretical paradigm in Cultural Studies. Perhaps, as part of the process of reinvention and reflection on social class within Cultural Studies we need to go back 'to that moment of "staking a wager" ... to those moments in which the positions began to matter' (Hall, 1992, p. 278). In terms of bringing class back into question, this return is a potentially important move. It is also one that Hall urges caution on. 'In the early stages perhaps we spoke too much about the working class, about subcultures. Now nobody talks about them at all. They talk about myself, my mother, my father, my friends, and that is, of course, a very selective experience' (1996, p. 402). The important methodological issue that Hall raises for Cultural Studies is the way in which personal experience 'can be used to theorise social positionality within structures that touches on questions larger than our own' (*ibid.*). Elspeth Probyn argues that 'it is precisely the level of the lived that we need to explore if we are to rethink and elaborate alternative enunciative positions in cultural theory' (1993b, p. 16). Probyn structures experience as working on two fronts at once – the ontological and the epistemological. If the experiential is deployed across these two fronts then it is never just about 'me', but works to address the politics of knowledge production, and to create alternative conceptual frameworks for understanding the ways in which social classifications are lived as difference. If we continue to rework the tensions between Marxism, political economy and the study of social class in Cultural Studies, together with the methodological problems attached to the use of personal narratives, then we can move forwards, and regenerate the terms of the debates on class – staking a wager, making class matter again.

As a means of bringing class back into question on the critical agenda, feminist writers from the late 1980s have also turned back to the experiential as the critical mode of address that helped shape the formation of British Cultural Studies. Using the complexities and contradictions embedded in their own working-class histories to frame working-class identity within a poststructuralist paradigm, they present these class identities as now fragmented, in flux, contradictory, performed, lived as narratives and fantasies. What I want to focus on here is the experience of finding a voice from which to speak in the wake of this work, and my relationship with some of the assumptions embedded in it. Carolyn Steedman writes that when 'I first came across Kathleen Woodward's *Jipping Street*, I read it with the shocked astonishment of one who had never seen what she knows written down before' (1986, p. 16). In 1990, as a 21-year-old MA student, overwhelmed by an influential programme in the Social

History of Art at Leeds University, and only beginning to realize that my feelings of dislocation were classed, the discovery of *Landscape for a Good Woman* and *Schoolgirl Fictions* were influential beyond my belief. Here, I could not only read about feeling out of place, but be offered conceptual frameworks for understanding and using feelings of dislocation. My discursive mothers offered me an experiential critical language that my real mother was not part of. I wrote Valerie Walkerdine fan letters; I cut out my own picture and stuck it on the cover of *Landscape for a Good Woman*. These confessions feel uncomfortable and immature. But such feelings of discomfort link in interesting ways to some of the existing critical work on fandom as a kind of pathology. Joli Jensen discusses the role of research on fans that distinguishes 'us', an elevated community of researchers (scholars, collectors, aficionados) from 'them' the fans, 'even though they engage in virtually the same kinds of activities' (1992, p. 19). Jensen goes on to argue:

> Am I suggesting, then, that a Barry Manilow fan be compared with, for example, a Joyce scholar? The mind may reel at the comparison, but why? The Manilow fan knows intimately every recording (and every version) of Barry's songs; the Joyce scholar knows intimately every volume (and every version) of Joyce's oeuvre. The relationship between Manilow's real life and his music is explored in detail in star biographies and fan magazines; the relationship between Dublin, Bloomsday and Joyce's actual experiences are explored in detail in scholarly monographs. (p. 20)

What Jensen is urging us to think about are the lines drawn between the differences and similarities of the fan and the scholar: passion versus rational evaluation, mass appeal versus cultural hierarchy.[7] Lisa Lewis maintains that 'we are all fans of something. We respect, admire, and desire. We distinguish and form commitments' (1992, p. 1) What is interesting about the ways in which academics tend to discuss their relationships to favoured texts is that the desire is written out of the equation in favour of respect and admiration, feelings which are much more acceptable in the academy. My fan impulse towards these texts manifested some interesting points of tension.

There is important work on the theorization of the process of being 'educated out' that does look at the perceptions of success and achievement placed on working-class academics by their families and their concomitant feelings of fraudulence.[8] Much of this work is insightful, located in the historical, material and cultural relations of escape, but it does not address the perceptions of success and achievement placed on the educated working-class academic. As an educated working-class woman still in the throes of being 'educated out', I felt that Walkerdine and Steedman had already arrived, had achieved, had power, and I wanted to be like them, to write like them. When Valerie Walkerdine wrote that 'I cannot explain what it feels like to be in another place because of that work, for embedded in it is the necessary fear of giving up, the terrifying doubts that very soon they will find out that you have no talent' (1990, p. 163), I identified with her, but I also envied her. Seemingly she had arrived at another place. It is possible to take account of generational difference and fantasy and perceptions of academic achievement to make the processes of being 'educated out' even more complicated. Louise Morley also argues that 'the academy, with its claims to authority and knowledge production, provides perfect preconditions for feelings of fraudulence' (1997, p. 115). What I desired was the institutional privilege (albeit relative in terms of the numbers of working-class women in positions of authority in higher education) that Walkerdine seemed party to. When she spoke of feeling fraudulent, I think that I was locating her as a successful woman talking about the difficulties that she had overcome, for she had moved beyond the rank and file of working-class anonymity. I could see that. It was aspirational. She had the 'made-for-TV' story that I wanted. What I constructed in the work of working-class educated feminists was the apparent degree of confidence beneath their (and my) fears of fraudulence.

What happens when we go to seek out the 'real' mother, the star behind the writing to supervise our research? How can these women live up to our expectations and the fantasies of success and achievement ascribed to them? My relationship with one of these working-class female academics did not end on good terms. I want to explore the dynamics of this, not to attribute blame, but rather to open up a critical dialogue that takes account of theoretical fandom, the fantastic construction of the achievements of the working-class feminist academic, and the place of these in the intense relationship between a supervisor and supervisee in the production of knowledge.

What I will talk about here are my significant fantasies of my supervisor. I worked with her because in a field where class was talked about so little, the women that took account of it so centrally, became my mentors. They represented productive spaces in which class could be explored through the personal. What is interesting is that the space of the personal and the emotional that had constituted such a significant moment in returning to questions of class, should also have become the location of unspeakable tensions in our relationship. I wanted her to like me, to approve of me, to support and praise me, and she did that. We could talk and work through our mutually terrifying feelings of fraudulence. What strikes me, as I write this, is that I wanted her approval of me as a person before (perhaps as a necessary addition to) her approval of my research. My supervisor nurtured me through three years of research, and then we sent the work out in the form of the finished thesis. I believed at that time that it, that I, was good enough. At the viva the thesis was referred with substantial changes. This experience is not unique to me, and the emotional fallout does not need to be dealt with here. What makes the experience important, in terms of the arguments that I am trying to make about generations of educated working-class academics and our worship of discursive mothers, are my feelings of anger and betrayal that I had been 'found out' and found wanting. I was a fraud. What Walkerdine (1990, p. 163) feared most had happened to me, and my supervisor had let it (at least that was what I felt). To borrow the metaphor that I set up earlier, the 'sonorous envelope' had become seriously unstuck.

I felt that I had betrayed and let down my family, and indeed the women upon whose lives the empirical research was based. My choice of research was motivated very strongly by feelings of nostalgia and loss of my working-class identity. Over the course of 1994 and 1995, I interviewed seventeen white working-class women in their homes about their relationships to Hollywood film musicals in Liverpool in the 1950s, paying particular attention to the significance of those memories in their lives today. The women I interviewed either had replied to a letter in the local paper or were members of a local history group that met once a week as part of a community education programme. The doctoral thesis produced out of this empirical research staged a series of questions around the function of qualitative empirical research on female audiences for film, and the interpretative breadth of cinematic meanings deployed in these working-class women's lives. What the thesis did not tackle (this was done as an aside in research diaries and margins) was *my* motivation for researching working-class women's lives in Liverpool as a means of holding onto my childhood, where the images of childhood existed through the 'structures of feeling' to which I belonged. This structure of feeling is a fantasy, and a problematic one at that; itself discursively produced by the privileges (and hindsight) of being 'educated out', it longs for an authentic and stable working-class identity (another kind of fantasy).

Jonathan Steinwand argues that nostalgia 'relies on a distance – temporal and/or spatial, separating the subject from the object of its longing' (1989, p. 9). He works nostalgia out as:

> a sort of homesickness, a pain or longing to return home or to some lost past. The distress that inclines one homeward uproots the relation to the present by drawing one toward where one remembers feeling a sense of wholeness and belonging. The homeward pain of nostalgia presupposes that one's present place is somehow not homey enough. (*ibid.*)

Nostalgia always returns us to the present. We go 'there' in order to come back. For me this meant a return to feelings of class dislocation, of not belonging. In my work I returned home in an attempt to nostalgically reconstruct some authenticity. I focused the empirical work on women of my mother's generation, many of whom grew up on the same streets. I looked at their relationships with a genre of film that had been particularly pleasurable to me when watching with my mother, her sisters and my grandparents as a child. In other words, I was using the women's memories to summon and frame my own memories. The resulting nostalgic fantasy of my childhood operated throughout the course as a place of retreat through which my feelings of dislocation as a doctoral researcher could be negotiated and made safe.

The choice and process of the research were already infused with emotional class 'baggage'. To have it marked not good enough, was to have myself marked not good enough. It was easier to work when the power perimeters between 'us' and 'them' were demarcated along the lines of those who had been working-class 'us' and those who had not 'them'. These lines became blurred for me in the post viva trauma. It prompted me to think more carefully about who 'we' are. I want to acknowledge that the methods of classification deployed in contemporary work produced on class and the transition into education, where 'they' are seen to be the middle-class 'other' onto which we transcribe a kind of 'proper envy' (Steedman, 1986, p. 14) are made more complicated when we have working-class academics who are well published and academically powerful onto which it is possible to transcribe our aspirational fantasies.

Hopefully this chapter has raised questions relating to the complexities of the process of being 'educated out', and addressed an envy and desire that is complexly determined by class and its specific relation to the production of theories on class within Cultural Studies. It has also addressed the role of the personal in the analysis of the lived difference of class, and indeed the production of explanatory frameworks for class as lived difference. It is intended to intervene in the ongoing tensions around 'the most difficult bit of theory' that is an inevitable part of Cultural Studies' past, present and future, through its attempts to figure a better way of talking about class beyond economic determinism. If we continue to acknowledge and rework the tensions between analytic frameworks for understanding class and 'really existing identities' (McRobbie, 1992, p. 354) that are complicatedly determined by class, we might maintain a changing profile of social class within the Cultural Studies' agenda, one that works with the experiential *across* the two fronts of the ontological and the epistemological.

Notes

1. See hooks (1984, 1989), Hull *et al.* (1982) and Parmar (1989a, 1989b).
2. To deploy a maternal metaphor means necessarily problematizing it. 'Mother' can mean so many things: safety, protection, and monstrous, suffocating, separation, irresponsible, something to be resisted and rebelled against. The meanings of the maternal are not fixed. It is differently constructed according to culture, context and time. I do not want to imply fixity to the term in my use of it here. The metaphoric construction of Walkerdine and Steedman's work operating for me as discursive mothers took place at a particular moment in my life, and in relation to a specific body of critical work. I openly acknowledge its specificity to me as a fantasy of the maternal.
3. I am a fan of the made-for-TV genre. I have been giving a lot of thought recently to the pleasures that I get from the narratives of suffering and overcoming that are so much a part of the narrative conventions of the films shown every evening on the satellite channel UK Living. UK Living markets these films as women's pictures. Certainly in their focus on women being trapped in circumstances beyond their control and eventually escaping them, they relate to many women's 'real-life' experiences. They appeal to me in a way that is determined by a knowledge and experience of working-class women's entrapment in 'structures of deprivation and hardship' (Skeggs, 1997a, p. 7) beyond their control, and my longing to see them free of those. They are hopeful, and escapist in the sense that they offer the possibility of something different that might be achieved through struggle.

4. This phrase has been used by Hoggart and Williams and later by Steedman (1986) and Walkerdine (1990) to name the passage of working-class children into grammar schools and higher education as a result of the 1944 Education Act. It is an important part of British Cultural Studies' history, inasmuch as it was founded as a discipline (in part) on the achievements of the 'scholarship boys' and their articulation of the sense of not quite belonging in the academy, of never quite shaking the 'scholarship boy' label. See Hoggart and Williams (1960) for an interesting exchange on these feelings of dislocation.

5. See in particular the essays by Reay (1997), Morley (1997) and Holloway (1997).

6. See Garnham (1997) and Kellner (1997) for a useful analysis of this.

7. Scholars are also salacious. Academic gossip about the private lives of theorists circulates, although not (as yet!) in the form of official publications. We love hearing that Althusser may never have read Marx, and that he pushed his wife out of a window. We may dress it up as something else, but the gossip enables us to access a 'real-life' realm beyond the texts.

8. See Morley (1997), Reay (1997), Tokarczyk and Fay (1993), Walkerdine (1990, 1992) and Steedman (1986).

Bibliography

Dahlgren, P. (1997) 'Cultural studies as a research perspective'. In J. Corner *et al.* (eds), *International Media Research: A Critical Survey*. London: Routledge.

Doane, M. A. (1980) 'The voice in the cinema: the articulation of body and space'. *Yale French Studies*, no. 60 (1980), pp. 33–50.

Ferguson, M. and Golding, P. (eds) (1997) *Cultural Studies in Question*. London: Sage.

Garnham, N. (1997) 'Political economy and the practice of Cultural Studies'. In M. Ferguson and P. Golding (eds), *Cultural Studies in Question*. London: Sage.

Hall, S. (1992) 'Cultural studies and its theoretical legacies'. In L. Grossberg *et al.* (eds), *Cultural Studies*. London: Routledge.

Hall, S. (1996) 'Cultural Studies and the politics of internationalisation: an interview with Stuart Hall and Kuan-Hsing Chen'. In D. Morley and K.-H. Chen (eds), *Stuart Hall: Critical Dialogues in Cultural Studies*. London: Routledge.

Hoggart, R. (1957) *The Uses of Literacy*. London: Penguin.

Hoggart, R. and Williams, R. (1960) 'Working Class Attitudes'. *New Left Review* 1 (January–February), pp. 26–30.

Holloway, W. (1997) 'Finding a voice: on becoming a working class feminist academic'. In P. Mahony and C. Zmroczek, (eds), *Class Matters: 'Working-Class' Women's Perspectives on Social Class*. London: Taylor & Francis.

hooks, b. (1984) *Feminist Theory: From Margin to Center*. Boston: South End Press.

hooks, b. (1989) *Talking Back: Thinking Feminist, Thinking Black*. London: Sheba Feminist Publishers.

Hull, G., Scott, P. and Smith, B. (1982) *But Some of Us Are Brave: Black Women's Studies*. New York: Old West.

Jenkins, H. (1992) *Textual Poachers: Television Fans and Participatory Culture*. New York: Routledge.

Jensen, J. (1992) 'Mapping "us" and "them" in fan research'. In L. Lewis (ed.), *The Adoring Audience: Fan Culture and Popular Media*. London: Routledge.

Kellner, D. (1997) 'Overcoming the divide: Cultural Studies and political economy'. In M. Ferguson and P. Golding (eds), *Cultural Studies in Question*. London: Sage.

Kristeva, J. (1980) 'Motherhood according to Giovanni Bellini'. In T. Gora, A. Jardine and L. S. Roudiez (eds), *Desire in Language: A Semiotic Approach to Literature and Art*. New York: Columbia University Press.

Kuhn, A. (1995) *Family Secrets: Acts of Memory and Imagination*. London: Verso.

Lacey, J. (1997) 'Seeing through happiness. Class, gender and popular film: Liverpool women remember the fifties film musical'. Unpublished doctoral thesis, Goldsmiths College, University of London.

Lewis, L. (1992) *The Adoring Audience: Fan Culture and Popular Media*. London: Routledge.

Mahony, P. and Zmroczek, C. (eds) (1997) *Class Matters: 'Working-Class' Women's Perspectives on Social Class*. London: Taylor & Francis.

McRobbie, A. (1992) 'Post-Marxism and Cultural Studies: a postscript'. In L. Grossberg *et al.* (eds), *Cultural Studies*. London: Routledge.

Morley, L. (1997) 'A class of one's own: woman, social class and the academy'. In P. Mahony and C. Zmroczek (eds), *Class Matters: 'Working-Class' Women's Perspectives on Social Class*. London: Taylor & Francis.

Parmar, P. (1989a) 'Other kinds of dreams'. *Feminist Review* 31, pp. 55–65.

Parmar, P. *et al.* (eds) (1989b) 'The past before us: twenty years of feminism'. Special issue of *Feminist Review*, no. 31.

Probyn, E. (1993a) 'True voices and real people: the problem of the autobiographical in Cultural Studies'. In V. Blundell *et al.* (eds), *Relocating Cultural Studies: Developments in Theory and Research*. London: Routledge.

Probyn, E. (1993b) *Sexing the Self: Gendered Positions in Cultural Studies*. London: Routledge.

Reay, D. (1997) 'The double-bind of the working-class feminist academic: the success of failure or the failure of success?' In P. Mahony and C. Zmroczek (eds), *Class Matters: 'Working-Class' Women's Perspectives on Social Class*. London: Taylor & Francis.

Seiter, E. (1995) 'Mothers watching children watching television'. In B. Skeggs (ed.), *Feminist Cultural Theory: Process and Production.* Manchester: Manchester University Press.

Skeggs, B. (1997a) 'Classifying practices: representations, capitals and recognition'. In P. Mahony and C. Zmroczek (eds), *Class Matters: 'Working-Class' Women's Perspectives on Social Class.* London: Taylor & Francis.

Skeggs, B. (1997b) *Formations of Class and Gender: Becoming Respectable.* London: Sage.

Sparks, C. (1996) 'Stuart Hall, Cultural Studies and Marxism'. In D. Morley and K.-H. Chen (eds), *Stuart Hall: Critical Dialogues in Cultural Studies.* London: Routledge.

Stanley, J. (1995) 'Pain(t) for healing: the academic conference and the classed/ embodied self'. In L. Morley and V. Walsh (eds), *Feminist Academics: Creative Agents for Change.* London: Taylor & Francis.

Steedman, C. (1986) *Landscape for a Good Woman.* London: Virago.

Steinwand, J. (1989) 'History, longing and nostalgia'. In C. Shaw and M. S. Chase (eds), *The Imagined Past: History and Nostalgia.* Manchester: Manchester University Press.

Tokarczyk, M. and Fay, E. (eds) (1993) *Working Class Women in the Academy.* Amherst: University of Massachusetts Press.

Walkerdine, V. (1990) *Schoolgirl Fictions.* London: Verso.

Walkerdine, V. (1992) Inaugural Lecture. Goldsmiths College, University of London.

Walkerdine, V. (1996a) 'Subject to change without notice: psychology, post-modernity and the popular'. In J. Curran, D. Morley and V. Walkerdine (eds), *Cultural Studies and Communications.* London: Arnold.

Walkerdine, V. (ed.) (1996b) 'Social Class'. Special issue of *Feminism and Psychology: An International Journal* 6(3).

Williams, R. (1958) *Culture and Society.* London: Chatto & Windus.

Williams, R. (1973) *The Country and the City.* Oxford: Oxford University Press.

Williams, R. (1976) *Keywords.* London: Fontana.

Williams, R. (1979) *Politics and Letters.* London: New Left Books.

Williams, R. (1989a) *Critical Perspectives* (ed. T. Eagleton). Cambridge: Polity Press.

Williams, R. (1989b) *Resources of Hope: Culture, Democracy, Socialism* (ed. R. Gable). London: Verso.

Williams, R. (1989c) *What I Came to Say* (ed. N. Belton). London: Hutchinson.

3

The Theme That Dare Not Speak Its Name: Class and Recent British Film

Roger Bromley

This chapter will argue that class has become the ghost in the machine of contemporary British politics, the great 'unspoken' which is the source of the fear and anxiety which seems to motivate much current political discourse. Euphemisms, sound-bites and neologisms constitute the vocabularies of welfare debates, law and order controversies ('tough on crime and tough on the causes of crime'), and educational rhetoric (exclusion, failing schools). In almost all cases, agency has effectively been removed from the subjects of these discourses, yet, invariably, almost all social problems are traced back to these same subjects in, what I would call, a process of pathologization and 'causality transference' – irresponsible parenting, poor teachers, truancy, lone mothers, estates from hell and so on. Curfews are proposed, work to welfare projects developed, lone parent benefits are reduced, and homework clubs are set up. These are all part of a symptom-led political programme which refuses to address inequality as the deeply structured and informing process which drives the distribution of power in contemporary Britain. In part, this programme is derived from the principles and practices of nineteenth-century liberalism, overlaid by contemporary American models of social reform. Linked with this is a rhetoric which has evacuated the concept of class, both as an analytical category and as a site of potential agency and empowerment. 'Affluence tests' and social exclusion units are the products of an under-researched and positivist think-tank mentality. The assumption is that change is a process of social and cultural 'engineering', a design problem, which can be solved by expert 'planning' procedures. A basic premise of this kind of thinking is that *adjustment* is the mechanism whereby a condition of relative material affluence can be achieved, a set of essentially middle-class values can be (re)established, and a stakeholder ideology widely absorbed, without any radical attention being paid to the fundamental and systemic causes of inequality, exclusion and dysfunctionalism.

Arguably, one medium where the issue of class is still alive is film. Many recent British films – including those which have achieved blockbuster status – are shaped by processes which have, however implicitly or idiosyncratically, a class-belonging nature. The fact that, in many instances, comedy is the generic form used is, itself, of particular interest. Comedy is, in some ways, an acceptable way of representing class if the situation is contemporary. Other representations of class – for example, in *Regeneration*, the Merchant Ivory films or *Land and Freedom* – are sanctioned by periodization or otherwise distanced in time (Ken Loach is the only current British film-maker using class in an explicit political sense). Although class has almost no political or academic salience in Britain at present, a highly stylized and stereotypical set of class images seem to be marketable as 'recognizably British' codes or markers for export to the USA and elsewhere. Class appears to have a brand or iconic function. Some films, like *Four Weddings and a Funeral*, *The Full Monty* or *Trainspotting*, have been widely consumed in both the UK and the USA, whereas Loach and Mike Leigh's work is regarded seriously in mainland Europe, but has limited distribution in the two countries mentioned.

In an ICM poll commissioned by the Radio Four *Today* programme early in 1998, 55 per cent of the people interviewed identified themselves as 'working class', 12 per cent more than in 1949. In a very general sense, as Andrew Anthony (1998) argues in his article on class in the *Observer*, class is a matter of perception, but it is nevertheless extremely surprising that, at a time when class seems to have almost no political salience and 'middle England' is seen as being virtually synonymous with being middle class, so many people should describe themselves as 'working class'. Maybe on the 150th anniversary of *The Communist Manifesto* (1848), the class antagonisms have become simplified again and society 'is more and more splitting up into two hostile camps' (Marx and Engels, n.d., p. 49). This is not very probable, as the term 'working class' is more likely to be seen as an occupational, gradational descriptor rather than as a relational feature of an antagonism or of a class struggle. Nevertheless, it does suggest perhaps that post-manufacturing capitalism with its emphasis on a 'service' class has proletarianized large sections of the white-collar workforce, especially those occupied by women. The phenomenal growth of 'call centres' is but one manifestation of this. It may also be that deepening insecurities around long-term employment and property ownership have led people to recognize that, notwithstanding their patterns of consumption or occupation, economically they are 'working-class'.

In 1998, as opposed to 1848, exploitation may not be experienced as 'naked, shameless, direct, brutal . . . ' (Marx and Engels, n.d., p. 52), but it is still experienced in some form or other. The four films I wish to concentrate on – *Ladybird, Ladybird* (1994); *Brassed Off* (1996); *The Full Monty* (1997); and *My Name Is Joe* (1998) – all feature class exploitation in different ways. The last three, in particular, deal, directly or indirectly, with the legacies and casualties of three major activities of industrial capitalism: coal mining, steel production and shipbuilding. The extent to which the changing interests of capital have become dominant is indicated by the absences in each film of effective organization at work or outside of work to challenge these. Marx's 'class for itself' is reduced to a sentimental and/or silenced presence. The apparently expanded middle class is an intermittent presence (vestigial only in *The Full Monty*), represented by intermediaries with varying degrees of expertise and authority who are at the class interface on behalf of an increasingly diffuse, impersonal and distanced dominant class. While each of the three films is set in carefully specified *locations*, the 'positively privileged class' (Weber's term) is disembedded and detached from the localized instances of its enterprises or industries. There is still evidence of conflict and of polarizations in the class structure, but the possibilities of class action are narrowed down to non-antagonistic and inward-looking gestures of resistance. In Loach's work and in *Brassed Off*, the existence of 'credentialized' figures who inhabit contradictory class locations by virtue of their role in shielding or deflecting the real patterns of class control, and because of their proximity to the local, substitute for the sources of class exploitation. The alliance of class fractions which represents the dominant power bloc is almost entirely invisible: we catch glimpses of this bloc in a film like *Four Weddings and a Funeral* – although only in its 'decorative' role – but part of the achievement of this bloc has been its ability to slip through the prevailing currencies – visual and narrative – of identity and representation. Dispersed, international, corporate and impersonal, it eludes figuration other than through the odd 'fat cat' caricature or the spectacular, hyper-real grotesque like Robert Maxwell. The power bloc's only consistent mediation is through the parasitic lens of 'celebrity', which focuses on lifestyle rather than on the specifics of its exploitative activities.

All the main political parties in Britain, as well as the state itself, represent the interests of capital, with varying degrees of emphasis and inflection. In the past twenty years, as Edgell and Duke's study of class consciousness and action under Thatcherism has shown (Edgell and Duke, 1991), the balance of power between capital and labour altered in favour of capital, and the 1997 Labour election victory has done, and will do, nothing to change this. If anything, it has confirmed class dealignment in political terms. So, although 55 per cent of people sampled in the ICM poll may identify as working-class, and 25 per cent of children are growing up in homes without a working adult, at the level of *values* the dominant class still dominates. Loach's most recent film focuses upon a fraction of the working class, negatively privileged by the distinctiveness of its poverty and diminished 'market chances' to a point where it is outside these values, but, at the same time, it is powerless to resist them in anything other than episodic, fragmented and often self-destructive ways.

The not-so-hidden injuries of class

In his most recent films, Loach is not claiming to depict *the* working class as such but is focusing upon a social issue or problem confronted by 'negatively privileged' individuals for whom their class position is a crucial dimension of their experience. In a way, the experience is both specific, and generic or emblematic; from the close-up a wider angle is developed on class conflict – in its localized form of the discourses of expertise and legitimation – so-called market choices, exploitation and the pathologization of impoverishment as moral failure. There is no homogeneous working class as such which is capable of representation, it has too many regional, ethnic and gender variations, but Loach is attempting to question how and why a relatively affluent society in the late twentieth century has managed to separate off and marginalize millions of people into what is mediated as an 'underclass' or through the category of 'social exclusion'. The effectiveness of capitalism depends upon its ability to accommodate every 'need', just as long as these 'needs have buying power' (Lyotard, 1992, p. 17). What Loach's films are now concerned with is those without buying power and for whom the familiar objects, social roles and institutions of capitalism have become 'derealized', so much so that realism as a mode of representation – with its unity, identity and secure closures – is no longer a viable option, hence the emphasis on those extremes and excesses which are no longer accessible to a credible meaning or 'communicative consensus' (Lyotard, 1992, p. 13). In *My Name Is Joe*, buying power is confined to the 'needs' of the addict for whom drugs and alcohol are the only means of decoding the images, syntax and sequences of a destabilized and derealized 'reality': a source of terror and suffering for figures who discover 'the *lack of reality* in reality' (Lyotard, 1992, p. 19). In *Ladybird, Ladybird, Land and Freedom* (1995) and *Carla's Song* (1996), class conflict and an exploitation-centred conception of class are given an historical and international articulation. Of contemporary directors working in English, only the American John Sayles has a similar preoccupation.

Ken Loach's unique contribution to British cinema can be summed up very easily – it is characterized by a consistently political analysis inflected through a particular aesthetics of film-making. He has developed a highly crafted and stylized mode of working which is marked by an apparent lack of style. This apparent artlessness is produced by a sophisticated grasp of character development and episodic narrative drive. This is especially true of the recent films which are distinguished by his trademark cutting and editing techniques, framing and shot composition, a particular use of script combined with improvisation, off-camera direction and distinctive performance styles.

His work began at a time when politics and class had a far wider reference and resonance than they currently do. Class has almost disappeared as a political category – certainly as part of orthodox political rhetoric, as it is rarely articulated in the sphere of party politics. The Office for National Statistics has just replaced the existing (since 1911) six categories of class (four of which were working-class) with a new seven-point scale, four of which are middle-class, three working-class. The Office says: 'Definitions like manual and non-manual have stopped being relevant. We have moved towards a service-based economy, and our social classifications have to adapt to that.' There is also an eighth category which has received little attention: that of non-workers and long-term unemployed. It is this category to which most of Loach's characters belong.

Without realizing it, of course, Loach's early work began to trace the beginnings of a process which, at the time, affected a relatively small number of people, and has now extended to whole zones of British cities and towns, particularly the inner cities. I am speaking of de-industrialization and de-skilling, casualization, insecure work, an informal economy, unemployment and pauperization. Whether this has produced an 'underclass' or 'zones of social exclusion', it is nevertheless true that, relatively speaking, it is a lot more expensive to survive if you are poor without access to bulk-purchasing, credit arrangements, direct debit facilities, a bank account and low interest loans.

The earlier productions alternated between a concern with exemplary social victims and the dramatization of forms of collective industrial and political action which, even if historical, were given a contemporary resonance. Post-Thatcher, the political culture of the working class has been partly destroyed and Loach has gone back to Spain in the 1930s, or out of Britain to the Nicaragua of the 1980s, for an exploration of a political culture based on collective action and forms of solidarity, but also crucially weakened by divisive internal conflicts and betrayals. Otherwise, the 1990s films have focused upon a range of exemplary social victims – exemplary in the sense that, for example in *My Name Is Joe*, in every other street in this area of Glasgow and in every town and city, there is a Liam and a Sabine (perhaps also a Joe).

I used the word 'victims', but Loach's recent films also attempt to give value and voice to those who are often denied both value and voice. He does this by immersion in the most minute details of his subject matter. The films are mosaics, episodic narratives, fragments of which are seen in close-up and magnified to a point of deliberate excess where we see not just case studies, outlines or abstract statistics, but in-lines and the close grain of lives lived under impossible pressures. As Loach has said: 'the essence is always to find the humanity in whatever situation you're exploring, and to find moments of resistance and moments of dilemma and choice in which there's inherent drama, inherent struggle' (Fuller, 1998, p. 115). The films *are* about choices; however, as Marx said, people make choices but not under the circumstances of their own choosing. To simplify for a moment, this is perhaps what the new seven/eight point scale classification is about: the top four are those with some power over their own circumstances (with, that is, economic, social and cultural capital), the bottom three/four are the disempowered and choiceless. He is not sentimental about these under-represented lives (see, for contrast, *The Full Monty* or *Brassed Off*) nor are they merely victims, as there is resilience, resourcefulness, wit, irony and self-mockery, loyalties and love – even residual efforts to be heroic in unheroic conditions. The consistent focus is on the human cost.

For all this, *My Name Is Joe* also shows us, not just the people fighting back, albeit in piecemeal and desperate fashion, but also the divisiveness of a violent subculture in which people fight the people fighting back. For all its narrative urgency, the film causes us to pause and reflect on the silences and the absences. The film is set in an area of Glasgow (with the highest incidence of intravenous drug use in Europe), a city with strong political cultural traditions, a powerful, skilled and organized working class: shipbuilders to the world – the site of Red Clydeside. These solidarities and collectivities have gone, they merely shadow the present. The solidarities have been thinned down to personal commitments, insecure and highly conditional: the infantilized males of the unemployed football team, the young couple (Liam and Sabine) rendered childlike by their fear, need and dependency. Sarah and Joe virtually 'mother' and 'father' these marginalized people, yet both have their own vulnerabilities, Joe, in particular, a recovering alcoholic haunted by the memories of his own, alcohol-fuelled violence. *My Name Is Joe* suggests a minimal, stripped-down identity, almost like a young child's early utterance. At least the footballers, however bad as a team, *are* a team; they inhabit spaces (but note, not grass surfaces) snatched from within a culture of poverty. The women lack even these spaces, they are rarely afforded any socialized outlets, there are no exits, no places to run to (Sarah is almost the only resource left for some). Nor do we ever see the 1990s Glasgow, the refurbished and affluent European city of culture. The editing and camerawork shut down, narrow and confine the spaces available into tight frames, soulless streets, increasingly ill-lit and enclosed and enclosing interiors: these are both material conditions and metaphors of inner impoverishments. Even when we see lochs, mountains and green spaces they are shot in a context of the negative, desperate and highly conditional.

The point of all this is that poverty is not just about being short of money. Loach takes material hardship, combines it with the black market in drugs, a closed door on education, a killed-off community (just lean streets and shabby interiors), a narrowed-down space for love and other human relationships, and shows us the hidden injuries and brutalities of class in the present – the physical, emotional, social and spiritual damage. The principal reason why Sarah breaks up with Joe is not that, ultimately, as a health visitor she reverts to her class belonging, nor only that he has run drugs for McGowan in order to pay off Liam's debts, but that he accepts an extra £500 from McGowan 'for himself', and buys Sarah earrings and a ring from this profit from a petty capitalist enterprise which is helping to destroy the very children she is charged with caring for. There are no simple answers, the film does not end, but *pauses* – on that pause we reflect on the absences and the unspoken, and on the possibilities of a political culture that does not look back to disappeared solidarities, or sideways to market forces, but which actively remakes, organizes and renews the potential of resistances but upon different kinds of foundations.

Loach has used Glasgow twice recently as a location, not just for its 'gritty northernness' but also because it represents a microcosm of contemporary forms of marginalization: 'There in Glasgow where we filmed it is very hard and it has the highest incidence of intravenous drug use in Europe. A lot of the people there are in a very bad shape. But, as you'd expect, there are also people there performing acts of heroism on a daily basis, just trying to make something viable happen' (Fuller, 1998, p. 110).

Ladybird, Ladybird (1994) is based on a true story, but it is a work of fiction and not a documentary. Loach's own distinction between the two modes is illuminating:

> Fiction is about more than a political analysis ... Fiction is about the expression or the lines on somebody's face when something happens. It's about the way light falls in a room. It's about the way people walk down the street after a lifetime's work. It's about how they live in their rooms, how they've got the food they put on the table. It's about the fabric of life, the product of all those details of the way we are. Politics is implicit in all that, but it can't be dragged out of it. (Fuller, 1998, p. 114)

At the outset of the film Maggie, a Liverpudlian living in London, is presented as a woman with four children, all with different fathers. She meets Jorge, a Paraguayan political exile, in a pub and they form a relationship. From this outline, Maggie would appear to be the feckless, irresponsible, sexually profligate single mother of contemporary media urban myth. The film uses flashbacks, and a series of set-pieces – an abused childhood, battering by a common-law husband, a fire in the refuge which injures her children, court appearances, the serving of a place of safety order and the seizing of one of her babies from the hospital – to build up an in-line profile which places in context Maggie's mood swings, her anger, pain, violence and deep love for her children, and the cycle of abuse and poverty in which she is enmeshed. She and Jorge are both displaced persons in many senses. In Paraguay, the country with the greatest disparity between wealthy and poor, Jorge worked in a home for people who needed shelter, witnessed the daily violence of a brutal regime in which the rich and powerful seized his family's land, and recognized that it was dangerous to speak out or to seek to alleviate suffering because, as he says, suffering has a job to do for government. In Paraguay, glimpses are afforded of a more visible power bloc and a situation in which antagonistic class relations are more transparent. The power bloc has not yet disappeared behind impersonal, dispersed, international corporate forms nor has it negotiated itself a set of hegemonic values. Loach is not arguing crudely that the Paraguayan and British dominant class alliances are the same, but Jorge's presence opens a window on a *structural* continuum of power which includes the invisible, absent and 'unrepresentable' forms of advanced capitalism and its more palpable third world military incarnations.

Maggie lives a life under siege. She is never able to slow down, relax or find a language of conciliation. We see her endlessly restless, constantly smoking, in perpetual motion – 'on the run' both from herself, and all that has contributed towards her complex situation, and from the 'enemy' – the authorities who have taken her children into care. Although she does not articulate it as such, Maggie is embattled, at the centre of a class war in which she is seen as 'inadequate', living in a series of abusive relationships (as if by choice), a 'loser' who is unable to provide her children with a stable environment. By officialdom she is constructed as though she has the power of agency and choice – the means of the 'positively privileged'. In the words of the judgement which confirms the place of safety order on the second child she has with Jorge, she is a woman of low intellect and little self-control, with a number of partners, who has put her children at the risk of violence. She is deemed to be beyond help and will never change. Seen from the perspective of the case conference and the court hearing, and from the point of view of social workers subject to instant media vilification if a child is placed at risk, the decisions seem justifiable on the basis of the 'objective' evidence.

What the film does most effectively is to juxtapose the credential-based experts (social workers, police, the judiciary and the medical profession) who act as 'brokers' for a class-based system of deeply structured inequality, with the relatively isolated and pathologized individual, 'failed' mother (with all the ideological ballast that carries in a patriarchal society) who is powerless, choiceless and 'illiterate' or inarticulate in the 'dialect' of the authorities. I use the word 'dialect' deliberately – idiolect may be even more precise – because one of the central contrasts in the film is between the spoken and body languages of bureaucracy and that of the embattled object of its attention. The experts of the new 'intermediate' class operate within a discourse of professionalism which, in some ways, is dependent upon both servicing and policing the 'negatively privileged'. Loach carefully stages the rhetorical differences and distances, the gaps in register and discourse, and the slow, controlled reasonableness of the body language of officialdom (masculine 'reason' confronts feminine 'emotion'). Terms like 'rehabilitation', 'assess' and 'statutory duty' all legitimize the actions of class brokerage – the 'reality' of capital – and transfer the problem to the victim. These very same terms represent precisely the 'derealization' for Maggie which was discussed earlier. The film's unasked questions – such as who was responsible for the leaking roof and defective wiring in the women's refuge, and whose family values left Maggie in an abusing home environment – are both articulate silences and the fabric of Maggie's 'real'.

There is an interesting moment when Maggie accompanies her solicitor to her first court hearing. Their dress is identical. In an act of professional mimicry, Maggie leaves her angry, passionate body language behind and dresses in the clothes of the expert: a semiotic 'truce'. Surrounded by expert testimony which grossly misrepresents her, she reverts to her own demotic, becomes 'irrational' and runs from the court, turning on her solicitor in the process (in her later court appearance she resumes the dress of her 'reality'). What Loach shows is that, in the end, the very system of representation (discursive 'realism') – plaintiff, defendant, solicitor, barrister, judge – even when it acts on behalf of the 'negatively privileged', merely serves to legitimize a hegemonic discursive regime which, in impersonal form, is based on class interests and power. In the absence of the real class 'enemy' which has delegated limited powers to managers, experts and the 'credentialized', Maggie's anger is relatively directionless and is randomly distributed towards social workers, the legal profession, the police (who, when appropriate, exercise their right to the monopoly of legitimate violence), neighbours, her adult relatives, Jorge and, ultimately, herself – but never, the film stresses, her children for whom she has unconditional love. Her anger and frustration are the products of love and powerlessness: there is no organized network or analysis, economic, political or professional, to which she has access.

What Maggie and, indeed, some critics 'misrecognize' is the 'persons' of the social workers, health visitors and so on, which she conflates with the *structures* they operate within and through. In themselves, they are relatively low-level white-collar functionaries, but they are on the class front-line, charged with delivering the policies and processes which, in part, are designed to obscure and misrepresent the 'naked, shameless, direct, brutal exploitation' of dominant class interests. They are the manifest, indirect and relatively powerless bearers of legitimation. Like Sarah in *My Name Is Joe*, they are caught in their own contradictory class locations, and are often deeply committed to supporting and defending their 'clients'. The point is made in the post-fiction, postscript caption to the film which tells us that 'Maggie' and 'Jorge' had three more children, all of whom still live with them.

Yeah. Like skateboards

The other two films which I wish to consider both operate within the same broad territory as Loach but use the forms of comedy. *Brassed Off* (1996; directed by Mark Herman) was a Channel Four film production. It used a popular, populist even, format with two or three star names and a host of British character actors. It is situated at a moment of closure of one of the Yorkshire coalfields, and works within a number of staple and formulaic conventions of working-class representation: regional, masculine, industrial, brass band. A number of rapid establishing shots – miners' helmets, light and darkness, the pithead, communal showers, men laughing and joking together, placards opposing pit closure – combined with the brass band soundtrack situate the themes of the film with the opening credits: a traditional way of life under threat.

The primary conflict is produced by the threatened pit closure and the imminent redundancy offer, but there are a number of secondary conflicts which are developed in sub-plots – marital, romantic, generational, gendered – related to the symbiosis of the pit and the brass band. Both are seen to be facing closure as there is no logic to having one without the other. To fit in with the comedy format, there is a gradual shift in scale and focus which effectively makes the band the principal issue: family and gender stand in for broader class conflicts which are only sketchily articulated. The band is seen as the cultural embodiment of the history and traditions of a community and an industry, its harmonies a class-specific form of solidarity in the face of a dangerous and exploitative occupation. This is pointed up by the way the band rehearsals are intercut with union–management meetings, and the different perspectives and distortions which various band members bring to the closure issue. In the initial stages, Danny, the conductor, is out of 'synch' with the rest of the band in so far as for him the closure is a minor issue compared with regional and national band competitions.

In the circumstances created after the 1984/85 national miners' strike, the miners are divided and insecure, the union is seen as weak and complicit with management, and the women picketing round the clock against closure are seen as 'pissing in the wind'. A number of slippages and displacements occur which trivialize the closure issue and render it simply as a backdrop. The band becomes a symbol for both the pit and the workforce, with the divisions and the emasculations of the latter being reflected in the poor performances at rehearsal and in competition. Part of the sentimentality of the film lies in the fact that, in its early stages, the only accomplished performer is Gloria, the granddaughter of a 'legendary' local miner but also, unknown to the other players, working for management. The bandsmen's sexism and vanity is lightly mocked when some of them decide to stay on in the band because of this very attractive young woman.

Family tensions and break-up reflect the internal conflicts in the band and the pit. In the context of insecurity, weakened leadership and relative isolation, people turn in on themselves. One example is provided by Harry – the euphonium player – and his wife Rita, who is an activist in the women against pit closures group. She says to Harry: 'Ten years ago before the strike you were full of fight, packed full of passion; now you just do nowt, just blow your bloody trumpet.' His response is: 'At least people listen to us.' It is an isolated exchange, a rare cameo in which the politics of the situation are foregrounded, but it is in a minor key in an otherwise depoliticized narrative. Phil, Danny's son, faced by mounting debts and loan sharks is forced to moonlight as a clown, Mr Chuckles. On the verge of a breakdown, torn by loyalties divided between his father and family, his furniture seized by 'bailiffs', he cracks up at a children's event: 'I'm a miner; you remember them, love: dinosaurs, dodos, miners.'

In attempting too much the film dilutes much of its political analysis – which is broad brush and gestural – as its primary articulation is at the level of individuals and families. It does show some of the human costs of closure in a number of powerful and moving scenes: Phil's breakdown and attempted suicide; the silence and funereal pace of the miners, with heads down and in 'mourning' after the 4:1 vote for redundancy; Danny's collapse and subsequent illness; the playing of 'Danny Boy' in the darkness of the hospital grounds with each player lit up by a miner's helmet lamp; and, above all, Danny's Albert Hall speech in which he brings to national attention the systematic and inhuman destruction of a community by Thatcherism. However, these are disaggregated and chart the mortality of a particular class struggle – masculine, industrial, obsolescent – by focusing on its symptoms. Management, cynical and self-serving, stands in for the class interests of capital but these are confined to its localized instance. Gloria steps outside of her complicit, credentialized role in management, resigns and hands over her severance money to fund the band's visit to the Albert Hall. Her class mobility gives her a power of choice which is exercised positively, whereas the workers are seen to have no choices, but it is her function as the 'love interest' – the Grimley 'Juliet' – which really motivates her actions, not any form of political understanding.

The raw material of the film – the pit closure, the weakened and divided solidarities, the pain and despair of redundancy, the self-contempt of scabbing and the destruction of community – has a profound and moving impact, but this is eroded by the manipulative and sentimental magical resolution in fantasy, reconciliation, victory and harmony. Defeated workforce, victorious band (the workers, defeated, will never be united: only in a brass band!). It is the latter which constitutes the film's dominant meanings. The playing of 'Land of Hope and Glory' outside the Houses of Parliament sends a number of mixed messages – it is triumphant but not ironic. The wake takes over from the funeral – the wicked witch (Thatcherism) is dead. The captioned postscript undercuts the comedy–fantasy to a certain extent: 'Since 1984, there have been 140 pit closures in Great Britain at the cost of nearly a quarter of a million jobs.' *Brassed Off* is a valedictory film, an epitaph and obituary for one of the most powerful sectors of the British male working-class movement and, as such, for all of its sentimentalization of class as essentially part of the recent past, is nevertheless a powerful tribute, impossible to watch without tears at times, to a dying way of life. Its formal unity, identity, populism and closure suggest no continuities, but an end-stopped, terminus film. It is a period piece, almost a costume drama, working within a long-established, descriptive and commodified cinematic frame of reference. For all the apparent signifiers of class, class remains essentially an absent content, evacuated from both work and outside of work as a mobilizing factor in organization.

Brassed Off was a commercially successful and popular film but had nothing of the phenomenal international impact of *The Full Monty*. The fact that the former was retitled *Thank You, Mrs Thatcher* in Italy, and the American version was shortened by cutting out the union meetings, underlines the point I have made above about its terminus, political costume-drama nature. The same director's *Little Voice* (1999) may have more of an international impact, partly because it is a Hollywood production, but also because of its highly eclectic package and re-mix of traditional working-class cultural forms at the level of theme and style – a veritable 'sampling' of the seaside holiday, a *tableau vivant* of figures from picture postcards, music hall acts and one-liners, petty capitalists, pigeon-fancying, cartoons. Blended in with this is a sense of the Americanization of popular culture, particularly of cars and music, knowing caricatures and stereotypes powerfully overplayed, a series of gay icon torch singers, a Romeo and Juliet love interest, pantomime, fairy-tale and fable, and a 'cod' Freudian sub-plot. *Little Voice* is an extended cameo, and somewhere inside it there is a sense of gender and class exploitation plus the use of entertainment as a means of class mobility, but despite some wonderful music and superb performances it is another 'end-of-pier' snapshot. It is a form of mock realism, over the top and nostalgic but, essentially, as Michael Caine sings: 'It's Over' – and he is not just referring to his own career.

The Full Monty (1997; directed by Peter Cattaneo) deals with the aftermath of the closure of the steelworks in Sheffield. A promotional film from 1970 is shown over the credits which speaks of a steel city, with night clubs, a city on the move, the beating heart of Britain's industrial north, the jewel in Yorkshire's crown, with 90,000 men employed in steel production. This is immediately and rather obviously contrasted with a derelict steel mill in the present day, rusted and obsolete, with the works band in rehearsal the only trace left, except for two former steelworkers 'liberating' a girder. Like *Brassed Off*, it is also a terminus film, the comedy format works with the notion of closure, but it is situated in a post-industrial context with an emphasis on gender politics. Peter Cattaneo says in the foreword to the published screenplay: 'Issues of male identity, gender roles, body politics and the effects of long-term unemployment are dealt with . . . ' (Beaufoy, 1997, p. vii).

A crisis in masculinity is linked to questions of fathering, the infantilization of unemployed males and sexual impotence. A number of traditional male attitudes to women are subject to criticism within a fairly limited framework. For example, women using men's toilets (all that are available in a working men's club) is seen as emasculating, as is the use of the club for a women-only event. The fact that the event is the Chippendales may mean a reversal of the male gaze, but the women are still passive and spectatorial, and paying. To a certain extent, and in different guises, each of the six principal male figures – one married, one divorced, one middle-aged, two gay and one black (unironically, politically correct) – has given up struggling or, in the case of Gerald, the former supervisor, is living out a 'mock' employment fantasy.

Implicitly, the film raises questions – neglected by Loach and Mark Herman – about how much the traditional working-class movement was based around unreflective assumptions about masculinity, the separation of public and private spheres, and the exclusion of women from work-based and non-work-based economic and political organizations. However, in appropriating the slogan 'the personal is political', the political has only a muted presence throughout. In the 1990s a major shift in employment patterns has taken place, with almost half the workforce now female, mostly in casualized and proletarianized forms of white-collar work, relatively low-paid, as well as a decline in traditional trade union membership. What the film does not acknowledge is the distinctive impact of race and ethnicity upon the shape of this 'negatively privileged' class.

Taking this shift in employment patterns, *The Full Monty* explores a series of role-reversals, with women beginning to enter spaces previously occupied by men and sometimes at the expense of men. The male responses are seen to be, variously, depressive, suicidal, child-like and regressive, self-pitying or fantasy-adjusted. As the writer of the screenplay points out, 'literally and metaphorically men were being told to shape up, get fit, get smart, and get sexy' (Beaufoy, 1997, p. x). One of the strengths of the film lies in the way which it acknowledges shifting gender roles and the need to confront traditional expectations by reinventing identities. Recognizing and valorizing gay sexuality is one such example, as is taking part in a 'feminine' activity like dancing; the latter is recuperated and re-masculinized, however, by the 'Arsenal offside trap' movement. This reinvention is also one of the weaknesses of the film as its foregrounding of gender and identity politics effectively removes class as a dimension of analysis, which means that the interests of capital in de-skilling, down-sizing and privatizing remain an 'absent content'. The only response is individual enterprise, finding a niche and increasing your market chances, although these six men do this in ensemble fashion, carving out new, but not necessarily gender exclusive, forms of bonding. What is not considered is how long the new self-respect and reflexivity will survive the sell-by date of their gimmick.

Initially, the men are fatalistic, resigned to the scrapheap (there are several puns referring to their former occupation in metal), 'genetic muta-tion', 'extincto', eclipsed by women, dinosaurs, doomed not to exist 'except in zoos', or, as Dave says, 'like skateboards'. Only occasional glimpses of their now superannuated skills-based, craft identities show through. They are men who have lived through and defined themselves by work, the illusory identity of alienated labour exploited, whilst their advanced skills were needed for a particular phase of the needs of capital. Ironically, and it is something the film makes nothing of, they come to be defined though their 'commodifiable' bodies, as women have been for centuries.

Home, previously an instrumental resource, now becomes a place of confinement or, for Gaz, exclusion. In his case, also, assumptions about the automatic right to the occasional, male-based activity of fathering are thrown into question. Even those in work, like Dave and Lomper, are security guards, one in a 'feminized' retail outlet, the other in a disused steelworks. The fact that in the final scene the men strip off security guard uniforms is a significant comment on one of the most parasitic growth industries of the past two decades – low-paid, non-unionized men employed to 'secure' inequality in the interests of capital (it is also, of course, about stripping off traditional male body insecurities). The role of the former supervisor, Gerald, is important because he derived his inter-mediate class identity from *not* being working class, distanced and detached by his quasi-managerial agency. His objective proximity to the people he supervised is made manifest by his unemployment, and a shift from surveillance to teaching as the group's 'choreographer and ballet master'. There is also a form of residual empowerment for the group in appropriating the disused steelworks for learning and rehearsing their new skills of movement, group cohesion and co-ordination. The use of these skills is more important in its modelling role than in their immediate application perhaps, but the film places all the emphasis on the latter. In the background of the rehearsals, however, the landscape of industrializa-tion is distanced, emptied and stilled. There is little sign of a reinvented identity in the form of 90,000 new jobs.

The Full Monty is, to date, the highest grossing British film of all time. It is extremely funny and developed from a witty conceit – the meta-phorical layerings of the idea of stripping. It demonstrates the need to deconstruct a whole set of masculine ideologies and anxieties about women and sexuality, and, as such, marks a growth in reflexivity and maturity. In the process of recovery and growth, however, the women remain secondary and shadowy, and having reinvented themselves the men have renewed their value, self-esteem and, for all the female gaze in the final scene (actually it is not even an all-female audience), are back where they belong, centre stage in the working men's club, off the hook perhaps and in control, even. The men are no longer marginalized in their own club (as in the opening scenes), nor are they laughed at, but laughed with. The final staging and choreography has been supervised and orchestrated by the men from start to finish, and there is even a parodic element in the use of the ageing macho Tom Jones. The decision to do 'the full monty' is made by the men on their own. This is all very different from female stripping: the men are back, forgiven, exposed in all senses of the word, *but on their terms*. Class is back there in the steel mills, rusted and obsolete. The unemployed 'boys' have become men again; once, and once only they will, because they now can, show their manhood in a public space again; they've got their ball(s) back!

While this chapter has referred to class as a determining absence in British politics and as a significant, if extremely ambiguous, presence in recent British cinema, it was not intended to reduce all the films to a crude, homogeneous formula. The differences are as important as the similarities, but it has been argued that class in recent British film, while it may be dismissed, laughed at as a 'peculiarity' of the British, localized or sentimentalized, deserves to be treated in ways which see it as much more than an obsolete economic classification, but rather as a condition of, what Raymond Williams called, a 'pre-emergence'. While appearing to be addressing residual characteristics of class, the films are, at the same time perhaps, indicative of emergent symptoms of the contemporary which are 'active and pressing but not yet fully articulated' (Williams, 1977, p. 126). While I have described class analysis, rather than class signifiers, as an 'absent content' in *Brassed Off* and *The Full Monty*, Loach's films were seen as being increasingly concerned with the marginalization of those without choices or buying power. This condition is an effect of the changing interests of capital in contemporary Britain, and of a shift of the balance between capital and labour. In recognizing the changing configurations of class, Loach is also concerned with the formal and representational challenge presented by a dominant power bloc that lacks visibility, presence and 'narratability'. While once there was a mill owner living in his mansion on the hill, today power is dispersed across many global mansions, often virtual; conceivable but unpresentable.[1] One of the triumphs of the ruling class is to avoid figuration or representation, and all that Loach is capable of doing is developing a technique of *allusion*: gaps, pauses and silences which point beyond the mediated, and class intermediaries, to the unpresentable absence. His films are formal attempts to represent, not the ideological currencies of 'reality', but the process of 'derealization' itself. In the process, his films are not realist but question the rules which govern popular images and narratives.

The challenge is not only aesthetic, but one which Cultural Studies itself faces. An over-concentration on the epiphenomena of culture has left the field ill-equipped to undertake an effective class analysis of the 'bigger picture', the deeper and wider cultural impact of violence, inequality, health and life expectations, educational disadvantage, patterns of subsistence consumption (not just a matter of lifestyle), inadequate housing, differential buying power, and impoverishment as forms of exploitation which serve the interests of capital and its class alliance power bloc. Additionally, of course, the field will also need to develop new models and definitions for undertaking an analysis appropriate to the changing configurations of class in contemporary society.

Note

1. This brief discussion of the 'unpresentable' is freely adapted from Lyotard (1992), pp. 20–4.

Bibliography

Anthony, A. (1998) 'What about the workers?', *Observer*, Review Section, 13 December 1998, pp. 2–3.

Beaufoy, S. (1997) *The Full Monty*. Eye, Suffolk: Screen Press Books.

Edgell, S. (1993) *Class*. London: Routledge.

Edgell, S. and Duke, V. (1991) *A Measure of Thatcherism: A Sociology of Britain*. London: HarperCollins.

Fuller, G. (ed.) (1998) *Loach on Loach*. London: Faber & Faber.

Lyotard, J.-F. (1992) *The Postmodern Explained to Children*. London: Turnaround.

Marx, K. and Engels, F. (n.d., first published 1848) *Manifesto of the Communist Party*. Moscow: Foreign Languages Publishing House.

Williams, R. (1977) *Marxism and Literature*. Oxford: Oxford University Press.

4

'This Is About Us, This Is Our Film!' Personal and Popular Discourses of 'Underclass'

Chris Haylett

Taking things personally

> We are people who are used to being represented as problematic. We are the long-term, benefit-claiming, working-class poor, living through another period of cultural contempt. We are losers, no hopers, low life, scroungers. Our culture is yob culture. The importance of welfare provisions to our lives has been denigrated and turned against us: we are welfare dependent and our problems won't be solved by giving us higher benefits. We are perverse in our failure to succeed, dragging our feet over social change, wanting the old jobs back, still having babies instead of careers, stuck in outdated class and gender moulds. We are the 'challenge' that stands out above all others, the 'greatest social crisis of our times'.[1]

I am the second daughter of a working-class girl of the 1950s who didn't pass her eleven-plus, and didn't then know why. My mother never did 'escape' from her class. I think she wanted something that wasn't on offer. She went on to have four children, to raise them on her own and to write poems. I am one of those children, brought up on benefits, on council estates, comprehensively educated at state schools. My politics are not derived from workplace, region or formal education. They are the politics of my home, of growing up through the 1980s on council estates in the south of England, talking back at the telly, sitting in waiting rooms of the Department of Social Security, and watching my mum go in and out of hospital. My class positionality is not only about a lack of money (although economically things aren't good enough), and it does not seek 'inclusion' to things middle class. In some respects my politics are private: a politics of finding pleasure in certain kinds of music and films as cultural affirmation of who I am, or imagine myself to be in relation to others. In other respects they are quite traditional: a politics of pride and anger, of personal and collective memory, a defence against division and against attack. I regard the contemporary moment of 'underclass' politics as such a moment of attack. My use of the term 'underclass' refers to a discourse whose language and ideas cannot, in practice, be separated from their material referent. Problems with the terminology of 'underclass' are well rehearsed with regard to its ideological motivation and its structural integrity as a residual class location (see for example Gans, 1993). 'Underclass' is generally held to refer to social groups at the base of the working class whose characteristics are those of long-term unemployment or highly irregular employment, single parenthood and criminality, where some or all of those characteristics are tendentially if not causally related.[2] This personal introduction is a situated starting-point to a discussion about contemporary representations of 'underclass' by someone who takes them personally and knows differently. In this chapter I'm going to talk about *knowing differently* via two films whose representations of working-class poverty contest some dominant meanings of 'underclass'. The chapter has two parts, the first of which is a critique of culturally dominant ways of seeing and knowing poor working-class people. In the dominant discourse of 'underclass', poor, working-class identities and places emerge through an aggregation of empirical characteristics about family, crime and work, inferentially linked to group attitudes and behaviours. The 'non-working' single mother and the young, unemployed male are central figures in this cultural landscape of amoral, anti-social council estate living. Such reductive typologies of identity and place could be met by an attempt to issue replacement 'truths' about these *sorts* of people and places. This chapter presents a case for refusing such a quest for truths about the working-class poor, and argues for an epistemology based on personal and popular experiences that are both real and imagined. My personal readings of two films – Mathieu Kassovitz's *Hate* (*La Haine*) (1995)[3] and Ken Loach's *Ladybird, Ladybird* (1994) – are presented as two such narratives.

The second part of the chapter discusses the relation between working-class subjectivity and collectivity in the two films. Their filmic space is presented as part of a popular cultural cartography which opens up different spaces of understanding about the working-class poor. 'Under-class' discourse is made up of more than one view and more than one knowledge: it makes multiple subject positions available, although they are not equally accessible, powerful or esteemed. Nevertheless, the discourse of 'underclass' is not 'one thing' that has negative 'effects'. It is partly constituted by representations which make positive subject positions available to the working-class poor and new understandings available to mainstream audiences. I am re-presenting *Hate* and *Ladybird, Ladybird* as popular, resistant discourses of 'underclass' based on subjugated knowledges of working-class poverty.

The stories told in the films are refracted through my own readings of them, based on identifications, recognitions and resonances that I am presenting as my part of a collective story of class and poverty. It is a purposefully strategic presentation of lives which are deemed to require exposure and social intervention in the contemporary period. The idea of the film as 'strategic defence' refutes others that have variously found favour in Cultural Studies: the idea that politically left-wing cultural representations habitually produce fictions of working-class heroism or solidarity, a kind of intense wishful thinking, or that they most readily settle on the idea of a working class politically destroyed by the dumbing diversions of popular culture. Mythologies of class produced within popular culture can instead be seen as a powerful strategic resource, part of the emotional and psychological struggles over class identity. My discussion of these films, as stories of working-class heroism, is a political attempt to redistribute some ideas about the lives of people represented as 'underclass'.

Ways of seeing and knowing the working-class poor

The underclass is not a degree of poverty; it does not refer to the poorest of the poor. It is a type of poverty: it covers those who no longer share the norms and aspirations of the rest of society, who have never known the traditional two parent family, who are prone to abuse drugs and alcohol at the earliest opportunity, who do poorly at school and who are quick to resort to disorderly behaviour and crime. (*Sunday Times*, 23 May 1995, p. 3)

During the 1990s the idea of a British 'underclass' emerged through a motif of decay and dereliction rotting the social fabric. Its production can be located in the realms of press and broadcasting media, often in relation to other authoritative representations in political discourse and academia. These productions exist as a visual regime of meaning, as particular ways of seeing people and places cast as 'other'. Visions of 'underclass' have become part of the personal, public and political imaginations of British culture in the 1990s. These are presented as entertainment in crime-genre television programmes, as CCTV evidence in factual documentaries or news items, and as the backdrop for announcements of new social policy initiatives. These kinds of representations are based upon reductive characterizations whose hallmark is a stamp of class difference as division from the rest of 'us'. This is a discourse of familial disorder and dysfunction; of dangerous masculinities and dependent femininities; of antisocial behaviour; and of moral and ecological decay. As a way of crystallizing a number of social, economic and cultural issues into one, 'underclass' is primarily about the problematic nature of long-term 'welfare dependent' groups in relation to the rest of society.

In *Outlaw Culture* (1994) bell hooks talks about representations which limit the possibilities of what it may mean to be poor and she puts forward the idea of an alternative regime of representation around poverty which would refuse worthlessness, shame, material status and the idea of perpetual aspiration:

> When intellectuals, journalists or politicians speak about nihilism and the despair of the underclass they do not link those states to representations of poverty in the mass media ... To change the face of poverty so that it becomes once again, a site for the formation of values, of dignity and integrity, as any other class positionality in this society, we would need to intervene in existing systems of representation. (hooks, 1994, pp. 169–71)

Hate and *Ladybird, Ladybird* act as such an intervention in the dominant regime of representation around working-class poverty.

Should we 'tell it the way it is'?

The study of relationships between class, culture and film has been most developed within Cultural Studies as an interest in the classed realities *produced* in films and the class nature of their *consumption*. Questions like 'how is the working class represented?', 'how do those representations relate to working-class histories and experiences?' and 'how do working-class people understand these films?' predominate. The nature of such work involves closely analysing text and filmic languages, and various kinds of 'audience research' to draw out sociocultural meanings.[4] Such prior-itization of evidence in the study of discursive meaning is rigidly tied to categorical notions of text and context, viewer and viewed. It holds the idea that with enough of the 'right sort' of evidence then the meaning, status and effect of representations can be 'known'. The rhetoric of evidence can only be a *claim* to knowledge, an *idea* which works to hierarchize particular sorts of meaning as more or less significant (where the subjective, personal or individual are less). That notion ignores the social aspects both of subjectivity and of the interpretative process itself.

Both *Hate* and *Ladybird, Ladybird* are explicitly concerned with the social significance of individual situations. Both deal with the character-istics of the dominant discourse of 'underclass'. Loach's *Ladybird, Ladybird* deals directly with social issues of state intervention by welfare professionals into the parenting practices of poor, single mothers, while Kassovitz's *Hate* deals with criminal justice issues of state intervention by the police into the lives of unemployed young men on 'problematic' public housing estates. Both directors have articulated commitments to the political representation of working-class experiences and manage to avoid an outsider's view of the working class, a middle-class idea of working-class difference. That perspective is achieved by installing the view of poor, working-class protagonists as the filmic view. Their filmic space is the antithesis of an observed space of working-class 'difference' and of middle-class 'truth' about that difference. It is a space of different possibilities, of recognitions and resonances, of real and imagined identifications, of personal and political connections. Its use to non-traditional social science epistemologies is to allow a different kind of approach to studies of working-class poverty: the *way* it represents working-class experiences of poverty allows different *kinds* of knowledges about them to emerge.

Hate and *Ladybird, Ladybird* map identities and places of working-class poverty to produce a popular cultural cartography rather than a traditional ethnography. If ethnography is understood as the traditional method of social scientific fieldwork based on the empirical observation of 'people in culture', then any sort of 'fiction' is decidedly non-ethnographic. On the other hand, if ethnography is understood as a reflexive method of creatively constructing reality, then there are some radical methodological implica-tions for ethnographic form. Writers inclined to pursue these implications have conceived of a 'poetics and politics of ethnography' opening up a new terrain of possibilities in which intertextual, plurivocal and interpretative forms and methods of practice take over from the scientific authorial voice (see Clifford and Marcus, 1986). Indeed, particular non-traditional ethnographic forms – such as poetry, novels and films – would seem to be well suited to express the 'happening-all-at-once' quality that constitutes social life. That fullness of meaning creates complexity which refuses both the viewer and the director absolute control over the subject's story.[5] These are meanings made in the conjunction of multiple events and non-events, conversations and interactions, looks and movements. Such meanings do not only exist in language and therefore cannot be conveyed in academic forms such as the research interview. They often cannot be repeated in speech, may be unspoken and are possibly unspeakable.

As representational spaces these films express possibility, they complicate and defend what they show and they do not leave their subjects exposed. They also give a cultural presence to the working-class poor that is not part of an injunction to tell: 'not telling' (to welfare professionals, to the Department of Social Security, to the police, in media confessionals, to researchers) is a strategic defence against confession and exposure. However, instead of withdrawing voice and visibility altogether, these films offer engagement on the terms of their protagonists. One good reason for preferring the representational space of the film over that of the empirical research space of the interview favoured by 'audience researchers', for example, is articulated in one of the 43 episodes of Edinburgh 'underclass' living found in Irvine Welsh's novel *Trainspotting* (1993). One of the main characters – Renton – is forced to discuss his identity with a counsellor. He reverses the relationship between the knowing 'interviewer' and the 'subject' of the interview as a refusal of the injunction to tell (the 'truth') and to be accountable:

> Sometimes ah telt the truth, sometimes ah lied. When ah lied, ah sometimes said the things that ah thought he'd like tae hear, n sometimes said something which ah thought would wind him up, or confuse him. (Welsh, 1993, p. 184)

Renton's refusal, together with the confusion it produces, results with him being sent for more counselling, an outcome that makes him think his mate got the easy option in being sent to jail. Nevertheless, he maintains a protective distance, a refusal to be convinced of the necessity to 'tell it the way it is' in order to be better *known*:

Once ye accept that they huv that right, ye'll join them in the search fir this holy grail, this thing that makes ye tick. Ye'll then defer tae them, allowin yersel tae be conned intae believin any biscuit-ersed theory ay behaviour they choose tae attach tae ye. Then yir theirs, no yir ain. (*ibid.*)

In *Hate* and *Ladybird, Ladybird* the main revelation is that whilst things are not all right for the protagonists, the reasons for things being as they are is to do with other social groups, *their* authority, *their* privilege, *their* values. Thus, a central part of the positive working-class affirmation offered by the films involves antipathy towards 'things middle class'. The films are pleasurable in being part of an insistence that parts of middle-class society should be made more accountable to the polity as a whole.

Raymond Williams describes a structure of feeling as the 'specifically affective elements of consciousness and relationships' (Williams, 1997, p. 132). The notion can work as a mediating category between social, experiential and representational practices. I have tried to structure some of that feeling in discussion of the relation between subjectivity and collectivity within the lives represented by the films. This theme is presented as a way of negotiating personal-political class meanings. It forwards an idea of *collective working-class subjectivities* as the core political meaning of the two films. In that idea is a link back to traditional Marxist theories of shared class interests and understandings (or consciousness), and a link forward to poststructuralist theories of the subject and the social in which 'class' is differentiated according to other social constructions (such as race and gender) and in which it is constituted by symbolic and affective elements of social being as well as by economic position.

Collective subjectivities

Both *Hate* and *Ladybird, Ladybird* tell stories about subjective experiences of poverty, class and oppression. The perspective is one-sided and angry, creating a political edge that forges subjective–collective meanings. Those meanings are not always articulated by the characters, are lived in myriad ways and are negotiated as matters of difference and belonging.

Hate chronicles 24 hours in the lives of three working-class friends from an outer Parisian housing estate in the aftermath of a riot. Vince, Hubert and Said wander the terrain of the night before, recalling its events, making small-time deals and trying to avoid the police and the television cameras. Much of the tension and dialogue centre on whether or not Vince will use a policeman's gun, found the night before, to revenge the police beating of a friend – Abdel – who now lies in a coma. The 24 hours are shown ticking by, a mixture of ordinariness and extremity. They are lived in a fantastical realm, through the projected images of middle-class others and through self-imaginings. Outsider views of Vince, Hubert and Said, from the media, law and welfare agencies which intervene in their lives, are overwhelmingly extrinsic, superficial and evidential. More than just reflecting a surface these views work to produce what they want to see: media cameras probe and provoke violent reactions, the police generate anger and hostility. The start of *Hate* is the media view of the riot: lads throwing missiles, running, setting fire to cars, fronting the police. A while later we see Vince waking up in his bedroom, looking the epitome of the sort of youth that would be associated with riots, with his skinhead haircut and knuckle-duster jewellery. A mirror scene which follows shows Vince getting ready to go onto the street. He performs like the hard-man contenders that he sees in American films, acting out adversarial street encounters. Later, Said does the same. The scenes show psychological and performative defences cultivated against violence and rejection, the importance of style as cultural capital and the power of American film culture to value macho masculinities. However, the behaviours of the young men from the estate are seen by outsiders as the direct expression of aggressive, violent and macho natures. They are divorced from the exigencies of their lives where status and credibility need to be created from limited economic resources for a positive degree of engagement with a wider culture. The struggle of Vince, Hubert and Said to make the grade is a struggle of identity within and between themselves. It is a struggle with drugs, violence and boredom, with unpredictable outcomes. Hubert, for example, is thoughtful and pragmatic, but in the end he is the one who 'kills the cop' in an impulsive yet principled reaction to the police shooting of Vince. Their behaviours do not fit the standard characterization of 'underclass' masculinity: one-dimensional 'no-hopers', dangerous or macho 'yobs'.[6] They are a part of young men with distinct personalities and talents whose subjectivities are enmeshed in social conditions and contingent situations.

Neither are the friends without self-understanding or insight into their lives. Still in Paris at 2.57 a.m., Vince, Hubert and Said sit on the roof of an old building, get stoned and reflect on their predicament:

HUBERT: The early bird catches the worm ... a stitch in time saves nine ... haste makes waste.

VINCE: Liberty, Equality, Fraternity – I save that one for special occasions.

They know that they cannot change their lives by believing in the sort of common-sense self-help implied in the simplicities of adages or ideological mantras. On the roof top where they sit, they have a view of both the city and how their lives on the estate fit into this bigger picture. They know that there is nothing much they can do to change this: there is no escape, only the mind-trick of hope reiterated by Hubert – 'so far so good, so far so good'. If that is an illusion, a fantasy, it is also all that is available to them, a psychological defence against admitting that one way or another they are not going to make it. In the meantime, Vince, Hubert and Said find togetherness in being hated and hating back. Vince is Jewish, Said an Arab and Hubert is black; theirs is an outcast solidarity. They exchange racial jibes, stripped of racist meaning, about each other's lack of racial 'authenticity'. The differences between them are both less meaningful to themselves and to outsiders who perceive them than what they have in common as poor, working-class young men from the estates.

The argument between them which runs the course of the 24 hours is about whether the police gun that Vince has found should be used to avenge Abdel's beating, but it also expresses a larger tension in their lives between subjective and collective interests. It is an argument within their group, with shared terms of reference, with no question as to who their adversaries are. Difference is expressed and negotiated within their group without detracting from the commonality based on the fall that they share, on lives that are part of each other's and, as Hubert's decision to kill and be killed for Vince finally shows, on inextricable feelings for each other. The tension between personal interests of survival and collective expressions of resistance has no easy resolution; as far as daily living and daily outcomes are concerned they are in it together. Hubert's final act disregards personal survival: it is an act of hate but also one of solidarity.

Ladybird, Ladybird is the story of Maggie Conlon, a single mother who has lost custody of her four children to Social Services after a fire in the women's refuge where she is staying. Whilst trying to get them back she meets Jorge, a Paraguayan refugee, who joins her fight against Social Services, and with whom she has two more children. As Maggie's behaviour and her past are used to mark her as an unfit mother, we witness the permanent removal of all of her six children, and the grievous anger that comes to define her way of being. Like the protagonists in *Hate*,

Maggie is cast as a caricature of disorder by professional outsiders – a woman of 'low intellect and little self-control'. This is her main burden. She cannot escape the professional image of her: she is fixed as a damaged person who will reproduce damage in her children. She selects bad partners, avoids and lies to officials, tries to run off with her children and refuses to practise birth control. The issue is not so much that Maggie is 'not really like that', but that her behaviour is so little understood and so readily pathologized by middle-class professionals. The Social Security's system of resource distribution is such that Maggie's definition of her interests in terms of basic needs provision cannot be met. Social workers are therefore paid to manage *her* as a problematic person: matters of personality, language and family culture are used to supplant issues of material need.

As a character Maggie is not a straightforward 'heroine' and in many ways that is the point: she is not there to please an audience of social workers or film-goers (some reviewers turned on her 'unlikeable' or 'unwatchable' nature; see, for example, *Guardian*, 1994, and *Independent*, 1995). She projects an image of being able to handle herself, admits to having loved her violent partner and is ambiguous as a 'victim'. Maggie's swearing, heavy smoking and refusal to use contraception make her an affront to a wide range of middle-class norms on 'good mothering'. Her choice of partner: multiple, bad and violent; her choice of having four children by four different fathers in poverty; and her refusal to stop reproducing even when her entitlement to mother has been officially withdrawn – these are the unacceptable face of motherhood. That symbolism subsumes Maggie as a person: she is a 'case', a list of disasters waiting to happen, a file of evidence, a failure of criteria, a risk. The objectivity of these 'facts' is ultimately a denial of her subjectivity. Although Maggie's isolation is at times stark, her predicament is clearly part of a collective story. Family courts, social work departments and ties with the police are shown ticking over on a daily basis. Channels are set up, ready and waiting: the system works against Maggie with ease, generating evidence and justification as it goes. Hers is just one story about how that system can work.

When Jorge enters her life, Maggie is able to share her experiences and feelings with someone who recognizes and validates them. Their relationship is forged on a mutual knowledge of oppression. Jorge is a political exile from Paraguay who has had to leave the country for setting up and writing about safe homes for children whose parents had been killed by the government for their land. When he first sees Maggie singing karaoke in a London pub, the poignancy and sadness of her song communicates her pain and loss, and speaks to his own suffering. At one point a social worker tries to suggest that because English is Jorge's second language there is a communication barrier between him and Maggie which undermines the suitability of their relationship. Maggie's reply that 'It's not only words you use to communicate' speaks of a shared empathy whose meanings are incomprehensible to the social worker. Rather than a divide, Jorge's ethnicity is a basis of understanding between them, not only because two of Maggie's first four children are black also but because she is well versed in the social relations of oppression. The issue of ethnic difference is only problematic for the authorities, who see Jorge as another choice of 'violent' partner because of his status as a political refugee. Whilst Maggie and Jorge react to similar experiences in very different ways, their basis of understanding remains intact. This kind of communication is alien to the authorities; in the professional languages which encode Maggie's life, nothing is understood outside of visible and spoken 'evidence'. Maggie and Jorge develop an explicitly political understanding of their situation which crosses cultural, ethnic and gender differences. They are both people on the run, intimidated and poor, denied basic rights, and they have both been terrified by a state of government-sanctioned siege. Jorge tries to describe the reason for their experiences based on what he knows in Paraguay, which is that fear prevents change: 'It's dangerous to alleviate suffering, suffering has a job to do for the government.' It is the only directly political line in the story, making connections between different kinds of oppression carried out against the working-class poor, in the name of government, for the good of the country.

Filmic discourse as politics

The focus and justification of intervention into the lives of Maggie, Vince, Hubert and Said are behavioural activities. The characters share an external mode of identification as problem and threat, and a social relation of impoverishment, brutality and disempowerment. In this respect, to conceive of collective relations between them is to suggest a shared, everyday political commonality which does not have to be articulated in a conventional 'political' language in order that it can be said to exist. Their struggle is not expressed polemically with the characters as political mouthpieces and their stories are not illustrations of any certain, monolithic political truth. Complex and changing working-class subjectivities are shown to be *part of* relations of class conflict and incommensurable differences with middle-class others. Distinction between groups of working-class people is the key tenet of the hegemonic discourse of 'underclass': the working class and the 'underclass', the deserving and the undeserving, the married and the single parent, male and female, young and old, black and white. To talk of the collective in this context is therefore a political refusal of the use of working-class differences as divides. Given the divisive nature of the hegemonic discourse of 'underclass', keeping hold of a notion of the collective would seem to be an important strategic resource. Race and gender specification is in no way antithetical to that notion; indeed, it is part of it in recognition that the working class is not just white and male, it is also female and male, black and white. Both *Hate* and *Ladybird, Ladybird* show how complex solidarities are lived as part of everyday experiences, where 'collectivities' are about strong interconnections and interdependencies rather than absolute sameness.

My main argument in this chapter has been for the epistemological value of *Hate* and *Ladybird, Ladybird*: that is, their value as a means of representing subjugated knowledges of working-class poverty which are so often reduced to journalistic snapshots or evidential scientific truths. A central element in my analysis concerns the relation between the material and symbolic aspects of existence – in this case the relation between poverty and representations of poverty. Rather than suggesting what 'outcome' of meaning may be made by those who watch the films (given that it is largely indeterminable anyway), my choice has been to say something about the experiences that they represent. Imaginative connections between subjectivities and collectivities produce political meanings. The stories of *Hate* and *Ladybird, Ladybird* as part of the discourse of 'underclass' provide a cultural and political representation of and for the working-class poor. They offer bold, alternative meanings about lives, people and places that have been largely rubbished in dominant representations. The films will not necessarily create strong sources of positive identification for poor working-class young men and single mothers on council estates. Neither will they necessarily change the attitudes of audiences with intransigent views of their own. My hope and feeling is that these stories of class and poverty are *likely* to ring true, for different audiences in different ways, and that for many these truths will echo the commonly expressed sentiment of those queuing from the estates to see *Hate*: 'This is about us, this is our film' (*Independent on Sunday*, 1995).

Notes

1. The 'challenge' of the 'underclass' is posed in Mandelson (1997), pp. 6–9 (his speech to the Fabian Society which launched the Social Exclusion Unit).
2. This group makes up about 10 per cent of the population, having doubled from 5 per cent in 1979. See Buck (1992).
3. For a discussion of the cross-cultural contexts of this French film, see Haylett (1998).
4. The text/audience relation has been opened up to a wider range of speculative and experiential readings through developments in postmodernism. See Crawford and Turton (1992).
5. It is important to note that the ethnographic value of film is very much contingent upon the view it constructs. For a discussion of the voyeuristic dangers realized in ethnographic films see Kuehnast (1992).
6. The commentator Charles Murray is a prime exponent of such views. See Murray (1994).

Bibliography

Buck, N. (1992) 'Labour market inactivity and polarisation'. In D. J. Smith (ed.), *Understanding the Underclass*. London: PSI.

Clifford, J. and Marcus, S. (1986) *Writing Culture: The Poetics and Politics of Ethnography*. Berkeley: University of California Press.

Crawford, P. and Turton, D. (eds) (1992) *Film as Ethnography*. Manchester: Manchester University Press.

Gans, H. (1993) 'From "underclass" to "undercaste": some observations about the future of the post-industrial economy and its major victims'. *International Journal of Urban and Regional Research* 17, pp. 327–35.

Guardian (1994) 'Rock steady'. G2, 29 September, p. 10.

Haylett, C. (1998) 'The making of a British "underclass" in the 1990s: a geography of power/knowledge'. University of Edinburgh (unpublished).

hooks, b. (1994) *Outlaw Culture: Resisting Representations*. London: Routledge.

Independent (1994) Film review, 30 September, p. 25.

Independent on Sunday (1995) 'Concrete jungle where life imitates art in the concrete jungle'. 11 June, p. 15.

Kuehnast, K. (1992) 'Visual imperialism and the export of prejudice: an exploration of ethnographic film'. In P. Crawford and D. Turton (eds), *Film as Ethnography*. Manchester: Manchester University Press.

Mandelson, P. (1997) *Labour's Next Steps: Tackling Social Exclusion*. London: Fabian Society.

Murray, C. (1994) 'The New Victorians and the New Rabble'. *Sunday Times*, 29 May, p. 12.

Welsh, I. (1993) *Trainspotting*. London: Minerva.

Williams, R. (1977) *Marxism and Literature*. Oxford: Oxford University Press.

5

Black Women and Social-Class Identity

Tracey Reynolds

Britain is a multicultural society comprised of a diverse number of ethnic and cultural groups. However, black and other minority ethnic people tend to be marginalized in academic debates on class (see Anthias, 1990; Mirza, 1992; Skeggs, 1997a). In instances where black people are represented in discussions of class, there is the assumption that black people share a collective working-class location. Furthermore, it is assumed that black people themselves are unconcerned about articulating a class identity, as race provides the defining characteristic in shaping their subjectivity. Through the narratives of twenty African-Caribbean women, this chapter re-opens the debate in order to identify the important influence social class has on the way in which black people in Britain understand their lives.

I begin by developing a discourse of social class which takes account of the racialized context of social class. The chapter then moves onto investigating the way that the varying expressions of racism that black people encounter and their strategies of resistance to challenge that racism is contingent upon social class. The final part explores a social group that is traditionally invisible in both class and race debates, i.e. the black middle class, in order to ascertain whether Britain, in a similar manner to the USA, can point to a growing and self-identified black middle-class cultural group.

Social class differences within a racialized context

Social class analysis which addresses working-class and middle-class positioning without also taking account of the interconnecting relationship of 'race' and gender as factors that shape individual subjectivity over-simplifies class debates. Black feminist research both in Britain (Anthias,

1990; Mirza, 1997) and in the USA (hooks, 1989; Hill-Collins, 1990) has given critical attention to the way that the interlocking factors of race, class and gender structure black women's experiences. As a consequence of this interconnecting relationship, black and white women's experiences of social class are racialized as well as gendered. The racialized context of social class acts to separate out black and white women who articulate similar middle-class and working-class identities because their racial ascription places them in different structural positions. Furthermore, as Patricia Hill-Collins (1990) suggests, this differing structural location that is underpinned by race translates politically into white women's racial privilege and a collective dominance over black women.

Beverley Skeggs' (1997b) re-evaluation of Pierre Bourdieu's theory of 'capital' (1989) is used to assess black women's racialized understanding of class. Skeggs advances Bourdieu's theory that capital is intrinsic to society. This capital comprises 'properties capable of conferring strength, power and consequently profit on the holder' (Skeggs, 1997b, p. 127). Four types of capital exist: cultural (made up of institutional, embodied and objectified capital); economic capital; social capital; and symbolic capital. Black women are able to access economic capital through occupational mobility into professional and managerial posts which result in relatively high income levels (see Modood, 1997). In addition, black women's access to a middle-class cultural capital is achieved through increased educational qualifications in higher education (see Mirza, 1995). As a consequence of racial inequality and disadvantage, however, black women's access to symbolic capital, which involves the legitimation of social, cultural and economic capitals, is limited. The limited access that black women, as well as black men, have to symbolic capital is similar to the limited access the white working classes have (Skeggs, 1997b; Reay, 1998). Black people's relationship to capital gives credence to the idea that black people share a collective working-class location. Often in class discussions a homogenous working-class location is implicitly assumed for black people. Heidi Mirza asserts that:

African Caribbeans living in Britain are no more homogenous in their class make up than their white counterparts, yet they are often discussed as one group. In the same way that class affects occupational location, access to economic, political and social resources, values and life-styles among the white British population, so too does it influence these factors for blacks. (Mirza, 1992, p. 166)

This assumption of a black working-class collectivity is primarily attributed to the colonial context of African-Caribbean migration to Britain and the developing patterns of employment amongst black people. The black migrants who first arrived in Britain from the Caribbean during the 1940s and 1950s were concentrated in areas of employment that were defined as traditional working-class occupations: unskilled and semi-skilled manual labour in public utilities and textile sector industries (see Foner, 1979; Fryer, 1984). The actual social class background of families who arrived in Britain were ignored. Studies show that migrants who occupied middle-class occupations and a middle-class status in the Caribbean were subsumed into the working classes (Foner, 1979; Bryan, Dadzie and Scafe, 1985). Racism prevented these earlier migrants from the Caribbean, as well as the Indian subcontinent, from securing the occupations that equalled their prior middle-class professional status. Thus, they were subject to downward reclassification (see Dodgson, 1984; James and Harris, 1993). The racialized nature of the labour market and the concentration of black people in specific areas of employment in routine clerical and manual occupations mean that black people today continue to be over-represented in occupations that are defined as working-class occupations (Modood, 1997).

Black women themselves have actively participated in promoting a black, collective working-class identity, and the black women's movements to emerge in Britain during the 1970s and 1980s invested greatly in the idea of a black women's collective working-class location (see Sudbury, 1998). Black women's struggles around racial and gender inequalities were defined in the context of wider working-class struggles. Organizations such as the Organisation of African and Asian Women of African Descent (OWAAD) highlighted the historical oppression of black women as underpinned by capitalism and imperialism. Both of these ideologies created the need for free and cheap labour (e.g. slavery and/or indentured labour in the Caribbean and later migrant labour in Britain), which led to the exploitation of black women as well as black men.

The African-Caribbean women that I interviewed[1] used 'objective' and 'subjective' definitions of social class to articulate a particular social class identity. 'Objective' understandings of social class were based upon conventional systems of classification such as that produced by the Registrar General based on occupation and income levels. The women's 'subjective' understandings of social class take their account of black racialized and gendered status in British society and the modes of inequality and exclusion this produces. How the women encounter, respond to and resist racism, together with the cultural, economic and social capitals they have at their disposal to do so, is also constituted in their 'subjective' understandings of class identity.

As a result of educational attainment, increasing numbers of black women in Britain are entering occupations identified as middle class: teaching, social work, housing management, healthcare management and other professional/managerial occupations (Bhavnani, 1994). However, the concentration of black women in such occupations does not automatically equate to large numbers of black women articulating a middle-class identity. Nearly two-thirds of the black women that I interviewed were in occupations traditionally defined as middle-class professions. Nevertheless, these women *rejected* a middle-class identity and instead they articulated a working-class status. Beverley, a divorced mother who is employed as a social work manager and lives in council accommodation, provides a case in point:

> People think that because of my job, I've made it, that I must be doing well for my family. But no, I'm working-class ... To be honest with you, every month is a struggle. When I'm in the position not to have to worry about making ends meet every month, than maybe I can say that I've reached a middle-class life.

The above comments show that income level is a salient feature in Beverley's articulation of a working-class identity. Another black woman, Cecile, expresses a similar viewpoint: Cecile is a teacher by profession, yet as a widowed [i.e. single] mother she survives on a limited income, lives in council accommodation and readily admits that 'things are tight financially'. These women's low income levels can be explained by the fact that social work and teaching, two feminine-gendered 'caring' professions, are notoriously low paid (Breugel, 1989). In addition, the racialized nature of the labour market means that black women are concentrated at the bottom of the occupational ladder, earning less salary than their white male and female and black male counterparts and in positions that offer fewer opportunities for occupational mobility (Bhavnani, 1994). Therefore as a consequence of their reduced earning potential, many black women in middle-class occupations, for all intents and purposes, live working-class lives in terms of 'objective' income levels and living conditions (see Reynolds, 1998).

These 'objective' means by which social class is assessed (occupation, income level and housing tenure) are also problematic in analysing black women's lives because these measurements assume that the head of the household is male and employed, and that women provide only a secondary income for the household. This marginalizes the experiences of black mothers who head households, or who are the primary financial providers (Mirza, 1992).

Racism, class difference and working-class strategies of resistance

Black women's collective experience and individual subjectivity are shaped by racism. Racism manifests itself through racist actions and practices that black women encounter as part of their daily lives. However, racism also acts to determine wider and pathological representations of black female identities in public discourse. Black women are constructed as the 'other', 'deviant' and 'sexually exotic' (hooks, 1992; Gilman, 1992). Representations of black women in the British media tend to identify them as the 'overachiever superwoman', the 'dominating matriarch' or the 'feckless single-mother', all of whom, these constructions suggest, produce dysfunctional families and juvenile delinquent children (see Reynolds, 1997). The different class experiences of black women are immaterial to the pathologized manner in which they are represented.

Black women's racialized class-positioning determines the various ways racism manifests itself. The following comments by Sharon, a low-income, working-class mother, and Camille, a high-income, professional middle-class mother, illustrate their understanding that membership of a working-class or middle-class location alters their experience of being black women:

SHARON: If you're black we all have to deal with the same things, don't we? But I suppose if you're educated they treat you differently. They may still be racist and think that they're better than you, but they will try to show it less, they won't be so up front about it ... They'd be polite to your face even if they don't like it and they'd have to respect you even if they are facety [rude] behind your back. With me though, because I'm low class, they're much more up front about it. There's this posh health visitor at the clinic, she looks down her nose at me like I'm a dirty smell or something. She talks to me like I'm stupid ... she thinks that because she is white she's better than me, but because I'm not educated she can get away with talking to me like that.

CAMILLE: Some people don't like to see black people getting too far, but the problem is that racism is so insidious that it sometimes difficult to pinpoint. You have to learn to read the signs. Sometimes what people don't say is more racist than calling you a black so-and-so. Where I live, some of my neigbours are definitely hostile to us; they don't like that we as a black couple can afford to live in a nice area in a nice house. They're nice enough to your face, but you feel that they're constantly watching you, just waiting for you to mess up. And another thing I've noticed is that during the summer months some of the neighbours will have barbecues and you see the other neighbours being invited. We've been living there for six years now and not once have any of them ever invited us, so you know they're racist even though they would never admit to it.

Both Sharon and Camille's comments suggest that a middle-class location produces less overt incidences of racism. The negative and abrasive way in which the health visitor responds to Sharon, the low-income black mother, is understood by her as representing a covertly racist encounter. This covertly racist attitude expressed towards her by the white health visitor is felt by Sharon to result from her lower-class status. Camille speaks of the subtle, almost invisible manner in which racism is commonly displayed to her as a result of her middle-class location.

These women's account of the class differences which affect expressions of racism is supported by race education research which identifies the significance social class location has on the way that racism is experienced by black children and their parents in their children's schooling. Diane Reay (1997), in her study of classroom interactions between teachers and black children, observed that social class difference affected the way teachers displayed racism towards black children. Reay argued that, in the middle-class teachers' interactions with black children and their parents, the racism was covert and manifested itself in a taken-for-granted attitude of racial superiority by the white teachers. Within the schools a 'colour-blind' approach to the teaching of black middle-class children was adopted. The black children's race and cultural difference were considered to be of little importance to the teachers and thus they were ignored. Christine Callender (1997) suggests that this 'colour-blind' approach to teaching is another marker of covert middle-class racism because it privileges white racialized identities as normative whilst silencing other racial categories.

In contrast to the covert expressions of racism experienced by black middle-class children and their parents, black working-class children and their parents have persistently encountered overt racism within the education system. This racist behaviour has ranged from being labelled as an academic underachiever, to experiencing high rates of school exclusion, and also verbal and physical racial abuse from white teachers (see Bryan, Dadzie and Scafe, 1985; Wright, 1988; Mirza, 1992; Gillborn, 1995).

However, black working-class women are not passive victims of these overt forms of racism. Instead, they have been using the resources that are available to them in order to fight back and resist the racist behaviour in stereotypical categorizations. Zora, a black working-class mother, exemplifies this resistance to racism:

ZORA: When I visit [my daughter's] school I make the effort to dress up a little bit more, wear a smart skirt or pair of trousers. I've noticed that when they can see you dress smartly and you speak correct English, the teacher's whole approach to you changes. It's like you're no longer the typical black mother they expect you to be. When I go to collect her, her teacher makes an effort to come up to me and tell me how her day has gone, what's she been up to, which she never did at first when she thought I was just a typical black mother.

TR: What's a typical black mother?

ZORA: Well the school she goes to, there are a lot of black children ... and some of the mothers are quite young, so I can just see them thinking in a certain way. I don't think it, but I think they see it as the single mother who doesn't know much about anything, who's ready to come up the school and fight you if you say anything bad about their child. So they [teachers] think it will cause too much hassle to go up and speak to you, it's best just to leave things. During her first week, I was off from work for a couple of days and so I was looking a bit rough. I could tell the teacher was a bit wary about approaching me. I bet she was thinking I'm one of those aggressive mothers ready to fight her if she says anything to me. I had to go up and speak to her; even then she was a bit funny, a bit distant. It was only after I told her I was a housing officer and she got to see me smartly dressed because of work, that she

relaxed a bit. Now she makes a point of talking to me every day;
acts differently to me now.

Zora's feelings suggest that white teachers make classed judgements about
black parents, and that they use these judgements in order to respond to
them. Zora believes that black mothers, who may themselves be single
mothers, but who are perceived by the teacher as having a middle-class
status or possessing middle-class aspirations, enjoy greater levels of contact
with the teacher than those who are perceived as working-class, low-
income single mothers. Consequently, Zora adopts what she considers to
be a middle-class appearance (e.g. wearing smart clothes) and behaviour
(e.g. speaking in standardized English) to establish a positive interaction
between the teacher and herself. In assuming these self-defined middle-
class signifiers, Zora is manipulating class divisions for her own benefit. It
does not necessarily, however, reflect a genuine desire on Zora's part to be
middle class. The fact that Zora even has to emulate a middle-class identity
to secure her objectives is telling in itself: it suggests that possessing both a
black racialized and a working-class identity equates to inferior values,
lifestyles and attitudes.

The black middle class

It is virtually impossible to locate research in Britain that develops discourses of a black middle class. However, research from the USA
addresses the ever-increasing black middle class, and some of the issues
raised can be tentatively applied towards the examination of the black
middle class in Britain. Robert Taylor (1997) suggests that the social and
economic resources of the affluent black middle class in America, in
addition to their values, lifestyles and attitudes, are now so different to the
black urban poor that it is no longer possible for black people to unite
around a collective racialized identity. Within black communities in the
USA, segregation between the middle-class and poor blacks along economic and social lines has now become commonplace. Two black
middle-class groups are identified. The first is the more established middle
class whose status followed on from the historical period of enslavement.
This group comprises the first black educators or landowners of post-
slavery who, with the collective effort of their extended family, were able to
build upon these social and economic advantages across successive generations (McAdoo, 1988). During this era, 'pigmentocracy', which affords

light-skinned blacks a higher status than dark-skinned blacks, also became the unspoken criterion for upward mobility into the middle class (Frazier, 1939). The second black middle-class group is the 'black bourgeoisie' whose economic wealth is derived from changes in US consumption patterns and the affirmative action[2] policies first advanced by the Civil Rights Movement.

Black people are prominent figures in sports and popular entertainment, and this has provided them with 'screens of opportunity' in which to acquire upward mobility to a middle-class location (McAdoo, 1988). Affirmative action policies in higher education and government offices have also produced trangenerational upward mobility for black groups in the USA in large numbers. As a result there exists in that nation a 'golden cohort' of black Americans comprised of young, university-educated men and women who are concentrated in professional occupations.

Black Britain has a considerable way to go before a black middle-class community is recognized as quite distinct and separate from a black working-class one. Many of the mechanisms that are in place for black people in the USA to achieve upward mobility in large numbers (and thus the establishment of black middle-class communities), such as affirmative action policies, are absent in Britain. Also, the geographical dispersal of black people in Britain makes it difficult to identify visible black middle-class communities in the way that can be done in the USA. The fact that the majority of African-Caribbean people in Britain have lived in the country for a relatively short period of time (from the 1950s onwards) has further inhibited the establishment of British black communities that are securely middle class.

It is clear, however, that, similar to the US debate on social class, black people in Britain are perceiving class differences, and in particular the articulation of a new black middle-class identity, to problematize the assumption of a common black unitary experience. Tanya, a black middle-class women, notes:

> There is a definite class divide amongst black people, which I notice is more so now than twenty years ago. There is a noticeable group of black professionals that are starting to earn good salaries and have a nice lifestyle ... Because of my line of work, you meet all sorts of [black] people that have it bad, their situation is hopeless ... It's like you can relate to them in one sense, but you also can't because their

world is so different – so I feel there is this divide between the classes and the gap is going to grow wider.

Not all of the women that I spoke too agreed with Tanya's comments that a black middle-class identity is a recent phenomena that has resulted from educational and occupational mobility. Such a viewpoint presupposes that black people in Britain all derive from a working-class historical location. Bryan, Dadzie and Scafe (1985) identify a visible black middle-class presence amongst the Caribbean migrants to Britain. Whilst migration forced downward economic mobility for the black middle-class migrants, many of the migrants still held onto their middle-class values and aspirations, which they communicated to their children. Thus, the black middle class is not such an emerging trend amongst blacks in Britain but has existed in different forms for at least fifty years.

Conclusion

The interviewees show that black people are very aware of class issues and, in conjunction with race and gender, they actively deploy this understanding in their daily lives. For example, the women articulate a middle-class or a working-class identity, within a racialized context, in order to explore commonality and difference between themselves and others who share a similar class location but a different racial or gender positioning. The women who express a working-class identity understand that societal privilege is afforded to a middle-class identity with its cultural and social capitals, and thus they emulate a self-defined middle-class identity and use middle-class signifiers as a strategy of resistance to racism. There are signs that there may be a consolidation of black middle-class identity in Britain as this group becomes more conscious of its own cultural capital, and continues processes of upward mobility and reclassification, causing new forms of black middle-class communities to emerge.

Notes

1. These interviews were undertaken as part of my PhD thesis, which explored an African-Caribbean mothering identity in Britain. During the period January 1996 to January 1997 I interviewed twenty African-Caribbean mothers within the south London area. The age of the mothers participating in the research ranged from 19 to 81 years. Access to my sample group was obtained through a 'snowballing' method (see Reynolds, 1998).

2. Affirmative action or positive discrimination involves the deliberate manipulation of employment or educational practices so that specific social groups (e.g. black people and women) have access to areas of employment and education that would be otherwise denied to them (Newson and Mason, 1986). American right-wing policy-makers such as Charles Murray (1985) have argued that the existence of a black middle class in the USA means that affirmative action is no longer needed. Since the 1980s there has been a gradual reduction of affirmative action policies in organizations and universities. This has led some commentators to claim that the black middle class in the USA will decline in the future as the routes that enable upward mobility for black people are diminishing (Roschelle, 1997).

Bibliography

Anthias, F. (1990) 'Race and class revisited: conceptualising race and racism'. *Sociological Review* 38, pp. 19–42.

Bhavnani, R. (1994) *Black Women in the Labour Market*. London: Equal Opportunities Commission.

Bourdieu, P. (1989) 'Social space and symbolic power'. *Sociological Theory* 7, pp. 11–24.

Breugel, I. (1989) 'Sex and race in the labour market'. *Feminist Review* 32, pp. 49–68.

Bryan, B., Dadzie, S. and Scafe, S. (1985) *The Heart of the Race: Black Women's Lives in Britain*. London: Virago.

Callender, C. (1997) *Education for Empowerment*. London: Trentham Books.

Dodgson, E. (1984) *Motherlands*. London: Heinemann.

Foner, N. (1979) *Jamaica Farewell: Jamaican Migrants in London*. London: Routledge and Kegan Paul.

Frazier, F. (1939) *The Negro Family in the United States*. Chicago: University of Chicago Press.

Fryer, P. (1984) *Staying Power: The History of Black People in Britain*. London: Pluto Press.

Gillborn, D. (1995) *Race and Anti-Racism in Real Schools*. Buckingham: Open University Press.

Gilman, S. (1992) 'Black bodies, white bodies: towards an iconography of female sexuality'. In J. Donald and A. Rattansi (eds), *Race, Culture and Difference*. London: Sage.

Hill-Collins, P. (1990) *Black Feminist Thought*. New York: Routledge.

hooks, b. (1989) *Talking Back: Thinking Feminism, Thinking Black*. London: Sheba Feminist Publishers.

hooks, b. (1992) *Black Looks: Race and Representation*. Boston: South End Press.

James, W. and Harris, C. (1993) *Inside Babylon: The Caribbean Diaspora in Britain*. London: Virago.

McAdoo, H. (1988) *Black Families*. Newbury, CA: Sage.

Mirza, H. (1992) *Young, Female and Black*. London: Routledge.

Mirza, H. (1995) 'Black women in higher education: defining a space/finding a place'. In L. Morley and V. Walsh (eds), *Feminist Academics: Creative Agents for Change*. London: Taylor & Francis.

Mirza, H. (eds) (1997) *Black British Feminism: A Reader*. London: Routledge.

Modood, T. (ed.) (1997) *Ethnic Minorities in Britain*. London: PSI.

Murray, C. (1985) *Losing Ground: American Social Policy, 1950–1980*. New York: Basic Books.

Newson, N. and Mason, D. (1986) 'The theory and practice of equal opportunities policies'. *Sociological Review* 32(2), pp. 132–46.

Reay, D. (1997) 'Feminist theory, habitus and social class: disrupting notions of classlessness'. *Women's Studies International Forum* 20(2), pp. 225–33.

Reay, D. (1998) *Class Work: Mothers' Involvement in Their Children's Schooling*. London: Taylor & Francis.

Reynolds, T. (1997) '(Mis)representing the black (super)woman'. In H. Mirza (ed.), *Black British Feminism: A Reader*. London: Routledge.

Reynolds, T. (1998) 'African-Caribbean mothering: reconstructing a "new" identity'. Unpublished PhD thesis, South Bank University, London.

Roschelle, A. (1997) *No More Kin: Exploring Race, Class and Gender in Family Networks*. Newbury Park, CA: Sage.

Skeggs, B. (1997a) *Formations of Class and Gender*. London: Sage.

Skeggs, B. (1997b) 'Classifying practices: representations, capitals and recognition'. In P. Mahony and C. Zmorczek (eds), *Class Matters: 'Working-Class' Women's Perspectives on Social Class*. London: Taylor & Francis.

Sudbury, J. (1998) *Other Kinds of Dreams*. London: Routledge.

Taylor, R. (1997) *Family Life in Black America*. Newbury Park, CA: Sage.

Wright, C. (1988) 'The relations between teachers and Afro-Caribbean pupils'. In G. Weiner and M. Arnot (eds), *Gender under Scrutiny*. London: Open University Press.

Part 2

Class, Taste and Space

6

Culture, Class and Taste

Jon Cook

> Aesthetics is naked cultural hegemony, and popular discrimination
> properly rejects it. (Fiske, 1989, p. 130)

The relation between class and taste has been a preoccupation of literary
fiction and cultural commentary from the eighteenth century onwards. A
standard argument is that distinctions of taste manifest distinctions of class
in the realm of leisure. As such they reinforce a class system that is initially
defined in relation to work. In this chapter I explore arguments about the
relation between class and taste which either confirm or challenge this
standard argument. But, as I want to show in my analysis of work in
Cultural Studies by Richard Hoggart, Dick Hebdige and Pierre Bourdieu,
the analysis of the relation between class and taste can itself draw on
judgements of taste. To understand something of what is at stake in
judgements of taste, I need briefly to return to the eighteenth century when
influential argument about the authority, logic and cultural form of judgements of taste begin to emerge. These arguments about good and bad taste
are part of the emergence of something like a modern market in aesthetic
commodities. From the outset they work as consumer guides. Yet this is
also and necessarily an episode in self-fashioning or subject formation: the
creation of the man or woman of taste, a process that continues through to
the present day.

The idea that judgements of taste are subjective is not new. Nor is the
idea that this fact makes it peculiarly difficult to decide on the rightness or
wrongness of judgements of taste. In his essay 'Of the Standard of Taste',
first published in 1757, David Hume begins by setting out what he takes to
be commonplace observations: judgements of taste are characterized by
their variety and by the role that 'sentiment' plays in formulating them:

> Beauty is no quality in things themselves: It exists merely in the mind which contemplates them; and each mind perceives a different beauty. One person may even perceive deformity, where another is sensible of beauty; and every individual ought to acquiesce in his own sentiment, without pretending to regulate those of others. (Hume, 1985, p. 230)

Hume's essay attempts to discover a 'standard' of taste in the midst of these different perceptions of 'deformity' and 'beauty'. He does this by describing the qualities and experiences that he thinks an arbiter of taste should have and by appealing to examples where judgements of taste coincide rather than disagree. So there is no point in setting yourself up as an arbiter of taste if you lack 'delicacy of imagination', or 'practice' in the art you claim to judge, or a long experience in discriminating 'beauty' from 'deformity'. It is not that judgements of taste can transcend subjectivity, Hume argues, but there can be a trained and discriminating subjectivity which carries authority in any dispute about taste. But Hume is a worldly philosopher. The intransigence of subjective preferences returns towards the end of his essay:

> But it is almost impossible not to feel a predilection for that which suits our particular turn and disposition. Such preferences are innocent and unavoidable, and can never reasonably be the object of dispute, because there is no standard, by which they can be decided. (p. 244)

So in Hume's world a little bit of what you fancy can do you good, and there is no one around who can tell you otherwise. His essay argues that there can be a standard of taste, and sets out the situations where it can be legitimately applied. But, and this is one of the important features of the realm of taste, there are always also going to be cases where the standard has no authority. Hume's problem is where to draw the line. His rhetoric is confident enough, but, conceptually, he wants it both ways: at once to acknowledge that the 'general principles of taste are uniform in human nature' and that there is real and significant variation from the 'different humours of particular men' and from 'the particular manners and opinions of our age and country'. The relation between the particular and the general is perilously close to an aporia in which particular cases elude the authority of 'general principles'. The essay's argument comes close to a paradox: in matters of taste, the standard is that there is no standard.

Hume's essay, and my sketch of its argument, may seem to have little to do with class in anything like its modern sense. In one way this is obviously true. Hume wrote before the historical making of the English or British working class and prior to the mainly nineteenth-century elaboration of a vocabulary which distinguished between middle and working classes, between the bourgeois and the proletariat. The very idea of a 'working-class culture' seems to have no place in his conceptual world. But there is another reading – one which discloses the links between taste and class – of the kind advanced by Terry Eagleton in his book, *The Ideology of the Aesthetic*. Here Hume's text is understood as one example of that conceptual reworking of the relation between law and pleasure which goes by the name of the aesthetic. And this reworking is part of the creation of a new kind of middle-class subject:

> If the aesthetic comes in the eighteenth century to assume the significance it does, it is because the word is shorthand for a whole project of hegemony, the massive introjection of abstract reason by the life of the senses. What matters is not in the first place art, but this process of refashioning the humans subject from the inside, informing its subtlest affections and bodily responses with this law which is not a law. It would thus ideally be as inconceivable for the subject to violate the injunctions of power as it would be to find a putrid odour enchanting. (Eagleton, 1990, pp. 42–3)

The exercise of good taste is what stands at this crucial junction point between law and pleasure, between what is right and what is enjoyable. Yet, as Eagleton stresses, the aesthetic is a volatile cultural form. If it holds out the opportunity for power, in the form of reason, law and its representatives, to invest itself in our sensuous and affective lives, it can also overturn the respect that power requires if it is to be properly powerful. What if the foundation of the law goes no further than what I happen to like? What if I find a putrid odour enchanting?

These problems were readily acknowledged at the time. They were repeatedly rehearsed and debated from the eighteenth century onwards. If, like Eagleton, we see this as part of a hegemonic project, the making of a social world fit for a bourgeois class, then it is the endless uncertainty of judgements of taste which is as striking as their authority. The connoisseur's gushing praise of beauty, the rhetorical hyperbole of literary reviews, even the avid talk of the fan, are so many signs of an anxiety about the difficulty of persuading others that what I like you should like too. Yet this very uncertainty is a mark of the power of taste. If laissez-faire economics and the iron laws of the market represent the hard face of bourgeois ideology, a life governed by implacable necessity, then the realm of taste is its gentle voice, questioning, adapting, finding value in what once had been reviled or ignored. It is not just an historical accident that John Maynard Keynes, the economist who tried to humanize the laws of the market, was also a founding father of the Arts Council.

Yet too strong an emphasis on this hard cop/soft cop view of bourgeois ideology can be misleading. It is a familiar point about a successful hegemonic project that it must have the means for inviting people to join in (Althusser calls it interpellation, Gramsci consent) as well as ways of making them obey the rules. The exercise of taste, the very heart of aesthetic judgement, can appear coercive as well as consensual, and it is clear that John Fiske sees it this way when he invokes the idea of the aesthetic as 'naked cultural hegemony' (Fiske, 1989, p. 130). The basic argument here, one that has been exhaustively pursued by Bourdieu in his book *Distinction*, is that judgements of taste are always imbricated in class. What we like to have in our living rooms, what music we hear or books we read, the style of clothes we wear, are not simply expressions of a personal preference, but declarations of class membership and status. According to this view, the pleasures of taste are never innocent of class. We enjoy what we enjoy not despite class but because it expresses our classed difference from others. The exercise of taste is constantly drawing and redrawing the boundaries between and within classes. It is a continuous and sublimated form of class struggle.

What this struggle enacts is something more complicated than the simple assertion or definition of aristocratic, middle-class or working-class taste. As Bourdieu has argued, the cultural logic of taste produces versions of aristocracy which do not have to do with principles of heredity and landownership. This picks out an important point about how taste manifests itself culturally. For the aristocrats of taste, good taste appears as a natural expression of personality. Bourdieu links this to the acquisition of positive educational titles, the means whereby modern societies declare that a cultured sensibility has been legitimately acquired:

Whereas the holders of educationally uncertified cultural capital can always be required to prove themselves, because they *are* only what they *do*, merely a by-product of their own cultural production, the holders of titles of cultural nobility – like the titular members of an aristocracy, whose 'being', defined by their fidelity to a lineage, an estate, a race, a past, a fatherland or a tradition, is irreducible to any 'doing', to any know-how or function – only have to be what they are, because all their practices derive their value from their authors, being the affirmation and perpetuation of the essence by virtue of which they are performed ... (Bourdieu, 1986, pp. 23–4)

What Bourdieu analyses are the conditions for the tautologous logic of 'good' taste: it is what tasteful people decide is tasteful. It is the result not simply of the sheer accumulation of cultural capital, but, as Bourdieu makes clear, the *manner* of its accumulation. Upon this depends 'the generalizing tendency of the cultured disposition', the capacity, that is, to make judgements and deliver opinions across a wide range of issues outside a particular area of expertise. This is summarized by Bourdieu in a trenchant contrast:

The reader of the popular-science monthly *Science et Vie* who talks about the genetic code or the incest taboo exposes himself to ridicule as soon as he ventures outside the circle of his peers, whereas Claude Levi-Strauss [anthropological expert on the incest taboo] or Jacques Monod [scientific expert on the genetic code] can only derive additional prestige from their excursions into the field of music and philosophy ... (pp. 24–5)

Bourdieu takes up a central classifying distinction in the realm of both artistic taste and intellectual culture more generally: that between the person who can 'truly' lay claim to authoritative judgement and those who can only pretend to it. The distinction is taken for granted in Hume's essay 'Of the Standard of Taste'. There are the few 'men of delicate taste' who 'are easily to be distinguished in society, by the soundness of their understanding and the superiority of their faculties above the rest of mankind', an eighteenth-century version, in effect, of Bourdieu's aristocracy of culture (Hume, 1985, p. 243). There are also 'these pretended critics' who will be readily seen through and judged, like Bourdieu's readers of *Science et Vie*, 'absurd and ridiculous' (p. 231). Hume is happy to accept the legitimacy of a process which Bourdieu wants to question. But, for all their differences, both see a cultural process which classifies through the use of ridicule.

Where does this leave the idea of taste as a marker of class? Bourdieu's sociological research suggests a systematic co-relation between economic class and taste. What the social elites like is high culture. What the working class likes is popular culture. These patterns are, in turn, systematically connected to what Bourdieu calls 'educational capital'. The more you have of this the more likely it will be that you will prefer Bach's *Well-Tempered Clavier* to Strauss's *Blue Danube*. These formations of taste are governed by protocols of entitlement. If you claim to like something or judge something without the appropriate entitlement you will be the subject of ridicule. Taste is not just systematically linked to class. It reinforces class distinctions. Moreover, the taste of the social elites is not organized according to the same assumptions about value as the taste of the working class. They have radically different conceptions of the role of art and culture in relation to daily life. In particular, working-class taste is governed by what Bourdieu calls an 'anti-Kantian aesthetic' (Bourdieu, 1986, p. 41). This gives a priority to what works of art are about over how they are formed. It refuses the idea that there can be a pure formal pleasure which constitutes its distinctive value. Art is valuable for the pleasurable or moral purposes it can achieve and these are intimately linked to its content. It is also tentative and provisional in its judgements, evidenced in a sample of reactions by working-class respondents to photographs:

> The insistence with which the respondents point out the limits and conditions of validity of their judgements, distinguishing, for each photograph, the possible uses or audiences, or, more precisely, the possible use for each audience . . . shows that they reject the idea that a photograph can please 'universally' . . . It is not surprising that this 'aesthetic', which bases information on informative, tangible or moral interest, can only refuse images of the trivial, or, which amounts to the same thing in terms of this logic, the triviality of the image: judgement never gives the image of the object autonomy with respect to the object of the image . . . (p. 42)

Bourdieu adds to this account the idea that the working-class 'aesthetic' is a dominated 'aesthetic'. It is aware of its impropriety and lack of authority in relation to an alien judgement world. This brings it close to Bakhtin's account of carnivalesque culture and, indeed, there are moments in Bourdieu's account where his way of describing popular culture is suffused with Bakhtin's language and, significantly, his sentiment:

popular entertainment secures the spectator's participation in the show and collective participation in the festivity which it occasions. If circus and melodrama . . . are more 'popular' than entertainments like dancing or theatre, this is not merely because . . . they offer more direct or immediate satisfactions. It is also because . . . they satisfy the taste for and sense of revelry, the plain speaking and hearty laughter which liberate by setting the social world head over heels, overturning conventions and proprieties. (p. 34)

What becomes evident across the whole span of Bourdieu's argument is that his social critique of taste is marked by its own aesthetic moments. The 'anti-Kantian' aesthetic is not simply presented as one further datum in the enterprise of the social critique of taste.[1] Bourdieu prefers it to what he presents as the emotionally cold formalisms of high bourgeois taste. He invites his readers to give new value to a mode of judgement which is presented as socially despised. He makes a judgement of taste between judgements of taste.

What happens in Bourdieu's text points to a large question in the analysis of the relation between class and taste. The effort to 'demystify' the authority of taste by connecting it to class formation runs alongside a process whereby class tastes themselves become the subjects of judgements of taste. What is ostensibly explained begins to direct the process of explanation. The analysis of a working-class aesthetic turns the working class into a subject of aesthetic pleasure.

This is not a new process. The antecedents of the industrial working class – the agrarian poor, for example – were made into art through the conventions of pastoral.[2] The question of whether and how laborious physical work might be represented was a recurrent topic in eighteenth-century debates about literature and painting. Contemplating bodies at work produces it own distinctive mixture of aesthetic observation and eroticism from the eighteenth century onwards:

Never, believe me, I knew of the feelings between men and women
Till in some village fields in holidays now getting stupid
One day sauntering 'long and listless' as Tennyson has it
. . . .
Chanced it my eye fell aside on a capless, bonnetless, maiden
Bending with three-pronged fork in a garden uprooting potatoes
Was it the air? who can say? or herself, or the charm of the labour

But a new thing was in me; and longing delicious possessed me
Longing to take her and lift her, and put her away from her slaving.
(Clough, 1968, p. 123)

This is from a mid-nineteenth-century poem, *The Bothie of Tober-na-Vuolich*, written by A. H. Clough. The fictional voice is that of the poem's radical, gentleman hero. As the context makes clear, it is a sign of his radicalism that he should confess to feelings of this kind. The 'charm of the labour' and his 'longing delicious' arise as a contrast with his judgement about the superficiality of 'our high-born girls'. The aesthetics as much as the epistemology of class arise out of explicit or implicit contrasts of this kind. This account does not exhaust the significance of this moment in Clough's poem as its tone of speculative uncertainty makes clear. But it is one example of a persistent cultural motif in the aesthetic observation of labour, one in which the very sense of class difference intensifies desire.

Cultural Studies announces its break with these modes of perception. In the opening chapter of one of the early and defining texts of cultural studies, *The Uses of Literacy*, Richard Hoggart cautions his readers against middle-class idealizations of the working class:

> From the pity – 'How fine it would be if only . . . ' – to the praise – 'How fine they are simply because . . . ' – here we encounter pastoral myths and 'Wife of Bath' admirations. The working classes are at bottom in excellent health – so the pastoral description runs – in better health than other classes; rough and unpolished perhaps, but diamonds nevertheless . . . (Hoggart, 1958, pp. 14–15)

Yet Hoggart's critical awareness, as he acknowledges, is not proof against the return of pastoral. His descriptions of working-class life show a taste for imagining the working class as the subjects for aesthetic contemplation, as in this account of a working-class girl's adaptation to married life:

> Watch the way a girl who, in view of the extent to which her taste is assaulted by the flashy and trivial, should have an appalling sense of style can impose on even the individually ugly items she buys the sense of what it is important to re-create in a living-room. Watch the way she handles a baby; not the more obvious features, the carelessness of hygiene and the trivialities, but the acceptance of child in the crook of the arm or in a bath by the fire. (p. 52)

This description belongs to an aesthetic sub-genre of working-class interiors. The rhetorical invitation to 'watch' establishes the ground for a voyeuristic pleasure; we see unseen. Yet aesthetic modes do not simply supply the framework for perception. Taste here is also what is being watched. The working-class girl is suddenly transformed into a middle-class housewife. Hoggart's language veers towards the idiom of a style manual or a version of a 1950s article in *The Lady* or *Good Housekeeping*. 'What it is important to re-create' is discreetly vague, but is animated by one of the basic principles of eighteenth-century aesthetics: beauty consists in the harmonious integration of detail with an over-riding order. And this taste, along with the capacity to be a working-class madonna with 'a child in the crook of the arm', is what is required if a house is to be a home.

The taste of this imaginary working-class woman is also a kind of overcoming. Hoggart's language makes this clear enough. An assault by 'the flashy and the trivial' which should degrade taste is surprisingly resisted. The 'flashy and the trivial' is a part of Hoggart's lexicon for all those aspects of modern media culture which *The Uses of Literacy* deplores. Hoggart's account of working-class taste has a different topography to Bourdieu's. The dominant in Hoggart's world is not a Kantian aesthetic but the advent of Hollywood cinema, figured in his famous description of the 'hedonistic but passive barbarian who rides in a fifty-horse power bus for threepence to see a five-million-dollar film for one-and-eightpence' (p. 250).

But this is not all that the working-class woman of taste overcomes. Her taste transfigures the material conditions of her classhood as well. The ugliness that surrounds and threatens her does not only come from the world of mass media. It comes from the ever-present threat of poverty and deprivation. Taste is at work in the midst of unpromising conditions and harsh necessities. Hoggart is again working his working class in terms of pastoral convention in so far as this overcoming of necessity is typically a device for creating working-class heroes and heroines (the structure of sentiment here can be roughly paraphrased as follows: 'Look how much they have to put up with and yet how well they do. Their sufferings remind me how fortunate I am. Thank God I'm not one of them, but they aesthetically offer me a lesson'). He is, as his chapter title indicates, viewing the working class as a 'Landscape with figures'. The title summons a tradition of pastoral literature and painting which had repeatedly placed its working-class subjects in the context of urban or rural landscapes.[3] Typical examples of working-class life are exhibited for our contemplation. The aesthetic frame is explicitly acknowledged.

Yet Hoggart's demonstration of a taste *for* class shows something about the relation between taste *and* class. If the young working-class woman, as well as her surprising tastefulness, is an expression of working-class taste, then taste, paradoxically, is also exhibited as a surpassing of class. At one level this has to do with a literary iconography of working-class women that finds one notable expression in D. H. Lawrence's novel first published in 1913, *Sons and Lovers* (1948). The novel is preoccupied with class and the aspiration to move beyond a working-class life. The family triangle of the Morels – mother, father and son – maps different relations to this issue. The father, a miner, accepts his class identity and takes pride in it. The mother aspires to another life, not least because she finds working-class life distasteful. The son follows his mother's aspirations for him to reclassify himself through education. In Bourdieu's terminology he becomes an accumulator of 'educational capital'.

Lawrence's imagination of the working class informs Hoggart's *Uses of Literacy*. In so far as we read Hoggart's text as autobiography, it is, like Lawrence's novel, an account of someone who has moved away from their class of origin. Such transitions can give a heightened, even exacerbated, awareness of questions of taste. And, of course, both texts reveal the intricate relations between class, taste and gender. In both the woman is presented as the bearer of good taste. In Lawrence's book this puts her at odds with her immediate class context. In Hoggart's work the sense of antagonism is less strong, but the woman is still imagined in terms of a special grace and presence (despite the difficulties with hygiene).

These examples raise a further question about the relations between taste and class. Taste becomes both aspirational and mimetic. It is a way of imagining oneself as being in another class, even a class apart. What taste does is imitate what is imagined as the taste of another class, a class which is felt to embody 'good' taste. This process has been a rich source of social comedy, whether in Jane Austen's novels or, more recently, in the BBC sitcom, *Keeping up Appearances*. The television series presents the contradictions in play with robust explicitness. The question of taste is again focused on the character of a woman, Hyacinth Bucket (pronounced 'bouquet'). She invests formidable energy in declaring her good taste by imitating the taste of what she imagines as the 'upper classes'. Her origins are working class, and these return, usually in the form of her family, to embarrass her efforts to be what she is not. The comedy of the series derives from her energetic obsession to maintain appearances and from the exposure of what those appearances are intended to conceal. Yet part of the power of the series is what it can tell us about a life lived in this way: being what you are not becomes a way of life and the aspiration to be tasteful maintains this being. The joke, at least for one part of the audience, is that to be so preoccupied with questions of taste is itself tasteless. Perhaps *Keeping up Appearances* is popular because its central character extravagantly displays and exorcises anxieties which run deep in the programme's audience.

Concepts of class and taste can, then, take two different forms: one, of the kind exemplified by Bourdieu, emphasizes the ways in which classes are distinguished one from another by their tastes. The other proposes an idea of taste as a way in which one class imagines itself as another. The first emphasizes the boundaries and antagonisms between classes. The second does not ignore these boundaries but inscribes them in a different way. Taste finds its social expression hierarchically. Those at the top of the hierarchy determine what is good taste, and those lower down imitate what has been decided by those above them. But hierarchy, at least in matters of taste, is also a process of circulation. Imitation does not simply work one way. High fashion designers adapt styles that originated in urban street cultures. The rich have been turning the clothes of the poor into fashion statements from the time of Marie Antoinette. The process works the other way round as well. In the 1950s Teddy Boys took over the styles of the upper-class Edwardian dandy, but their imitation was also an exaggeration, imprinting upon the upper-class original the signs of a different taste.

The imitative moment in the circulation of taste is complex. It may come from a desire to emulate what is felt to be a superior original; here imitation works to reinforce social hierarchy. But what is copied can also be transformed and appropriated. The style of one class can be made over into the style of another. There is something like a trade in taste, an exchange of styles going on across boundaries of class. And this points to a further possibility: that judgements of taste fracture class boundaries; that what taste creates are molecular and volatile communities, tangentially related to class, perhaps, but not explained by the monolithic orders of upper, middle and working class.

Dick Hebdige's subcultural kids may seem to be a case in point. Certainly they appear to be a world away from Richard Hoggart's young working-class wife, at once bound by her class world and bringing an unexpected taste to it:

It was during this strange apocalyptic summer [of 1976] that punk made its sensational debut in the music press. In London, especially in the south west and more specifically in the vicinity of the King's Road, a new style was being generated combining elements drawn from a whole range of heterogeneous youth styles. In fact punk claimed a dubious parentage. Strands from David Bowie and glitter-rock were woven together with elements from American proto-punk (the Ramones, the Heartbreakers, Iggy Pop, Richard Hell) ...
Not surprisingly, the resulting mix was somewhat unstable: all these elements constantly threatened to separate and return to their original sources. Glam rock contributed narcissism, nihilism and gender confusion. American punk offered a minimalist aesthetic (e.g. The Ramones' 'Pinhead' or Crime's 'I Stupid') ... (Hebdige, 1979, p. 25)

The working-class home and neighbourhood of Hoggart's description have been replaced by a different kind of urbanity. Hebdige's punks represent the apogee of subcultural style. They draw their energy from the media culture that Hoggart deplores. They define themselves apart from the continuities of the family which are, for Hoggart, a cherished part of working-class life. The concepts which sustain Hebdige's analysis and his sense of cultural value are avowedly different from Hoggart's. In the first chapter of *Subculture* Hebdige announces his break from Hoggart's model of Cultural Studies. This break has centrally to do with the renewed authority that Hebdige gives to Marxism, and, hence, an emphasis on culture as an arena of conflict rather than consensus. Hoggart's commitment to protect the integrity of a traditional working-class culture is replaced by Hebdige's search for an energetic style which will break open the false consensus of the bourgeois myth world, an energy which can remind us that the world we live in is not the only world there can be.

Yet, as Hebdige acknowledges, there is a continuity between his work and Hoggart's. This is formulated as the attempt to mediate between two different definitions of culture: one which establishes a standard of value in terms of which, for example, the taste of a culture can be judged; the other concerned with the understanding of large processes of cultural change as described, for example, by Raymond Williams:

an emphasis [which] from studying particular meanings and values seeks not so much to compare these, as a way of establishing a scale, but by studying their modes of change to discover certain general causes or 'trends' by which social and cultural developments as a whole can be better understood. (Williams, 1965, p. 58)

A revised form of Marxism, according to Hebdige, can mediate between these two imperatives of evaluation and description in so far as it offers at once a method for understanding large-scale change and a political criterion of social justice against which change can be evaluated.

But the tidiness of this conceptual order is deceptive. There is another kind of continuity at work between Hebdige and Hoggart and one that is not explicitly acknowledged. This has to do with the role that judgements of taste play in cultural description and evaluation. Hebdige's punks are evidently players in the game of judgements of taste, if only by the way they systematically violate what is held to be in good taste. Again, they may seem to be the very antithesis of Hoggart's working-class wife. But, however doubtful their parentage may be, they are still imagined as 'figures in a landscape', as the appropriate expressions of their setting: that 'strange apocalyptic summer'. This motif is, perhaps, only residually at work in Hebdige's prose, but the aesthetic attractions of youth subcultures, the fact that they are to the writer's taste and should be to ours, is evident in other ways. Hebdige describes them as producing a 'genuinely expressive artifice; a truly subterranean style' (Hebdige, 1979, p. 19). He finds analogies and anticipations of punk in the work of rebel hipster artists like Jean Genet and William Burroughs. The purpose of *Subculture* is to make us admire punk as well as understand it.

Hebdige knows this, of course, as the conclusion to *Subculture* makes clear. His argument here is uncannily like Hoggart's in 'Who are the Working Classes?', the first chapter of *The Uses of Literacy*. There is the same cautionary note about the dangers of succumbing to 'romanticism', the same anxiety about the gulf between the writer and his subject. Hebdige appears worried about his relation to different forms of judgement. His subcultural subjects will reject his book as yet another effort on the part of the straight world to understand them. Sociologists will find his work lacking in a comprehensive analysis of the 'various agencies of social control (the police, school, etc.) which play a crucial role in determining subculture' (p. 138). He has to guard against a mistaken political judgement, finding revolutionary potential in his subjects when none is in fact there. There is a sense of steely prohibitions at work here as though the author has been found guilty of celebrating his subject.

The tensions enacted in the closing chapter of *Subculture* have to do with the relation between different kinds of judgement. Judgements of taste lead Hebdige to a celebration of subcultural creativity. Punks become the makers of their own eclectic style. They are admired in the way that artists might be admired for both the unpredictability and the cultural significance of what they invent. They create a culture which becomes powerful enough to be imitated.

Sociological judgement points in another direction. Here youth sub-cultures are understood as symptomatic responses to changes in the condition of the working class in Britain after the Second World War. These include the destruction of the older forms of working-class neigh-bourhood celebrated by Richard Hoggart in *The Uses of Literacy*; the emergence of mass consumer markets, including markets oriented towards the young; and the pervasive idea that Britain is moving towards a classless condition. In this argument style is connected to class as an unconscious response to change. Youth subcultures are not aware of the significance of the styles they adopt. They need sociologists to explain that to them and to us. Hebdige is ambivalent about the authority of these sociological judge-ments. He wants to acknowledge their authority, and, hence, find a means of connecting taste to class. Subcultures find their proper parents in the working class. Their taste can be held and decoded in this context. Yet Hebdige is uneasy about making the connection too determining, not least because it conflicts with the account of subcultures derived from judge-ments of taste. It is not just that media play as important a role as class in creating subcultural style. Hebdige does not want his subjects to lose their identity as hipster artists in the face of a sociological judgement which would make them into cultural robots acting out the tensions inherent in a class-divided society.

Political judgement points in another direction. Marxism provides the context of this judgement. Its background assumption is a politics of revolutionary struggle, the moment when an exploited working class rises up and vanquishes the class that exploits it. But, of course, the revolution has not taken place, at least not in the right place or the right time. The working class has failed to fulfil its revolutionary role. While Hebdige finds a subversive energy in youth subcultures lacking in their parent working-class culture, he does not want to translate style into revolutionary politics. An aesthetics of subversion is not the same thing as a politics of militant class consciousness. Subcultural style may defy class but it cannot van-quish it:

I have tried to avoid the temptation to portray subculture . . . as the repository of 'Truth', to locate in its forms some obscure revolutionary potential. Rather, I have sought in Sartre's words, to acknowledge the right of the subordinate class (the young, the black, the working class) to 'make something of what is made of (them)' – to embellish, decorate, parody and wherever possible to recognize and rise above a subordinate position which was not of their own choosing. (pp. 138–9)

These differences of judgement are not the sign of a logical failure in Hebdige's book. They are the sources of its intellectual energy, each one constituting its subject differently: as aesthetic self-fashioner, as a manifestation of tension within a social structure, as militants who didn't quite make it. A happy pluralism which decrees that all these judgements are true, that they do justice to the rich complexity of their subject, is likely to ignore their incompatibility and division. If they are all true, then the subject they are true of is radically divided between being part of a class and not part of it, between being a free agent and the prisoner of a social structure, between the possibility of revolutionary action and its certain loss.

Subculture provides a further version of the relation between class and taste: the idea of a taste which defies class, not in the name of another class's superior taste but, perhaps, in a longing to be rid of class altogether. As such it can be set alongside the two other versions of the class/taste relation presented in this chapter: taste as the manifestation of class, and taste as a negotiation across class boundaries. What links these three versions is not so much a conclusion as a further question about the role of judgements of taste in Cultural Studies. Cultural Studies may be embarrassed by its own immersion in judgements of taste. Yet it can readily become a form of connoisseurship, taking as its objects not works of fine art but the multiplication of styles, artefacts and expressions characteristic of a media culture which voraciously converts politics into aesthetics.

Notes

1. *Distinction* is, amongst other things, a sustained critique of the aesthetic theories of the eighteenth-century German philosopher, Immanuel Kant. Bourdieu regards Kant as the main architect of bourgeois taste, particularly in his notion of the 'disinterestedness' of aesthetic judgement: works of art are

valued for their own sake alone and not because they achieve a moral or political purpose beyond them. For a detailed exposition see Caygill (1989).

2. William Empson provides a useful summary of the relation between pastoral and class: 'The essential trick of the old pastoral, which was felt to imply a beautiful relation between the rich and poor, was to make simple people express strong feelings (felt as the most universal subject, something fundamentally true about everybody) in learned and fashionable language (so that you wrote about the best subject in the best way)' (Empson, 1968, p. 11). This could be done in ways that acknowledged the artificiality of the form. From the eighteenth century onwards there was an increasing tendency to make pastoral realistic, rather than acknowledge it as artifice. See Empson (1968) and Barrell (1980).

3. Examples here would include the novels of Thomas Hardy (see in particular *Tess of the D'Urbervilles*, Chapter 14) and the paintings of L. S. Lowry.

Bibliography

Barrell, J. (1980) *The Dark Side of the Landscape*. Cambridge: Cambridge University Press.

Bourdieu, P. (1986, first published 1979) *Distinction* (trans. by R. Nice). London: Routledge.

Caygill, H. (1989) *Art of Judgement*. Oxford: Blackwell.

Clough, A. H. (1968) *Poetical Works*. Oxford: Oxford University Press.

Eagleton, T. (1990) *The Ideology of the Aesthetic*. Oxford: Blackwell.

Empson, W. (1968, first published 1935) *Some Versions of Pastoral*. London: Chatto & Windus.

Fiske, J. (1989) *Understanding Popular Culture*. London: Unwin Hyman.

Hebdige, D. (1979) *Subculture: The Meaning of Style*. London: Methuen.

Hoggart, R. (1958, first published 1957) *The Uses of Literacy*. Harmondsworth: Penguin.

Hume, D. (1985, first published 1777) *Essays, Moral, Political and Literary* (ed. E. F. Miller). Indianapolis: Liberty Classics.

Lawrence, D. H. (1948, first published 1913) *Sons and Lovers*. Harmondsworth: Penguin.

Williams, R. (1965) *The Long Revolution*. Harmondsworth: Penguin.

7

Escape and Escapism: Representing Working-Class Women

Steph Lawler

> Oppressed groups, such as the working class, have to survive in a way
> that means that they must come to recognise themselves as lacking,
> deficient, deviant, as being where they are because that is who they are,
> that is how they are made, an insidious self-regulation, while individual
> effort is allowed to those clever enough to plan an escape, an escape
> only to be pathologised by others who romanticise the oppression in
> the first place. (Walkerdine, 1997, p. 39)

In 1984, watching a production of Willy Russell's 1975 play *Breezeblock
Park*, I felt an almost physical shock of recognition on hearing Sandra's
speech in which she expresses her desires for a different kind of life to that
of her working-class family. The life she desires is characterized, not
(ostensibly) by more money, but by the artefacts of middle-class existence
which Bourdieu metaphorizes as (legitimated) cultural capital – books on
the shelves, red wine and different kinds of cheeses on the table, conversation. The shock came from recognizing my own desires publicly
represented. In 1984 I had never heard of Bourdieu or of cultural capital;
but I did recognize something in that speech which spoke of the inequities
of a classed system which are not reducible to economic exchange – the
'hidden injuries of class', as Sennett and Cobb (1977) describe them – and
something, too, of the desires around class which, I now know, are so easily
trivialized and pathologized. These desires may centre around the desire
for 'escape', but what happens to those who don't escape? Are they without
desires, without complexity, without authenticity? Are they to be condemned for their failure to 'escape'?

This chapter is an attempt to deal with some of these issues through looking at representations of working-class women in *Breezeblock Park*. The chapter is centrally about the representation of desires – women's desires for material and symbolic goods which are marked by class, whether those desires are realized or thwarted.

I want to emphasize at the outset that my critique of the play is not on the grounds that it represents working-class women 'negatively';[1] but nor am I attempting to uncover some form of resistance on the part of the working-class female (or male) characters represented within the play, which would then serve to 'ennoble' their lives. As Pamela Fox comments, such a reading tends to 'approve' only certain forms of behaviour:

> *Contestation, disruption, opposition, transgression, subversion* – all have become keywords in our profession for describing practices by which a range of marginalized groups can suggest some sense of both action and refusal. But refusal of what? Despite their attentiveness to (and frequently direct experience with) class-based cultural differences, resistance theorists tend to answer that question by proceeding from what are essentially dominant assumptions and values ... The Left stamp of approval thus falls on those behaviors, tendencies and gestures which not only resist domination but do so for decidedly progressive aims. (Fox, 1994, p. 8)

My aim, rather, is to show the ways in which *Breezeblock Park* provides deeply ambiguous representations of working-class women. At the same time that the play foregrounds the classed desires and fantasies of these women, it ultimately contains these desires within the trajectory of a plot which normalizes some desires and pathologizes others.

Breezeblock Park is set in the present, on two houses on the same council housing estate; the action takes place on Christmas Eve and Christmas Day. Although the stage directions do not indicate a specific geographical location, the characters' accents and verbal idioms indicate that it is (at least as written) set in Liverpool. The central characters of the play are Sandra, a woman of nineteen, and Betty, her mother. Other characters are relatives (Sandra's father, Syd; Betty's brother, Tommy; her sister, Reeny; Tommy's wife, Vera; Reeny's husband, Ted; and their son, John, who is slightly older than Sandra) with the exception of Tim, Sandra's student boyfriend. As we will see, the fact of Tim's being a student, and the signifiers of middle-class status with which he is marked in the play, are extremely important in the development of Sandra's own character.

As the play opens, the tensions between Sandra and Betty become apparent: Sandra does not participate in the celebration of Christmas in which the rest of the family is engaged: she criticizes the artificial Christmas tree her mother is decorating; and her mother's rebukes make it clear that Sandra is less than fully involved in family life. As the rest of the family arrive, Sandra leaves, to return with Tim. It is clear Tim and Sandra have some announcement to make: Sandra's attempts to get Tim to make this announcement repeatedly fail, until she herself tells her mother (and the rest of the family) that she is pregnant. Betty's reaction is ambiguous: she says little, she is clearly ashamed and, as the first act ends, she screams at her family to leave.

By the second act, set on the following day, Betty has come to the terms with the pregnancy; more than this, she is planning Sandra and Tim's wedding, where they will live, the name of the child, and his (it seems she has decided it is to be a boy) education. Betty has turned her shame into pride. Indeed, the whole family has accepted this shock revelation, and the men are concerned that Tim will 'do the right thing' by marrying Sandra. But Sandra disrupts these efforts at incorporation of her pregnancy: she refuses to marry Tim, and to live in her parents' house with him, even when Tim attempts to insist on this. She ends the play by breaking through the circle of family members who surround her and walking out of the house and into the night. Significantly, it is her mother – with whom Sandra has repeated angry disagreements throughout the play, and who is, in many ways, the Other to Sandra's character, the 'constitutive outside' to her self (Hall, 1996, p. 3) – who steps outside to let her out of the familial circle. It is as if Betty recognizes the need for Sandra's 'escape', and recognizes, too, that Sandra will escape and she will not. Sandra's desires for escape can only be achieved by the non-fulfilment of Betty's desire to keep her daughter within the family.

Class and capitals

The 'escape' which is named in the title of this chapter is Sandra's (potential, desired) escape from a respectable working-class position to a specific form of educated middle-classness. Her desire to escape from one class position to another centres, not primarily on the attainment of economic wealth, but rather around cultural and symbolic artefacts of class which Bourdieu (1977, 1986, 1993) metaphorizes as cultural and symbolic capital: 'tasteful' possessions, education, knowledge. For Bourdieu, cultural capital refers to a specific form of knowledge which, as Johnson puts it, 'equips the social agent with empathy towards, appreciation for or competence in deciphering cultural relations and cultural artefacts' (Johnson, 1993, p. 7). Cultural capital is accumulated over a lifetime, and is transmitted through numerous processes of formal and informal education and membership of social groups (Bourdieu, 1986, 1993).

Not all cultural capital can be 'traded' on equal terms, however (Skeggs, 1997). It is only when cultural capital is sufficiently legitimated that it can be converted into symbolic capital – the prestige or recognition which various capitals acquire by virtue of *being* (socially) recognized, 'known' and approved as legitimate. It is only the cultural capital of the middle classes which is legitimated in this way: their tastes and dispositions are coded as *inherently* 'right', *inherently* 'tasteful'. In this way, class distinctions are simultaneously at work and obscured: they are at work through the distinctions drawn between the cultural competencies attached to different social class positions, and they are obscured because they become, not a matter of inequality in legitimated forms of knowledge and aesthetics, but, precisely, knowledge and aesthetics themselves. To not possess symbolic capital is to 'fail' in the games of aesthetic judgement, of knowledge and of cultural competence.

Bourdieu's analysis is useful here in that it both highlights and overturns conventional assumptions about cultural competencies and cultural knowledges. These competencies and knowledges are not usually seen as social mechanisms: rather, they are assumed to inhere within the self, and this has specific social and cultural effects. Hence, taste, knowledge and other forms of cultural competency are coded as something innate – something one *is*, rather than something one *has* (Bourdieu, 1986; Lury, 1996). So, working-class and middle-class cultural competencies and knowledges (and hence, working-class and middle-class selves) are not socially constituted as 'equal but different': they are arranged hierarchically, with working-class people's difference from middle-class people being *made into* inequality (Walkerdine and Lucey, 1989; Blackman, 1996).

The 'working classes' have been the source of much disappointment and disgust for the middle-class observers who have studied them, and, in large part, this is marked out through the lack of legitimacy granted to working-class cultural capital. Roberts (1999) notes how sociological accounts of working-class life have historically positioned working-class people as untrustworthy, disgusting, apolitical (or right-wing) and chaotic. They do not *know* the right things, they do not *value* the right things, they do not *want* the right things. Similarly, Walkerdine argues that 'the working-class' has come to be the repository of desire, horror and fascination for middle-class people. Asking, 'What are the fantasies proved time and again in empiricist social science?', she argues:

> There are too many to name, but those of us who have grown up as any of those Others know exactly how we have become subjected. We are the salt of the earth, the bedrock of the revolution; we are working-class women with big hearts, big arms, big breasts; we are stupid, ignorant, deprived, depriving; we are repressed, authoritarian, and above all we voted Thatcher into her third term of office. We are revolting, anti-democratic. We suppress our children and do not allow them autonomy. How many more of these truths will there be? (Walkerdine, 1990, p. 206)

Sandra's potential class movement, her desires and fantasies, take place around specific configurations of cultural competency and cultural knowledge which are coded as 'middle class'. Her character is impelled through the plot through her desires for these competencies and knowledges. Yet it is important to emphasize that these cultural artefacts should not be somehow *set against* material goods: they centrally involve the ownership of specific kinds of 'things'.[2] However, and as later sections of this chapter will elaborate, not only does 'taste' mark out some people as better than others, but 'tasteful' possessions can also be marked as hardly possessions at all.

Competing desires: authentic and inauthentic selves

> Class is something beneath your clothes, under your skin, in your psyche, at the very core of your being. In the all-encompassing English class system, if you know that you are in the 'wrong' class, you know that therefore you are a valueless person. (Kuhn, 1995, p. 98)

Themes of desire and longing are recurrent in Russell's plays,[3] and are central to *Breezeblock Park*. The plot revolves around the characters' desires for specific kinds of material goods, which are culturally marked as either 'tasteful' or 'tasteless', as well as desires for specific sets of know-ledges and cultural competencies. These desires in turn centre around the characters' perception of the self, and their desires for particular *kinds* of self.

If cultural and symbolic signifiers of class are constituted as inhering within the self, then the movement from a working-class to a middle-class existence must involve (perceived) changes in the self, as the self becomes more knowledgeable, more 'tasteful'. *Breezeblock Park* deals with the il/legitimacy of desires, and the implications of these desires for the self.

Sandra's escape takes place around the defiance of convention, not because she is pregnant,[4] but because she wants a different life to that mapped out for her by her family. She wants to leave behind the world and the class inhabited by her parents. And she has a comparison, since her relationship with Tim has provided her with an insight into 'another world' – a world of middle-class existence. In dialogue with her aunt, Sandra points to her family's lack (and Tim's family's possession) of legitimated cultural capital, through contrasting the ways in which the two families will spend Christmas:

> SANDRA: They won't spend Christmas stuck in front of the telly. They'll get a big massive table out in the drawing-room.
>
> VERA: Are they old-fashioned? No one has drawin' rooms now.
>
> SANDRA: They do. And a big fire in the grate. And they'll have lots of people round, interesting people, round to dinner. And it'll be a proper dinner, a special dinner, like an event and it'll take hours to get through ...
>
> VERA: Ooh, I'd hate to do the washin' up in their house.
>
> SANDRA: And candles on the table, and wine, and all the people will sit round the table afterwards and talk and tell stories and laugh. All the people that Tim knows are like that, Aunty Vee.
>
> VERA: They sound like snobs to me. (Russell, 1996b, p. 44)

We do not know, of course, how far this is Sandra's fantasy around Tim's family and how far it is based on what he has actually told her: there is no indication in the play of her having actually met them. The point is, though, that she has a (real or imagined) scenario which she knows to be in every way preferable to the world inhabited by her own family. Although

Vera presents an alternative understanding of this kind of world ('they sounds like snobs to me'), the two women's perceptions are not culturally marked as equivalent, but take place within a set of understandings which constitute Sandra's understanding of Tim's family as the 'right' one. The symbolic and material goods which Sandra wants are already marked by their superiority. Her family's inability to 'see' this is one of Sandra's major frustrations. It seems that the members of Sandra's family simply cannot see that they are 'wrong'.

Sandra's escape is set in relief by those who fail to escape; those around her whose only recourse is *escapism*. Betty dreams of owning her own home, 'A little house I could do up on me own, without having to get the Council's permission' (Russell, 1996b, p. 83); Tommy dreams of an escape to New Zealand[5] (but will never go); Ted dreams of writing a book and lavishes attention on his car. Sandra's cousin John, probably the most violently escapist character in the play, engages in secret acts of sabotage as, every night, he tears apart the new three-piece suite his parents have bought, seemingly in silent protest at the impositions, restrictions and demands of his parents.

For me, however, the most powerful scene in the play centres around the contrast between Sandra's potential escape and her mother's escapism. Sandra's desires for a different world are set against Betty's desires for respectability, convention and a nice home. The showdown between the two women takes place around this question of competing desires:

SANDRA: I want a *good* life, Mother. I want something that's got some meaning left in it. I want to sit around and talk about films and – and music. I want a house where we don't have the telly on all day, where we don't worry about the furniture. I want books on the shelves, Mother – and – oh – for God's sake, I want paintings on the wall and red wine on the table and lots of different cheeses. I want – I want – I want . . .

BETTY: Want – want – want! And what about what *I* wanted?

SANDRA: What you wanted, you got! Y'got it all, Mother – y'three-piece suites, y'fridge, y'plastic pedal bin. What you wanted – you got!

BETTY: You begrudge me every bit of pleasure I have ever had – don't'y? Well, let me tell you – it's more than pleasure – much more . . . Let me tell you, Lady Muck – if it wasn't for the things I buy – I would

have cut my throat years ago! ... I wouldn't mind, but I'm not askin'
for very much, am I? I live on an estate that's like a – a camp for
refugees, me only entertainment's a Saturday night in a social club, I
work forty-nine weeks of the year doin' a job that took me half a day to
learn ... Well, I'm tellin' you, Miss Criticize – many's the time, many's
the time that a trip round the supermarket and a new find on the
shelves has stopped me goin' home and puttin' my head in the gas
oven. (Russell, 1996b, pp. 90–1)

Betty's response speaks of her desires as compensation for her life. In
contrast to Sandra's desires, which are not elaborated or fully explained,
Betty's appear coherent *only* because of the exigencies of her life. Her
character is, to some degree, dignified through an appeal to an understanding of the repetitive monotony of her life. Her desire for material
goods and for respectability become coherent through this appeal, and she
becomes, in many ways, a more sympathetic character through the invoca-
tion of a life in which there are 'few pleasures'. In many ways, it could be
seen as 'not her fault' that she wants these material goods. They provide
the escapism that she needs. But why should she not want them? Why do
they have to be explained in this way? Is it because the things she wants are
deemed to be *inauthentic*? Is it because she does not have the 'taste' to know
this?

Much of what impels the plot of *Breezeblock Park* is the rivalry between
Betty and Reeny, her sister. The two women are constantly trying to outdo
one another in terms of their homes, their furniture, the behaviour of their
respective children, and so on. The competition, then, takes place around
two axes – that of material goods, and that of less tangible phenomena such
as respectability. As such, it takes place around the axes of material and
cultural artefacts. Yet it is these women's desire for material goods which is
foregrounded within the play. For Russell, one of the themes of the play is
'the families' refusal to confront, how feelings and passions and needs were
sublimated or stifled or perverted into concern for purely material matters'
(Russell, 1996a, p. xvi). The association of working-class existence with
crass materialism is a pervasive one (Walkerdine, 1990, 1997). But Betty is
not the only one who wants things: Sandra, too, wants things – she wants
paintings, specific types of food, books, a particular kind of house, a real
Christmas tree. For Sandra, these material goods signify desires for a better
life, just as they do for her mother, but what she wants is coded as
inherently better than the plastic pedal bins, fridges and three-piece suites

she derides and criticizes as meaningless. While Betty's desires could easily be characterized as inherently trivial, Sandra's are not: they are the 'high art', as it were, to Betty's mass culture. More than this, Betty's desires are marked as material(istic) in ways Sandra's are not. 'Tasteful' (middle-class) consumer goods, then, can be coded as hardly material at all.

'Who does she think she is?': between being and seeming

The desire for goods marked as 'tasteless' is not only coded in terms of crass materialism but, often, in terms of pretentiousness also. Betty's pretentiousness is reinforced again and again, and provides much of the humour. She has bought a three-piece suite costing £220; throughout the play, the price gets progressively inflated until she tells Reeny it cost over £1,000. She describes her former job as a nursing auxiliary as 'much higher' than an SRN.[6] Her concern for sexual and domestic respectability underlines the humour that attaches to her character.

Indeed, both Betty and Reeny are marked by pretentiousness as they vie with each other over their houses, their furniture and so on. But they are also marked as pretentious in pretending to know what they do not. Just as Ted's exposure of the flaw in *Waiting for Godot* (he foresees that Godot will not appear when he reads the programme and sees that there is no cast member playing him) makes his ignorance apparent through his desire to affirm his intelligence, so too with Betty and Reeny. Betty believes that the vibrator bought for her by Tommy is a 'drinks mixer' and, in conversation with Tim, who comes from Stafford, says, 'All those hops!' (Russell, 1996b, p. 40). Reeny, explaining why it is 'flyin' in the face of nature' for men to be present at childbirth, asks, 'Why, since the beginnin' of time, have they always built waitin'-rooms at the side of labour wards? See my point?' (Russell, 1996b, p. 87). So it is not just consumerism, but these characters' tenuous hold on knowledge which renders them 'pretentious'.

Bourdieu defines pretension as 'the recognition of distinction that is affirmed in the effort to possess it' (Bourdieu, 1986, p. 251). Pretensions, according to Bourdieu, provoke 'calls to order'; 'Who does she think she is?' (Bourdieu, 1986, p. 380). 'Pretentious' is a charge levelled at people in whom what they *seem to be* is not (considered to be) what they *are*: in whom there is a gap between *being* and *seeming*. 'We' (the audience) can see this gap, as we 'see through' the characters' inauthenticity. Who does she think she is? indeed.

Sandra's desires, by contrast, are marked as always-already legitimate, not only because she wants material and cultural goods which are held to be superior, but also because she expresses desires for a closure of the gap between being and seeming – to 'really' be a different person, rather than to seem to be one. The closure of this gap evokes an authenticity in the self; it is the real, authentic self which is to be actualized through Sandra's escape, and, conversely, the real self which is represented as stifled within the exigencies of working-class life. It is the self, itself, which has to be realized,[7] to escape from the fetters of working-class existence – an existence which is repeatedly represented as robbing the self of its actualization, in a kind of grinding-down process. Escapism, then, is represented in the play as the (pathologized) solution to a working-class life.

Classed femininities

Class ... plays a central role in the regulation of femininity, and the production of Otherness. (Walkerdine, 1997: 171)

Sandra's desired escape is an escape, not just from a working-class existence, but also from a rigid set of gender roles. Indeed, the two are intertwined throughout the play as Sandra's desires encompass, not only desires for the artefacts of a middle-class existence, but also desires for a less demarcated model of gender. Against this, Sandra's working-class family is represented in terms of a rigid and oppressive set of gendered conventions: they are appalled, for example, at Sandra's announcement that she is going to the pub to join Tim and the men in her family. As they explain to her, 'they'll be in the bar' – clearly not a proper place for a woman. Consider, too, this interchange between Ted and Vera:

TED: ... [T]he mind, the human mind is a vast warehouse of ideas!
VERA: I suppose so. If y'a feller, like. (Russell, 1996b, p. 35)

Vera bursts the bubble of Ted's pomposity, but only through a characterization of women as unthinking. The rigid distinction between and separation of the sexes is reiterated throughout the play. For example, as the male members of the family discuss Sandra's pregnancy with Tim, her uncle tells Tim:

TOMMY: [Pregnancy] really does mean joinin' a club. Sandra's never been part of the women's club before, well not a full member anyway;

so she probably can't see the benefits. But she'll be able to become a part of it now – now that you've given her the membership card. Girls are always moanin', but once they become women they're different altogether. (Russell, 1996b, pp. 71–2)

Sandra, however, is characterized as defying gender conventions and gender segregation by speaking out about her opinions and by resisting the demarcation along gender lines imposed by her family. She (in some cases literally) steps out of her place. She questions their received wisdom through an appeal both to an understanding of women and girls as able to think, and to a characterization of her relationship with Tim as one which is, at least potentially, marked by reciprocity and mutuality.

As such, Sandra can look like a feminist heroine, and there is much to admire in her rebellious and outspoken character. However, the intertwining of a rigid class and a rigid gender system makes the character much more problematic for a feminist analysis. This representation suggests that it is (a specific, educated form of) *middle-class* (and heterosexual, and white) femininity which is to be aimed for. That this can be so easily represented as a kind of freedom from gender roles is an indication of how normalized, how naturalized, middle-classness has become, and, conversely, of the degree to which working-class existence is pathologized. Sandra's sympathetic and positive characterization is enabled by the negative characterization of the other women characters.

I noted earlier how working-class people are, in many contexts, Othered and pathologized within middle-class culture. But working-class *women* stand in a specific relationship to this pathologization. The work of authors like Skeggs, Steedman and Walkerdine indicates how working-class women are particularly marked as 'Other'. Eulogized in the figure of 'Our Mam' (Steedman, 1982, 1986), or pathologized as bad and insensitive mothers (Walkerdine and Lucey, 1989; Walkerdine, 1990), or laden with sexuality and dirt (Skeggs, 1997), or displaying the wrong amount and type of femininity (Walkerdine, 1997), these women are constituted as exotic and repulsive Others when observed from a middle-class perspective. They are also positioned as particularly disappointing from the standpoint of Left politics: they are the cultural dupes who want the trappings of capitalism at the expense of the real class struggle. These women become objects in a plot in which the only position for them to occupy is one of pathology.[8]

Skeggs (1997) notes how 'woman' has historically developed as a classed sign, with white, middle-class women able to claim a proximity to this sign, and working-class women positioned as at a distance from it. As she argues, 'Working-class women – both Black and White – were coded as the sexual and deviant other against which femininity was defined' (Skeggs, 1997, p. 99). This historical legacy continues, according to Skeggs, with white and black working-class women being constituted in terms of excess, vulgarity and sexuality, rather than in terms of the containment, taste and asexuality (or restricted heterosexuality) associated with femininity.

It might, then, appear contradictory to see Sandra as escaping femininity through becoming middle class. However, this classed movement has also to be seen in terms of notions of individual and social *progress*. In some, at least, middle-class milieux, certain forms of (individualized) gender freedom are marked as 'progressive', against a 'retrogressive' view of the sexes belonging in different spheres, of there being distinct men's and women's roles and so on. This is part of a wider characterization of middle-class existence as more knowing, more up-to-date, more forward-thinking, than working-class life (Rose, 1991). Rigid concepts of masculinity and femininity can be seen to be associated with working-class people, who are then constituted as lacking the 'knowledge' about more up-to-date understandings of gender. This does not mean that middle-class culture is in any 'real' sense more 'feminist' or 'liberated' than working-class culture. Rather, it is that the (gendered) behaviour of working-class people can all too easily be characterized as retrogressive, pre-feminist, repressive, while the (gendered) behaviour of middle-class people can be characterized as either not gendered at all or gendered in a more acceptable, liberating way. Sandra is not characterized as shedding femininity; rather, she aspires to a different form of femininity.

So, working-class women are distanced from 'real' femininity, but the meanings attached to femininity can be unstable. In this context, the women in Sandra's family who attempt to enforce gendered roles and gendered behaviour can, indeed, be seen as *not* feminine. Their pretensions, their attempts to assert authority, can all be characterized as 'unfeminine', partly *because* they attempt to enforce gender segregation. If 'real' women are middle class, and if middle-class culture has come to embrace some rhetorical commitment to a gender mutuality and reciprocity, then behaviour which accentuates gender antagonism and gender segregation can be coded as unfeminine.

In addition, working-class women can become 'monstrous' through an association with the desires for the (material and cultural) objects of middle-class existence. This relates to my earlier point about the relationship between class and materialism, but adds a further dimension in terms of classed femininities. To want and to envy the markers of a middle-class existence is to be in a peculiarly vulnerable position, especially for women, who already stand in a specific relationship to those desires. As Carolyn Steedman comments, in Britain at least:

> there is no language of desire that can present what my mother wanted as anything but supremely trivial; indeed, there is no language that does not let the literal accents of class show, nor promote the tolerant yet edgy smile. (Steedman, 1986, p. 113)

What Steedman's mother wanted was 'fine clothes, glamour, money, to be what she wasn't . . . things she materially lacked, things that a culture and a social system withheld from her' (Steedman, 1986, p. 6) – desires, in other words, for specific forms of femininity which were not available to her. Women's desires for and envy of respectability and material goods are marked as apolitical, trivial, pretentious (Steedman, 1986; Fox, 1994). Yet, as both Steedman and Fox point out, these desires, this envy, should be situated within *political* struggles around dispossession and exclusion. Why should people not envy what 'a culture and a social system' withholds from them? Indeed, how could they not, when what is withheld is constituted as *inherently* desirable and *inherently* normal? And why are desires like this trivialized? Is it because they are represented as peculiarly 'feminine' affectations? Is it because they stake a claim on an existence to which you have no 'right'? The behaviour in which characters like Betty and Reeny engage is not the parodic distancing suggested by Russo (1994) as being a constituent of the 'female grotesque': these characters are grotesque because they apparently want to be taken *seriously* (see Skeggs, 1997). Parody and excess simply do not have the same meaning if the joke is on you.

Conclusion

In its avoidance of any glamorizing of working-class existence, *Breezeblock Park* avoids, too, a neglect of the costs of being working-class and being excluded from a range of categories characterized as 'normal' (see Fox, 1994). However, in representing Sandra's real, authentic self as realized through the attainment of knowledge and taste, and through the casting-off of gendered conventions associated with working-class existence, the naturalism of middle-class life is reinstated at the end of the plot. Sandra's oppositional strategies are easy to recognize and approve, but what about the oppositional strategies of those women who fail to escape? Are they to be always condemned for a preoccupation with material goods, with respectability? Are they to be condemned as apolitical because middle-class observers do not approve the forms their class strategies take? As Skeggs argues:

> Within the field of cultural criticism working-class people have come to be seen as bearing the elemental simplicity of class consciousness and little more. They have always been the site for the projected longings of the rebellious middle classes who put their investment in change in others rather than themselves. (Skeggs, 1997, p. 95)

Yet, at the same time, and as both Walkerdine (1997) and Roberts (1999) note, the answer to the 'problem' of working-class people has convention-ally been to make them more like their middle-class counterparts.[9] Is this why escape is heroic, while escapism can only be seen as failure?

Notes

1. This is one of the grounds on which Russell has been criticized: as he says, at the opening of *Breezeblock Park*, he had 'been approached by members of the Workers Revolutionary Party and warned that "to present the proletariat in such an unflattering and demeaning light was to undermine the class struggle" ' (Russell, 1996a, p. xiv).
2. Indeed, the conventional split between the cultural and the material falls down when one considers the very materiality of cultural assets. Even education, which can seem 'abstract', can be traded on the jobs market for material, as well as cultural, rewards.
3. See, for example, *Stags and Hens, Blood Brothers, Shirley Valentine, Educating Rita*.
4. And is therefore both struggling towards and embodying a 'new life'.
5. Another kind of 'new world', of course.
6. SRN refers to the (now defunct) nursing grade State Registered Nurse – a qualified nurse. A nursing auxiliary is generally regarded as doing unskilled work (and is certainly more badly paid).
7. The realization or achievement of the 'authentic self' is enabled, according to Paul Ricoeur, by the conventions of narrative. He comments of contemporary

narrative forms that narrative configures an identity through a movement towards self-actualization: the hero *becomes* who s/he *always was* (Ricoeur, 1980, 1991; Somers and Gibson, 1994). In this context, it configures an identity in which Sandra (potentially) realizes her 'true self' through becoming middle-class.

8. For example, Pamela Fox (1994) notes how the genre of the working-class novel of the late nineteenth to mid-twentieth centuries frequently positions women in terms of desires for respectability in the artefacts of the domestic world, desires which are constituted as disreputable and apolitical. Posed against the 'nobility' of the male manual worker, women within these plots are frequently represented as frivolous and pretentious. Walkerdine argues that, in the 'rags to riches' films of the 1950s (such as *My Fair Lady*), 'the working-class girl is given nothing to be proud of, even to like about herself' (Walkerdine, 1997, p. 97).

9. Yet, as Roberts notes, working-class people are often seen as also getting this 'wrong'.

Bibliography

Blackman, L. (1996) 'The dangerous classes: retelling the psychiatric story'. *Feminism and Psychology* 6(3) (special issue on social class), pp. 355–79.

Bourdieu, P. (1977) *Outline of a Theory of Practice* (trans. R. Nice). Cambridge: Cambridge University Press.

Bourdieu, P. (1986) *Distinction: A Social Critique of the Judgement of Taste* (trans. R. Nice). London: Routledge.

Bourdieu, P. (1993) *The Field of Cultural Production: Essays on Art and Literature* (ed. and introduced by R. Johnson). Cambridge: Cambridge University Press.

Fox, P. (1994) *Class Fictions: Shame and Resistance in the British Working-Class Novel, 1890–1945*. Durham, NC: Duke University Press.

Hall, S. (1996) 'Who needs "identity"?' In S. Hall and P. du Gay (eds), *Questions of Cultural Identity*. London: Sage.

Johnson, R. (1993) 'Editor's introduction'. In P. Bourdieu, *The Field of Cultural Production: Essays on Art and Literature*. Cambridge: Cambridge University Press.

Kuhn, A. (1995) *Family Secrets: Acts of Memory and Imagination*. London: Verso.

Lury, C. (1996) *Consumer Culture*. Cambridge: Polity Press.

Ricoeur, P. (1980) 'Narrative and time'. *Critical Inquiry* 7(1), pp. 169–90.

Ricoeur, P. (1991) 'Narrative identity' (trans. D. Wood). In D. Wood (ed.), *On Paul Ricoeur: Narrative and Interpretation*. London: Routledge.

Roberts, I. (1999) 'Bring 'em back alive'. In H. Beynon and P. Glavanis (eds), *Patterns of Social Inequality*. Harlow: Longman.

Rose, N. (1991) *Governing the Soul: The Shaping of the Private Self*. London: Routledge.

Russell, W. (1996a) 'Introduction'. In W. Russell, *Plays: 1*. London: Methuen.

Russell, W. (1996b) *Breezeblock Park*. In W. Russell, *Plays: 1*. London: Methuen. (First produced in 1975.)

Russo, M. (1994) *The Female Grotesque: Risk, Excess and Modernity*. New York: Routledge.

Sennett, R. and Cobb, J. (1977) *The Hidden Injuries of Class*. Cambridge: Cambridge University Press.

Skeggs, B. (1997) *Formations of Class and Gender: Becoming Respectable*. London: Sage.

Somers, M. R. and Gibson, G. D. (1994) 'Reclaiming the epistemological "Other": narrative and the social constitution of identity'. In C. Calhoun (ed.), *Social Theory and the Politics of Identity*. Cambridge, MA: Blackwell.

Steedman, C. (1982) *The Tidy House: Little Girls Writing*. London: Virago.

Steedman, C. (1986) *Landscape for a Good Woman: A Story of Two Lives*. London: Virago.

Walkerdine, V. (1990) *Schoolgirl Fictions*. London: Verso.

Walkerdine, V. (1997) *Daddy's Girl: Young Girls and Popular Culture*. London: Macmillan.

Walkerdine, V. and Lucey, H. (1989) *Democracy in the Kitchen*. London: Virago.

Acknowledgements

My thanks go to Sally Munt, both for her editorial comments and for giving me the opportunity to write this chapter. Thanks also to Mariam Fraser for her comments, and for our many discussions about the issues raised here, and to Celia Lury for inspiring the title.

8

The Appearance of Class: Challenges in Gay Space[1]

Beverley Skeggs

Appearance has always mattered. It is the means by which others are recognized and it is part of the way we want ourselves to be recognized. But this is not just a matter of interpersonal, even dialogical construction of subjectivity; it is a matter of how symbolic violence may or may not occur. Appearance and recognition are central to the processes by which some groups are denied access to economic and cultural resources because they are not recognized as being worthy recipients. Appearance is a central marker in the ability to make use of our cultural capital in matters of economic and symbolic exchange. Appearance is also central to how we know others as belonging or not belonging; it is part of the rhetorics that legitimate space. It is crucial to social order that we know our place and the places of others. Appearance as part of the scopic economy is one of the main reproductive practices of classification. It is the means by which knowledge about class, race, sexuality and gender is produced and values attributed to the bodies that appear in a certain way. It is the visible mechanism of evaluative classification. Appearance exposes the way in which every body becomes its gender (Butler, 1998) and its class.[2]

Mary Ann Doane (1991) argues that judging by appearances performs the colonialist gesture where visible markers function as signs of unknowability and exclusion from the logic of the subject. It is to assume that the judged subject is other, excluded, different and is not even worth knowing. When the judgement fits into forms of symbolic legitimation, recognition of oneself as judged acts to demarcate social and physical space. It reproduces the historical legacies of exclusion and being made nonsubject. It is a judgement of the valuelessness of the person being judged. Appearance questions the boundaries of the subject; the object which can be seen becomes the scene of the play of difference and lack. Appearance is a boundary issue, holding or containing the subject within a certain contour, keeping the subject inside (Ahmed, 1998a). Appearance is central to legislation – not as obvious as in the seventeenth century when dressing outside one's class was legislated against (Creed, 1995), or in the 1950s when anti-crossdressing ordinances were put into effect in New York (Nestle, 1987) – but as Young (1990, 1996) and Williams (1991) note, appearance is a crucial aspect of criminalizing and entry or not into public space. Appearance can operate as a form of evidence legislating against certain forms of social presence.

It is through appearance that recognitions are made and subjectivity is enabled. Recognition, both Nancy Fraser (1995, 1997) and Charles Taylor (1994) argue, is the new 1990s grammar for political claims-making. To be recognized as something has been used by certain groups, e.g. the debates on multiculturalism in the USA (see Goldberg, 1994) and on gay politics (see Berlant and Warner, 1998), to mobilize claims for political recognition. Framed within the language of bourgeois individualism and inevitably tied to formulations of identity politics (Brown, 1995), the shift from the politics of redistribution to the politics of recognition has produced significant consequences for the politics of class.

Drawing on previous ethnographic work, published as *Formations of Class and Gender: Becoming Respectable* and a current collaborative research project on 'Violence, Sexuality and Space', this chapter will explore the different possibilities that are offered by the constitutions and disruptions of class and sexuality. It will explore the differences between straight working-class women who do not want to be recognized as the identity position to which they are regularly consigned and lesbians who have carved out a space for reclaiming a positive identity. However, before that can take place some scene setting is necessary. The signifiers that enable the conditions of possibility for identification or dis-identification are historically produced. In this production, systems of value and classification are generated. The political battles that we fight in the 1990s are strongly framed by these historical articulations.

Historical articulations

The middle class, Finch (1993) shows, came to recognize themselves through difference: a difference they produced through the generation and distribution of representations of different, identifiable 'others'. The conceptualizations of the middle classes were enabled by particular

Enlightenment technologies, such as social surveys, observation, photography and ethnography, which were part of a project to develop a science of society, constituting 'reason' through the classification of observable behaviour. These provided the means for interpretation and recognition of others. These forms of recognition were moral references containing an implied judgement; the act of observation was always an act of interpretation. The importance of the use of moral categories to define an observable 'other' class, Finch (1993) argues, is that it placed women (their bodies and practices) at the centre of the discursive construction of class because it was women who were predominantly observed. They came to be recognized, by those with the power to put their conceptualizations into circulation, through their appearances and through the interpretation of their practices. So it was not just a straightforward imposition of a representation. It was the production of forms of interpretation which then enabled the understanding of particular representations *and* practices. These were used by those who could not tell the difference, by those who knew no other, by those who thought that the technologies of observation were objective, reliable scientific sources of truth. They had access to no other ways of knowing, unlike those who were the object of the visual scrutiny and interpreted themselves and their own behaviour very differently. They produced boundary markers based on class as a way of learning to know themselves.

Because of the lack of bourgeois discursive creativity coupled with a fear of that which was not known, degeneracy and danger became the dominant motifs of those distanced from the bourgeois ideal (McClintock, 1995). In this way the different categorizations of race, gender, class and sexuality were interlocked and articulated through the generic definition of 'dangerous classes'. Ware (1992) describes how modes of colonial white femininity were defined in relation to particular constructions of black femininity and white masculinity. These enabled the construction of a sexualized other from which respectability could be measured against and distanced from. Definitions of sexuality became deeply linked to class and 'race' because 'Sex is regarded as that thing which *par excellence* is a threat to the moral order of Western civilisation. Hence one is civilised at the expense of sexuality, and sexual at the expense of civilisation' (Mercer and Julien, 1988, pp. 107–8). The practice of sex came to be designated as a practice of the 'other', a practice of the uncivilized, the one without civility and respectability. The structuring of official discourses through a series of binary oppositions – vice/virtue, filth/cleanliness, animality/civilization –

was raced as well as classed, and made through the designation of sexuality. As Gilman (1990) shows, black female sexuality became equated, in the nineteenth century, with white working-class prostitution, and Hart (1994) explores the discursive dilemma that was produced through this alignment in the historical recognition of the lesbian. Naming the activity threatened to produce the category, and thereby to mark a site that could actively be assumed. She notes how the entry of the lesbian into discourse not only pathologized and criminalized her, but also displaced the threat of women's sexual 'deviance' onto women of colour and working-class women: 'Lesbianism was recognised as prevalent among women of color and working-class women: foreclosure would "properly" pathologise it in order to obviate the "contagion" of the White, middle-class European female' (Hart, 1994, p. 14). One reason for the discursive act, she argues, was to maintain a category of 'woman' that was purified and unmixed with racial and class differences. White middle-class women were located within a pure and proper femininity, precisely because black and white working-class lesbians and straight women were defined and designated as unpure, dangerous and sexual (Ware, 1992).

Lesbians have always occupied an ambiguous position in relation to class, initially being marked as working class but then movement being enabled by the amount of literature and science which made visible the upper- and middle-class lesbian.[3] This was consolidated by the liberalism of the 1970s, where expressions of sexuality became a radical bourgeois practice (Marshall, 1981; Evans, 1993) and feminism which, as a predominantly middle-class movement, consolidated the representational space for some lesbians to move away from designations of the degenerate classes (see Case, 1989). The powerful and pervasive discourse of individualism enabled some forms of sexuality to become de-sexed, as in the case for recognition struggles waged by middle-class lesbians through the concept of 'romantic friendships' (see Faderman (1985) and sexology battles in Doan and Bland, 1998). The positioning of middle-class women with femininity and against sexuality has always represented particular problems for the articulation of lesbianism.[4] The key to recognition by appearance and subsequent classification and evaluation is still, however, the evacuation of femininity – although this is hotly contested by femmes who sustain and use the masquerade of femininity (Case, 1989; Blackman and Perry, 1990). This discursive movement is very different from the male homosexual subject, which, White (1980) argues, has become *the* sign of sex, always dangerous and always contagious (Mort, 1987). The difference in the way that respectability intervenes in the discursive alliance between masculinity and class and femininity and class means that the distance drawn from sexuality enabled by middle-class femininity does not work in the same way for masculinity, which historically has not been generated through association with purity. In fact, the struggles between black and white masculinity suggest a precarious association to sexuality has been produced through fear of the othering generated by the designation of black men as hyper-sexual (see Skeggs, 1994).

The historical representational embodiment of purity in the middle-class white woman, however, continues to be reproduced (Dyer, 1993) and the evacuation of sexuality from recognitions of value, respectability and legitimation is the mechanism by which the heterosexual (and often lesbian) middle-class body comes to be known (visualize 'Laura Ashley' clothes). Subjecthood is not located in embodied sexuality but in the distance that is drawn from it – what Bourdieu (1986) defines as the 'sublimated, refined, disinterested, distinguished' aesthetic eye in which the mind is distinguished from the body. There is, however, a continual, wilful, resistant response to this discursive positioning and judgement by those positioned at a distance from it, often taking the form of investments in respectability (Stacey, 1975; Steedman, 1986; Walkerdine and Lucey, 1989; Duneier, 1992; Gray, 1992; Seiter, 1995; Skeggs, 1997) and always with the uneasy sense of standing under signs to which one does and does not belong (Butler, 1992).

By the end of the nineteenth century 'the working class' had become a knowable, measurable and organizable category. Its members could be recognized, evaluated and judged and they could learn to recognize themselves as working class through categorization: a categorization which initially had no meaning for them and continues to remain problematic, but a category infused with sexuality and degeneracy. It began the process of being positioned within an uninhabitable categorization (Doane, 1991; Butler, 1992).[5]

This is also gendered through femininity and masculinity. The appearance of women, via their lack of/or associations with femininity, is often the means by which class becomes read as embodied. The body of the working-class woman is always read through femininity (Tyler, 1991); yet as Nead (1988) and Poovey (1984) have shown, femininity is a sign that was made for and only fits the middle-class woman. Rowe (1995) argues that working-class women have often been associated with the lower unruly order of bodily functions, such as that of expulsion and leakage (and reproduction), which signified lack of discipline and vulgarity. Historically, the division between the sexual and the feminine was most carefully coded at the level of conduct where appearance became the signifier of conduct; to look was *to be*. Subjectivity was read off from the interpretations of representations that were produced to consolidate the identity of others. Appearance became conduct, the key marker of respectability, of class. Interestingly, this concern with appearance has been reproduced through certain forms of feminism where concentration on appearance is seen as a sign of immorality (see Wilson, 1986). In this way it parallels the bourgeois concept of possessive individualism in which identity is constituted as a property of the person that can be read off from visible signs (Abercrombie, Hill and Turner, 1986).[6]

It is therefore rather ironic that some feminists have used femininity as the visible sign of otherness, a measure of the proximity to patriarchy, a signifier of investment in heterosexuality. Or that some have only recently recognized femininity as a masquerade, the mimicry of a projected signifier. Working-class feminist and lesbian writers have long drawn attention to femininity as a form of cultural capital, a local necessity, a game (see McRobbie, 1981; Steedman, 1986; Case, 1989; Walkerdine, 1990; Albrecht-Samarasinha, 1997), and *not* as a property of the self. The women of my previous ethnographic research saw femininity as something that they could produce on their bodies, but also as something that could be discarded, especially with age and other responsibilities (Skeggs, 1997). As Tyler notes:

> Theories of mimicry reinscribe white, middle-class femininity as the real thing, the (quint)essence of femininity ... Miming the feminine means impersonating a white middle-class impersonation of an 'other' ideal of femininity ... Feminist theorists of mimicry distinguish themselves from 'other' women even as they assimilate the latter by romanticising them, assuming the 'other' has a critical knowledge about femininity because of her difference from what counts as natural femininity: white, Anglo, bourgeois style. It is only from a middle-class point of view that Dolly Parton looks like a female impersonator. (Tyler, 1991, p. 57)

The articulation of feminism from the perspective of individualism continues to reproduce working-class women as the site of the other. The mimicry of femininity by working-class women is often not recognized as such; it is often read as exactly what it is not: a display of femininity. Or, even worse, their fabrication is seen as a display of the authentically heterosexual with all the subsequent pathological baggage that this judgement carries. Working-class women have rarely had the conditions of possibility that enable a possessive relation to femininity. What they appear to be is rarely what they are. Historical signifiers only work for those who have come to recognize and accept their positioning.

Political claims-making

To challenge representational positioning and to begin to re-signify pathological signs, access is needed to the forms of capital that count. That is, working-class women, black, white, straight, lesbian, need access to the circuits of distribution that enable symbolic capital to be generated; those that enable them to be recognized as non-pathological. To engage in the politics of recognition is to convert cultural capital into something more, something that has a wider value than the local cultural arena; something that can be recognized by others, including powerful others. It is a means of gaining legitimacy and also, as Connell et al. (1982) argue, a means for putting a floor on downward spiralling circumstances. It is about surviving, not thriving.[7] Bourdieu (1979, 1986, 1987, 1989) suggests a model of class which is based on 'capital' movements through social space. The structure of this space is given by the distribution of the various forms of 'capital', by the distribution of their properties, properties which are capable of conferring strength, power and consequently profit on their holder. This model can be put together with the historical analysis by seeing class as an arbitrarily imposed definition with real social effects (Moi, 1991). Bourdieu identifies four different types of capital:

1. Economic capital. It includes income, wealth, financial inheritances and monetary assets.
2. Cultural capital. This can exist in three forms: in an embodied state, i.e. in the form of long-lasting dispositions of the mind and the body; in the objectified state, i.e. in the form of cultural goods; and in the institutionalized state, resulting in such things as educational qualifications. Cultural capital only exists in relation to the network of other forms of capital.
3. Social capital. This is resources based on connections and group membership. It is capital generated through relationships.

4. Symbolic capital. This is the form the different types of capital take once they are perceived and *recognized as legitimate*. Legitimation is the key mechanism in the conversion to power. Cultural capital has to be legitimated before it can have symbolic power. Any capital has to be regarded as legitimate before it can be capitalized upon.

People are distributed in the overall social space according to: first, the global *volume* of capital they possess; second, the *composition* of their capital, that is the relative weight of the different forms of capital; and third, evolution in time of the volume and composition according to their *trajectory* in social space.

When we are born, we enter an inherited social space from which comes access to and acquisition of differential amounts of capital assets. Each kind of capital can only exist in the inter-relationships of social positions; they bring with them access to or limitation on which capitals are available to certain positions. Gender, class, sexuality and 'race' are not capitals as such. Rather, they provide the relations in which capitals come to be organized and valued. Our social locations influence our movement and hence our ability to capitalize further on the assets we already have. In my previous study the working-class women had, by the age of sixteen, only limited capital to trade. When they traded their appearance on the marriage market, they were able to negotiate some interpersonal power rather than gaining access to wider institutional power. The trading of appearance, however, also involves them as the object of the exchange.

To live in 1990s Britain as black or white working class is to be continually judged and found lacking, to have one's cultural capital not recognized as having value and therefore being unable to trade, or being recognized as a worthy recipient.[8] Judgements are still made on the basis of appearance *and* read as conduct. For working-class women, judgements are often made on the basis of the control of sexuality and/or through maternal practices and the capacity to care and observe the social limits established by the state. McNeil (1998) goes so far as to argue that the 'lone mother' has become the sign of gendered class (articulated in the USA via the code 'Welfare Mothers'). On all of these counts the judged are given responsibility for the judgements of others. This imposes limits on what they can do, how they can move through social space and how they can convert their cultural capital into something that counts.

This continued pathological marking imposes severe limits on the political claims-making that can be made. The lack of investment in and unwillingness to take on the sexed and raced sign of the working-class woman led in my ethnography to multifarious attempts by the women to dis-identify because they felt mis-recognized on a daily basis. The mis-recognition takes the form of being mistaken as the sign of pathology whereas the women see themselves as respectable. To be mis-recognized Fraser argues:

> is not simply to be thought ill of, looked down on, or devalued in others' conscious attitudes or mental beliefs. It is rather to be denied the status of *full partner* in social interaction and prevented from *participating as a peer* in social life – not as a consequence of a distributive inequality (such as failing to receive one's fair share of resources or 'primary goods') but rather as a consequence of *institutionalized* patterns of interpretation and evaluation that constitute one as comparatively unworthy of respect or esteem. When such patterns of disrespect and disesteem are institutionalised, for example, in law, social welfare, medicine and/or popular culture, they impede parity of participation, just as surely do distributive inequities. (Fraser, 1995, p. 280)

Mis/recognition through appearance is never an innocent act. It is to participate in a system of judgement and classification. It always involves evaluation and, as Berlant argues, pain:

> Yet if the pain is at the juncture of you and the stereotype that represents you, you know that you are hurt not because of your relation to history but because of *someone else*'s relation to it, a type of someone whose privilege or comfort depends on the pain that diminishes you, locks you into identity, covers you with shame, and sentences you to a hell of constant political exposure to the banality of derision ... Pain thus organises your specific experience of the world, separating you from others and connecting you with others similarly shocked (but not surprised) by the strategies of violence that constantly regenerate the bottom of the hierarchies of social value you inhabit. In this sense subaltern pain is a public form because its outcome is to make you readable, for others. (Berlant, forthcoming)

The gap between recognition and mis-recognition, between identification and dis-identification is due to the gap between representation and experience, between positioning and response, or in Gramsci's (1971) terms between hegemony and lived culture. It is a gap in interpretative strategies and it is the result of the historical generation of the term 'class', which was used to shore up and consolidate the identity of the bourgeoisie and had no meaning for those to whom it was applied. The desire not to be identified and not to make identifications has a subsequent impact on the political claims-making that can be achieved. If it is being carved out of a positive-identity politics, then this has severe implications for those who do not identify with the signifier that was used to keep them in their place.

Some attempts have been to re-signify the sign class; US theorists have reclaimed the term 'white trash' (Wray and Newitz, 1997) as an incitement to critical thinking, attempting to undermine the projections of the powerful and force a recognition of the racialized production of class. Their arguments intervene in the 'vulgar multiculturalism' debates that always assumes a homogeneity to whiteness in terms of terror and racism (Wray and Newitz, 1997).

This form of intervention is different from the 'positive images' politics that were made in the 1970s such as 'Black is Beautiful', 'Black and Proud' and the 1980s queer 'We're here, we're queer'. The first is an attempt to dismantle the representations of power from a dual position of partial normalization and pathology (i.e. white *but* working class), whereas the others speak from one stake in a marginalized identity (either black or gay). Both strategies have as their aim correction to mis-representation and mis-recognition. The latter have been successful in providing a cultural space for those previously marginalized to 'be something' positive, to partake in identity politics, to spatialize identities and to articulate demands through the 1990s politics of recognition (remembering that claims for recognition are usually precursors to or accompany claims for redistribution). Claims for recognition can be generated by groups who feel proud to be recognized as 'something' (insert as appropriate categories of sexuality, race, gender, disability, nationality), who have an investment in the system and who want access to the resources available. These claims are usually made in the singular of political claims-making, reinforcing differences and often employing the 'strategic essentialism' that Spivak (1990) has suggested necessary for some political struggles. However, this represents problems for those who desire dis-identification, for whom the judgemental weight of the sign they are positioned by offers little possibility for articulating any recognition politics.

Dis-placing others and others

Lesbian and gay politics (and to some extent queer) have been generated primarily through identity politics, through a struggle for recognition, for visibility, for legitimacy, for the conversion of cultural into symbolic capital and economic capital. These have taken place on many fronts: generating significant awareness of the positive aspects of standing under the sign lesbian/gay/queer. This battle had enabled the conversion of cultural capital into the economic as evidenced in the territorialization of spaces as recognizably gay (such as Soho in London; Christopher Street and Park Slope, Brooklyn, in New York; Castro in San Francisco; Dupont Circle in Washington; Cabbagetown in Toronto; Amsterdam; and areas in Manchester, Vancouver, etc.). These spaces have often been more successfully generated by gay men whose relationship to capitalism, hedonism and pleasure was less mediated by radical feminism,[9] yet they have been important to staking a claim for a spatialized, recognizable identity.[10] The recent research by Les Moran, Carole Truman, Paul Tyrer, Karen Corteen, Lindsay Turner and me[11] into the gay village in Manchester suggests that there is something of a struggle occurring in the established gay space over issues of class, gender and sexuality which is being formulated through the processes of identification and the desires for visibility/ invisibility, recognition/avoidance of positioning. These struggles are spatial and temporal, presenting examples of how different identity positions can disrupt others in claims for space, safety and legitimacy.

The ethnographic research showed how, as a way of escaping the continual pathological sexualization they experience as young, straight working-class women, they use Manchester's gay clubs to become invisible:

The best thing about gay clubs is that you just aren't noticed. There is something completely liberating about not being gawped at all the time. Like you can walk around the whole club without anybody batting an eye. It's like you're invisible. I'm sure it would get to you if it happened every day of your life but every now and again it's very refreshing. (Karen, 1992)

It's great, nobody notices you, nobody's going to say 'who's that drunken tart over there' or come on to you. They just leave you alone. You're either ignored, but not in a bad way, or it's dead friendly and you get to chat and share poppers and that. It's really liberating. You feel safe and you feel you can behave as mad as you like. I'd be there every night if I could afford it. (Val, 1992)

Both women note the liberating effect of the safety in the space to behave badly. They are less likely to be judged by hedonistic gay men as irresponsible or lacking in respectability – they can just have a good time. They move into a culturally compatible class space to defend against heterosexualizing. The space is not used to articulate a political identity but to defend against continual marking. It is a respite from heterosexual masculinity and all the judgements that usually keep the working-class woman in her place. This, however, has displacement effects for others, in this case lesbians, whose entitlement to use the space has been hard fought for:

They've no idea how to behave when they're on somebody else's territory. (Maxine, 1997)

We need another ghetto, we need to re-ghettoize ourselves. We've become too big and sort of like , I don't know I think the market's taken over. We need to like ... we'll probably happen again. I'm sure wherever we move to we'll get followed ... (Chris, 1997)

Yes. And when you're in a toilet queue and you've got all these women with like big platform shoes and little short skirts and loads of make-up, and you just, but you do really feel like you're in a minority ... you feel really invaded in your own space and they can't wait to get out again to be with the gay male friends who they think they're really safe with. (Maxine, 1997)

I was stood in the queue at Manto, I was watching one of those little micro-skirted girls and every lesbian that came out was like with their head down, oh you know ... Wouldn't dream of looking. Sort of like, just felt like, you know, just trying to take up as little space as possible. This is a gay space and yet these women ... (Joan, 1997)

The straight working-class women's desire for invisibility, invariably because of their normalization by heterosexuality, re-heteros the gay space. It is not just about escaping hetero-boys but escaping the continual classificatory effects of classed heterosexuality. Here they are positioned as irresponsible, for using space to which they should, on the basis of sexuality, have no entitlement. Chris's point about being followed illustrates a strong sense of never being able to escape from the clutches of heterosexuality, even in a space marked gay. It also shows a strong parallel to work on the physicality of shame when the head is lowered. It is lesbians who are made to feel out of place. It is a reproduction of the affect produced by the lesbian inside/outside structure (see Munt, 1998).

The lesbian group, who in this limited and limiting example[12] are older professional women, have been able to spatialize their identity (if only momentarily) through their use of the conversion of oppositional sub-cultural capital into a legitimate symbolic public space (not of course without struggle and continual maintenance). They have also been able to use their class position to defend their sexuality. This is obviously not the case for all lesbians, some of whom cannot even afford to use the 'village', or do not have access to any subcultural capital. But what is interesting is how the invasion of embodied heterosexuality is being articulated here in gendered-class terms.

The straight women are infantilized *and* sexualized by such comments as 'those little micro-skirted girls', 'loads of make-up' and 'big platform shoes'. They also proceed to talk about big hair, which as Ortner (1991) has shown, is one of the main signifiers of white trash in the USA. They are not dissimilar to the straight middle-class women's comments about the hyper-sexuality of working-class women (Ortner, 1991). It is the use of space that has generated this linguistic deployment. The comments also suggest how significant appearance, bodily dispositions (and conduct) is to identifying others.

But how can we ever be certain of identities? Femmes, for centuries it seems, have been mis-recognized; in fact the straight women's presence disrupts the recognition of femmes. A politics constructed through visible identity is always looking for the fix. It is a desire to maintain the place that is known. It offers no transitional space. Femininity is read as complicity with heterosexuality, based on the prior assumption inherent in reading the femme that every visible form of femininity is straight until proven other-wise (Butler, 1998). The appearance comes to signify subjectivity: to look is to be. Garber describes the 'desire to see and interpret otherness in order to guard against a difference that might otherwise put the identity of one's own position into question' (Garber, 1991, p. 130). In this case the visible appearance of class and the mistaken historical association of class with femininity is used as the marker to establish difference and distinction. Walker (1993) notes how in lesbian theory and forms of interpretation, the femme is the paradigmatic figure of exclusion from the theory which privileges the butch and reads off lesbian from butch appearance (the evacuation of femininity). She shows how privileging the visible is a way of taking part in the discourses that naturalize socially constructed categories of difference and that this privileging elides other identities that are not constructed as visible. The paradigm of visibility is totalizing, she argues, when a signifier of difference becomes synonymous with the identity it signifies.[13] Moreover, Hart (1998) illustrates the problems with talking about lesbian identity when questions are always mired in terms of 'who we are' rather than 'what we do'. This results in emphasis on appearance and narrative, rather than sexual practice, reproducing the discursive regulation of appearance = being.[14]

But lesbians know that rarely do they have power to put these judgements into effect. In fact, as Joan notes above, they are the ones who are made to feel out of place, who keep their head down. Both groups of women have only limited entitlement to the space because of their gender. This is partly because the village bar scene which is of interest to straight women is one based on glamour, hedonism and pleasure. It is a particular sort of culture that requires particular cultural competencies and capital. It is a culture that many lesbians have never belonged to, have disinvested from or have only partial interest in (see Wolfe, 1992; Valentine, 1993; Rothenberg, 1995; Retter, 1997) or have diversified from (Ross, 1990). It has an appeal to the young, the clubbers, the hedonists, what Whittle (1994) describes as the hegemony of the young, beautiful people (see Whittle, 1994 for a scathing description of Manchester's gay village). It is a culture that Wolfe (1992) argues has never had much to offer to lesbian life, or what Grant (1997) calls the 'not-quite-as-visible-as-we-might-be-lesbians'. The formations of lesbian identities have only rarely been hewn out of inner-city club culture. Yet it is a culture that has many parallels to that of young, straight working-class women. The labour and skill required in working-class women's culture to be glamorous is given validation here (unlike, say, the middle-class student clubs where dressing down is a sign of cultural capital). In fact not only is it legitimated, it is celebrated and this produces a sense of entitlement that is rarely enacted by working-class women. They seem to have found a place where they fit in more comfortably than spaces which are heterosexually designated for them. They are less uncomfortable with gay men than they are with middle-class women. It is a temporal-cultural alliance. Their limited cultural capital enables them to make momentary raids into the space of the othered: what de Certeau (1988) calls the tactics of powerlessness. But this is against the sense of entitlement that is a similarly rare experience for lesbians.

Different capitals are being used to make different claims: one for spatialized recognition, one for invisibility. Both are precarious.

Only rarely in the village do lesbians have the ability to turn their subcultural capital into the symbolic and economic[15] in the same way as the gay men who have been able to occupy and develop that space. And it is gay men who have enabled the production of a subcultural capital, through the commodification and popularizing of certain aspects of gay male identity. Studies of lesbian space show a move towards the outskirts of the city, towards neighbourhoods (e.g. Adler and Brenner, 1992; Wolfe, 1992; Rothenberg, 1995; Bouthillette, 1997), towards access to less economic capital and a different way of making contacts with one another – not a culture based on cruisy bars.

Conclusion

If the shift that Fraser (1995) and Taylor (1994) have suggested from redistribution politics to recognition politics has taken place in the 1990s, then this has significant implication for the politics of class; a politics hewn out of sexuality and race but which seems to be creating disjunctures and distinctions rather than alliances. The central problem with a politics based on recognition is that it fixes and excludes, it draws on historical legacies of the imperialists and bourgeoisie and it reproduces them through judgements made on the basis of appearance. If recognition politics is the grammar and the frame, then only those who can symbolically convert their capital and legitimate it will have a chance. For those who want to avoid misrecognition the possibilities are severely curtailed. They will be further marginalized and silenced, their cultural capital devalued even more. They will be unable to trade at all. Recognition politics also means that little re-signification will occur and that working-class women (straight or non-identified lesbians) will continue to be judged as what they are not.

Appearances are not just clothes, they are skin-deep and like race, but, unlike femininity, classed dispositions cannot be so easily discarded. The bodily dispositions we learn as a result of positioning bear the markers of class as effectively, if not more so, than clothes themselves as Bourdieu (1986) shows. To be classed is to embody a physicality which will always be a means of recognition (of either similarity or difference). It is far easier to recognize class (if one knows the national codes) than to recognize sexuality, partly because class is not illegal and partly because class passing rarely works where sexual passing frequently does (Skeggs, 1997). Working-class clothing and bodily dispositions seal in class, just as skin colour works for recognitions of race. In the seal, Ahmed (1998b) argues, lies the threat of contagion, disruption and ungovernance.[16] Bodies are the transporters of other categorizations. To others, white working-class women's bodies are symbolically read as the carriers of heterosexuality and femininity. To other working-class women, they expose the constructions and disruptions of these categories; how bodies become what they have to be categorically.

The singularity, exclusion and adoption of historically pathological models of interpretation close down the possibilities of political change. Appearance is promoted as a form of being, as an 'authentic subjective experience'. It enables people to be mis-recognized, and draws boundaries around what a particular category should look like. It does not recognize the disruption but looks for closure, for the easy fix. It is an easy palliative to ontological insecurity. It is about being a subject, about belonging, about being able to move in different social spaces, about not being limited, contained or made vulnerable. It is about mis-recognizing difference and reading bodies as inhabitable by only one category.

The struggles over space are struggles not just for identity but also safety and legitimacy. Reading these as a struggle in identity politics is to ignore the processes by which identity is enabled and who can and cannot forge an identification with something. Whilst identity politics has been critiqued scathingly from every angle possible, it is still being enacted on a daily basis. This enactment enables some groups to spatialize their claims for legitimacy and enter into the political claims-making arena of recognition, others cannot.

Whilst political struggles have to be conducted on a variety of levels and spaces, and for some identity politics is an entry point into dignity and recognition, Phelan (1993) has shown how a politics of unmarking threatens the stability of historical articulations and generates more damage for the signified positions than recognition politics which is usually reproductive, assimilative and framed by the discourse of individualism. To continue to carve a politics out of the limitations imposed by categorical judgements is to constrain interconnections, to fix and to frame. Fragile senses of entitlement are pitted against each other as power remains intact. Lesbians are able to make identity claims through recognition politics but are unable to spatialize these claims. Straight women are unable to make identity claims but are able to temporarily spatialize their presence through reiterative heterosexuality. If space is central to instantiating political claims, then both groups are excluded through the new grammar of political claims-making which is based upon spatializing visible presence. If recognition politics renders some lives intelligible, lives which are consistently removed from perception and liveability (Butler, 1998), then it also captures the intelligibility in a constraining political discourse; one which may be known in theory but limiting in practice.

Notes

1. With thanks to Jon Binnie, Sally Munt, Les Moran and Karen Corteen for their critiques. The space under discussion is commercial, predominantly male, gay space in the 'Gay Village' in Manchester, UK.
2. See Munt (1998) for the erotic interpretation of appearances as constitutive of visible sexual styles of butch/femme.
3. There is a debate about the initial class marking: see Hart (1994) and Munt (1998).
4. See Kirkham and Skeggs (1996) and Smart (1992).
5. This does not mean that the middle class neatly inhabit their classificatory positioning. This is always disrupted by gender, race, generation, etc.
6. Lury (1998) shows how consciousness and memory are also necessary for a person to claim a separate status as an individual.
7. Thanks to Karen Corteen for this succinct remark.
8. Although exploitation is always possible as in the use of 'black culture' as a signifier of authenticity to make objects of consumption more desirable (see Gilroy, 1990).
9. See Weston and Rofel (1997) and Wilton (1996).
10. See Berlant and Warner (1998).
11. On 'Violence, Sexuality and Space' and funded by the ESRC as part of the 'Violence Initiative'. The research is funded for 30 months to explore the impact of 'safe gay space' on the formation of sexual identities. The pilot focus group transcript used here was conducted by Lucie Scott and Carole Truman.
12. In the future, after further research, comparisons will be drawn between working-class lesbians who use the village and middle-class professional, straight women to see how the articulations alter. Hopefully, the identity categories we are deploying will also be broken down through nuanced complexity. But we are not at this stage yet.
13. Thanks to Karen Corteen for drawing my attention to Walker's argument.
14. Hart (1998) argues that this is because of an understanding of desire which is optical and object-oriented. If desire is a scene, a setting, a location, the place

of fantasy rather than the pursuit of an object, which is what she argues, then understanding spaces of desire becomes even more significant.

15. Although not known for her political campaigning from an identity politics, one of the main movers and shakers in the village is Carole Ainscow, who co-owns a bar and an apartment block.

16. For black women and men, Ahmed argues, skin is seen as a stained physical 'reality' that cannot be transformed or contained. It is *the* physicality.

Bibliography

Abercrombie, N., Hill, S. and Turner, B. (1986) *Sovereign Individuals of Capitalism*. London: Allen & Unwin.

Adler, S. and Brenner, J. (1992) 'Gender and space: lesbians and gay men in the city'. *International Journal of Urban and Regional Research* 16(1), pp. 24–34.

Ahmed, S. (1998a) 'Tanning the body: skin, colour and gender'. *New Formations* 34, pp. 27–43.

Ahmed, S. (1998b) 'Animated borders, skin, colour and tanning'. In M. Shildrick (ed.), *Vital Signs: Feminist Reconfigurations of the Bio/Logical Body*. Edinburgh: Edinburgh University Press.

Albrecht-Samarasinha, L. L. (1997) 'Gender warriors: an interview with Amber Hollibaugh'. In L. Harris and E. Crocker (eds), *Femme, Feminists, Lesbians and Bad Girls*. New York: Routledge.

Berlant, L. (forthcoming) 'The subject of true feeling: pain, privacy, politics'. In S. Ahmed, J. Kilby, C. Lury, M. McNeil and B. Skeggs (eds), *Transformations: Thinking Through Feminism*. London: Routledge.

Berlant, L. and Warner, M. (1998) 'Sex in public'. *Critical Inquiry* 24(2), pp. 547–67.

Blackman, I. and Perry, K. (1990) 'Skirting the issue: lesbian fashion for the 1990s'. *Feminist Review* 34, pp. 67–79.

Bourdieu, P. (1979) 'Symbolic power'. *Critique of Anthropology* 4, pp. 77–85.

Bourdieu, P. (1986) *Distinction: A Social Critique of the Judgement of Taste*. London: Routledge.

Bourdieu, P. (1987) 'What makes a social class? On the theoretical and practical existence of groups'. *Berkeley Journal of Sociology*, pp. 1–17.

Bourdieu, P. (1989) 'Social space and symbolic power' *Sociological Theory* 7, pp. 14–25.

Bouthillette, A.-M. (1997) 'Queer and gendered housing: a tale of two neighbourhoods in Vancouver'. In B. G. Ingram *et al.* (eds), *Queers in Space*. Seattle: Bay Press.

Brown, W. (1995) 'Wounded attachments: late modern oppositional political formations'. In J. Rajchman (ed.), *The Identity in Question*. New York: Routledge.

Butler, J. (1992) 'Contingent foundations: feminism and the question of "postmodernism" '. In J. Butler and J. Scott (eds), *Feminists Theorise the Political*. London: Routledge.

Butler, J. (1998) 'Afterword'. In S. R. Munt (ed.), *Butch/Femme: Inside Lesbian Gender*. London: Cassell.

Case, S.-E. (1989) 'Toward a butch-femme aesthetic'. In L. Hart (ed.), *Making a Spectacle*. Ann Arbor: University of Michigan Press.

Connell, R. W., Ashenden, D. J., Kessler, S. and Dowsett, G. W. (1982) *Making the Difference*. Sydney: Allen & Unwin.

Creed, B. (1995) 'Lesbian bodies: tribades, tomboys and tarts'. In E. Grosz and E. Probyn (eds), *Sexy Bodies: The Strange Carnalities of Feminism*. London: Routledge.

de Certeau, M. (1988) *The Practice of Everyday Life*. London: University of California Press.

Doan, L. and Bland, L. (1998) *Sexology in Culture: Labelling Bodies and Desires*. Oxford: Polity Press.

Doane, M. A. (1991) *Femmes Fatales: Feminism, Film Theory, Psychoanalysis*. New York and London: Routledge.

Duneier, M. (1992) *Slim's Table: Race, Respectability and Masculinity*. Chicago: University of Chicago Press.

Dyer, R. (1993) 'A white star'. *Sight and Sound* 3(8), pp. 22–4.

Evans, D. (1993) *Sexual Citizenship: The Material Construction of Sexualities*. London: Routledge.

Faderman, L. (1985) *Surpassing the Love of Men*. London: Women's Press.

Finch, L. (1993) *The Classing Gaze: Sexuality, Class and Surveillance*. St Leonards, New South Wales: Allen & Unwin.

Fraser, N. (1995) 'From redistribution to recognition? Dilemmas of justice in a "post-socialist" age'. *New Left Review* 212, pp. 68–94.

Fraser, N. (1997) 'Heterosexism, misrecognition, and capitalism: a response to Judith Butler'. *Social Text* 52/53, 15(3–4), pp. 279–88.

Fryer, P. (1984) *Staying Power: The History of Black People in Britain*. London: Pluto Press.

Garber, M. (1991) *Vested Interests: Cross-Dressing and Cultural Anxiety*. London: Routledge.

Gilman, S. L. (1990) ' "I'm down on whores": race and gender in Victorian London'. In D. T. Goldberg (ed.), *Anatomy of Racism*. Minneapolis: University of Minnesota Press.

Gilroy, P. (1990) 'One nation under a groove: the cultural politics of "Race" and racism in Britain'. In D. T. Goldberg (ed.), *Anatomy of Racism*. Minneapolis: University of Minnesota Press.

Goldberg, D. T. (ed.) (1994) *Multiculturalism: A Critical Reader*. Oxford: Blackwell.

Gramsci, A. (1971) *Selections from the Prison Notebooks of Antonio Gramsci* (edited, Q. Hoare and G. Nowell-Smith). London: Lawrence & Wishart.

Grant, A. (1997) 'Dyke geographies: all over the place'. In G. Griffin and S. Andermahr (eds), *Straight Studies Modified*. London: Cassell.

Gray, A. (1992) *Video Playtime*. London: Routledge.

Hart, L. (1994) *Fatal Women: Lesbian Sexuality and the Mark of Aggression*. London: Routledge.

Hart, L. (1998) 'Living under the sign of the cross: some speculations on femme femininity'. In S. R. Munt (ed.), *Butch/Femme: Inside Lesbian Gender*. London: Cassell.

Kirkham, P. and Skeggs, B. (1996) 'Pedagogies of pornography'. *Jump Cut* 42, pp. 14–20.

Lury, C. (1998) *Prosthetic Culture: Photography, Memory and Identity*. London: Routledge.

Marshall, J. (1981) 'Pansies, perverts and macho men'. In K. Plummer (ed.), *The Making of the Modern Homosexual*. London: Hutchinson.

McClintock, A. (1995) *Imperial Leather: Race, Gender and Sexuality in the Colonial Context*. London: Routledge.

McNeil, M. (1998) 'Lone mothers'. Paper presented to Women's Studies Research Institute, Lancaster University, June.

McRobbie, A. (1981) 'Just like a *Jackie* story'. In A. McRobbie and T. McCabe (eds), *Feminism for Girls: An Adventure Story*. London: Routledge & Kegan Paul.

Mercer, K. and Julien, I. (1988) 'Race, sexual politics and black masculinity: a dossier'. In R. Chapman and J. Rutherford (eds), *Male Order: Unwrapping Masculinity*. London: Lawrence & Wishart.

Moi, T. (1991) 'Appropriating Bourdieu: feminist theory and Pierre Bourdieu's sociology of culture'. *New Literary History* 22, pp. 1017–49.

Mort, F. (1987) *Dangerous Sexualities: Medico-Moral Politics in England since 1830*. London: Routledge & Kegan Paul.

Munt, S. R. (ed.) (1998) *Butch/Femme: Inside Lesbian Gender*. London: Cassell.

Nead, L. (1988) *Myths of Sexuality: Representations of Women in Victorian Britain*. Oxford: Blackwell.

Nestle, J. (1987) *A Restricted Country*. Ithaca, NY: Firebrand Books.

Ortner, S. (1991) 'Reading America: preliminary notes on class and culture'. In G. R. Fox (ed.), *Recapturing Anthropology: Working in the Present*. Santa Fe, NM: School of American Research Press.

Phelan, P. (1993) *Unmarked: The Politics of Performance*. London: Routledge.

Poovey, M. (1984) *The Proper Lady and the Woman Writer: Ideology as Style in the Works of Mary Wollstonecraft, Mary Shelley and Jane Austen*. Chicago: University of Chicago Press.

Retter, Y. (1997) 'Lesbian space in Los Angeles, 1970–1990'. In B. G. Ingram *et al.* (eds), *Queers in Space*. Seattle: Bay Press.

Ross, B. (1990) 'The house that Jill built: lesbian feminist organising in Toronto, 1976–1980'. *Feminist Review* 35, pp. 75–91.

Rothenberg, T. (1995) 'Lesbians creating urban social space'. In D. Bell and G. Valentine (eds), *Mapping Desire*. London: Routledge.

Rowe, K. (1995) *The Unruly Woman: Gender and the Genres of Laughter*. Austin: University of Texas Press.

Seiter, E. (1995) 'Mothers watching children watching television'. In B. Skeggs (ed.), *Feminist Cultural Theory: Process and Production*. Manchester: Manchester University Press.

Skeggs, B. (1994) 'Refusing to be civilised: "race", sexuality and power'. In H. Afshar and M. Maynard (eds), *The Dynamics of Race and Gender*. Basingstoke: Taylor & Francis.

Skeggs, B. (1997) *Formations of Class and Gender: Becoming Respectable*. London: Sage.

Smart, C. (1992) 'Unquestionably a moral issue: rhetorical devices and regulatory imperatives'. In L. Segal and M. McIntosh (eds), *Sex Exposed: Sexuality and the Pornography Debate*. London: Virago.

Spivak, G. C. (1990) *The Post-Colonial Critic: Interviews, Strategies, Dialogues* (ed. S. Harassym). London: Routledge.

Stacey, M. (1975) *Power, Resistance and Change*. London: Routledge & Kegan Paul.

Steedman, C. (1986) *Landscape for a Good Woman: A Story of Two Lives*. London: Virago.

Taylor, C. (1994) 'The politics of recognition'. In D. T. Goldberg (ed.), *Multiculturalism: A Critical Reader*. Oxford: Blackwell.

Tyler, C.-A. (1991) 'Boys will be girls: the politics of gay drag'. In D. Fuss (ed.), *Inside Out: Lesbian Theories, Gay Theories*. London: Routledge.

Valentine, G. (1993) '(Hetero)sexing space: lesbian perceptions and experiences of everyday space'. *Environment and Planning D: Society and Space* 11, pp. 395–413.

Walker, L. M. (1993) 'How to recognise a lesbian: the cultural politics of looking what you are'. *Signs* 18(4), pp. 866–90.

Walkerdine, V. (1990) *Schoolgirl Fictions*. London: Verso.

Walkerdine, V. and Lucey, H. (1989) *Democracy in the Kitchen: Regulating Mothers and Socialising Daughters*. London: Virago.

Ware, V. (1992) *Beyond The Pale: White Women, Racism and History*. London: Verso.

Weston, K. and Rofel, L. B. (1997) 'Sexuality, class and conflict in a lesbian workplace'. In A. Gluckman and B. Reed (eds), *Homo Economics: Capitalism, Community, Lesbian and Gay Life*. London: Routledge.

White, E. (1980) *States of Desire*. London: André Deutsch.

Whittle, S. (1994) 'Consuming differences: the collaboration of the gay body with the cultural state'. In S. Whittle (ed.), *The Margins of the City: Gay Men's Urban Lives*. Newcastle: Athenaeum Press.

Williams, P. (1991) *The Alchemy of Race and Rights: Diary of a Law Professor*. Cambridge, MA: Harvard University Press.

Wilson, E. (with A. Weir) (1986) *Hidden Agendas: Theory, Politics and Experience in the Women's Movement*. London: Tavistock.

Wilton, T. (1996) *Finger-Licking Good: The Ins and Outs of Lesbian Sex*. London: Cassell.

Wolfe, M. (1992) 'Invisible women in invisible places: lesbians, lesbian bars and the social production of people/environment relationships'. *Architecture and Behaviour* 8, pp. 137–58.

Wray, M. and Newitz, A. (eds) (1997) *White Trash: Race and Class in America*. London: Routledge.

Young, A. (1990) *Femininity in Dissent*. London: Routledge.

Young, A. (1996) *Imagining Crime*. London: Sage.

9

Children's Urban Landscapes: Configurations of Class and Place

Diane Reay

Different kinds of narrative map out and construct particular relationships to 'the urban' (Sennett, 1990). While these relationships are gendered, racialized and classed, within children's peer-group cultures topographies of safety and danger are powerfully influenced by social class in ways that have been neglected in academic writing. Although feminist work within geography has addressed the myriad ways in which space and place is gendered (Rose, 1993), apart from a tokenistic side glance at class, the geographical literature is insufficient on the extent to which the *experience* of inhabiting places is shaped by social class. This chapter focuses on children living in a predominantly working-class inner London area, and examines how the experience of growing up in a specific urban locale shapes individual orientations to mobility. Tales of geographical mobility and immobility are intertwined with histories of social mobility. Many of the children in the research study live on 'sink' council estates and the range of tactics they utilize to separate out a positive sense of self from negative emplacement are discussed.

The research study

The children who are the subjects of this chapter all attend Seagrove, an inner London primary school.[1] It is bounded by two busy roads and surrounded by modern council estates from which most of its intake is drawn. However, to the south of the school lies an area of private housing, comprising terraced rows and some Georgian detached and semi-detached houses, which provides the school intake with a small number of middle-class children. The school has just under 60 per cent of pupils receiving free school dinners on roll and a significant minority of refugee children, mainly from Somalia, Eritrea and Bosnia. The locality has a reputation as a working-class neighbourhood, characterized by deprivation, urban blight and social problems.

I spent one day a week from April 1997 until June 1998 observing classrooms and playgrounds, a process which generated extensive field-notes on both children's interactions and their perspectives on those interactions. Additionally, I interviewed children aged from eight to ten in both focus group settings and individually.[2] In all 46 children were involved in one or both types of interview. I designed mapping activities which focused on the locality, as well as involving the children in word association and brainstorming exercises. These were intended to both help children articulate how they perceived their locality and to elicit their symbolic as well as their geographical landscapes. It is this varied mix of data that I have drawn on in an attempt to unravel these children's conflicted relationship to space, and the potency of class within their understandings of the locality and their place within it.

Space, place and working-class landscapes

Space is a complex web of relations of domination and subordination within which place can be envisaged as a more tightly constrained local pattern (Massey, 1994). Linda McDowell distinguishes between space as relational and place as a location or a structure of feeling centred on a specific territory (McDowell, 1996; Williams, 1977). Spaces and places are not simply sets of material social relations; they constitute cultural objects and as such are invested with powerful associations and emotive resonances (Entrikin, 1991). In particular, places form an important source of meanings for individuals which they can draw upon to tell stories and thereby come to understand themselves and their place within wider society. 'Thus place and identity are inexorably linked' (Thrift, 1997, p. 160). But just as the places we grow up in shape the people we become, understandings of 'our sort of place' provide a sorting mechanism, sifting out the type of people we are not (Massey, 1995). However, to the children I interviewed, 'our sort of place', especially if it was one of the high density council estates, presented them with a dilemma. The 'sort of people' who lived in 'our sort of place' were pathologized in both the national and the local media, and the children were often caught up in dominant imaginary constructions of the urban poor at the same time as they tried to convey their own different, locally constructed realities.

Carolyn Steedman has described the attribution of psychological simplicity to working-class landscapes (Steedman, 1986, p. 12). Later in the same book she writes:

> Working-class childhood is problematic because of the many ways in which it has been pathologized over the last century and a half . . . the children of the poor are only a measure of what they lack as children: they are a falling short of a more complicated and richly endowed 'real' child. (Steedman, 1986, pp. 127–8)

I want to argue that the complicated selfhoods of working-class children such as those in my study have not adequately informed either psychological or psychoanalytic theorizing. We need a much more sophisticated understanding of social jealousy, fear, denial, longing and envy which, far from pathologization, would view such psychological responses as the logical inheritance of the poor: 'Exclusion is the promoter of envy, the social and subjective sense of the impossible unfairness of things' (Steedman, 1986, p. 111). In *Landscape for a Good Woman* Steedman reconstitutes envy as the rightful inheritance of the poor and, using Steedman's premise, I have attempted to analyse envy and related feelings of longing and jealousy as quintessentially normative in contexts of urban deprivation.

Class and mobility

Power and self-determination over one's space and place is a major advantage in the negotiation of contemporary society. The extent to which children feel in control of or controlled by cultural geography is powerfully influenced by additional social positionings such as gender, 'race' and disability, as well as being integrally linked to familial resources and income. For example, ten-year-old Richard (white, middle-class) communicates a sense of control and confidence in relation to space and place:

> I like travelling around the tube and I've nearly finished all the lines now. I've done all the Piccadilly, the Victoria, the Bakerloo and the Northern and I'm doing the Circle now.

As with other middle-class children in the study, the world 'out there' does not represent so much danger, as opportunity and excitement. What is a landscape of constraint for many of the working-class children is redefined as a landscape of mobility and possibility by Richard. He is laying claim to outside territory. He is engaged in a process of making distant horizons accessible:

> I've been to four other countries, France, Germany, Italy and Brazil. I was only a baby when I went to Brazil, but my grandparents are missionaries there so I count it as one of my family's countries.

In contrast, Lisa, a white working-class girl with an agoraphobic mother, has a very limited sense of accessible and safe space:

> LISA: I mainly go shopping on Fentham Road with my auntie, but I have been down to Oxford Street once on the 14 bus. Lots of people get mugged there.
>
> DIANE: On Fentham?
>
> LISA: No, Oxford Street.
>
> DIANE: More than in Fentham?
>
> LISA: Loads more.

The relationship of Richard and Lisa to space is somewhat different: the one venturing out with a degree of control and confidence; the other far more circumscribed and fearful.

Perhaps these two examples are too polarized, extremes within the sample, yet the white, indigenous working-class children in my study do have a different relationship to geography from either the middle-class children or the children whose families have migrated to London from abroad. For many children within the middle classes, particularly those like Richard who belong to the white male constituency, the rest of London is within easy reach, horizons are simultaneously expanded and compressed. The city is out there in the sense of adventurous project according to the way Richard describes the London Underground. There are resonances here with Michael Bell's ethnographic findings of class differences in Childerley, the rural village he lived in for eight months. He writes of the local and highly interactive habitus of the working-class villagers which contrasted with the more impersonal, but much wider horizons of middle- and upper-class villagers (Bell, 1994).

Horizons are configured very differently if you are working-class. For some of the working-class children who either are refugees or have one or both parents born abroad, there is a sense of connection, however tenuous, with places far away. But for most white, indigenous working-class children, anywhere outside the immediate urban locale is strange and unfamiliar. Their relationship to the wider world, geographically, socially and psychologically, is characterized by boundaries rather than accessible horizons. The wider world is either a fantasy realm laden with threat or sometimes an idealized hyper-fantasy (such as Disneyland, mentioned by many of the working-class children as their most desirable destination).

David Sibley writes about the liminal zones existing for children within their homes (Sibley, 1995). Yet there are also liminal zones, spaces of anxiety for children, outside in the streets and on the estates. In contrast to media images of rough, uncontrollable, working-class kids bunking off school and staying out late at night in order to roam the urban landscape and indulge in acts of petty crime (Holland 1992), the majority of the working-class children are domestically constrained. Both boys and girls talked in terms of both internally and externally imposed limitations on their movements. Sammy, a black working-class boy, describes the strait-jacket of parental concern which constricts his out-of-school activities:

Well, I'm not allowed out because like, my parents care about me. And even though most of the time like, I always want to go out, but I never get the chance to.

Sammy is allowed out, but only when his father is working on the family car outside their flat. The circumscription is even greater for a number of black and white working-class girls, some of whom seem to choose self-imprisonment. As Alice comments: 'I'm allowed to play out, but it's boring so I never do.' Doreen Massey describes the intricate web of power relations which make up urban places as 'power geometries' (Massey, 1993). These power geometries are not merely concerned with who moves and who doesn't, but are also linked to differential degrees of control and confidence in relation to mobility. The 'power geometry' of this urban locale, its flows and interconnections and the impact of age, gender and class, has 'effectively imprisoned' a number of these black and white working-class children.

Working-class legacies? Fear, shame and envy

Most of the children say very positive things about themselves. Both boys and girls use terms like 'clever', 'creative' and 'thoughtful' – words which appear sharply at odds with their descriptions of the locality and many of the other people who live there:

DIANE: What are the people who live in your flats like?

MICKA: They are nasty.

EMMA: Yeah, they're nasty.

MARK: Mostly nasty.

MICKA: Some of the gangs are horrible.

While many of the working-class children appear to manage the tension between positive self/degraded place, there are costs. These costs are most apparent in children's processes of displacement. The 'gangs' become repositories for all that is bad and negative about the estates. Then the boys, in particular, have to negotiate a difficult conundrum because gang membership represents a site of dangerous, yet desired, male subjectivity that evokes both terror (in the invasion of gangs from other areas and estates) and safety (in the enviable membership of such a gang).

Unsurprisingly, the children talk of escape – to idyllic green pastures or the seashore. Fantasies of escape are important tactics in many of these children's desperate efforts to separate out a worthwhile estimable self from a degraded, harshly judged context in which you are implicated as 'no better than where you come from' (Skeggs, 1997). These children are bombarded with shameful recognitions: they have to contend with seeing their estates labelled as 'hotbeds of crime', 'drug ridden' and 'full of problem families' in the local press. Also, as is very evident in their accounts, they have to negotiate a welter of fear: outsiders' fear of contamination, as well as the fear of others inside, particularly the old, towards them. The children themselves expressed a lot of fear about living on the estates, often depicting them as danger zones.

Conceptualizations of fear in relation to space and place are powerfully differentiated by class. The psycho-spatial dynamics of estate living generate a culture of fear which is very immediate, while middle-class fear appears more ephemeral and divorced from its immediate context. In contrast, for these working-class children and their families, fear is far more tangible; it is a fear of what is already inside, occupying the same space, an ever-present fear that does not need to be conjured up ideationally because it occupies the same space psychically and physically. Yet, paradoxically, it is proximity which offers the prospect of resolution as Sarah's account demonstrates:

> Nothing will happen to me because it is so safe around my flats for me. Even though they take drugs and that, it is really safe cos they all know me so they wouldn't do anything.

She, like all the other children living on these estates, talks in terms of gangs, drug dealers and drunks, but because she is known by, and knows, many of the other families on her estate she and it are perceived as safe. This is not to dismiss working-class fears and anxieties about middle-class spaces, but the focus of both middle- and working-class children's fears implicated primarily working-class spaces. Yet there remains something complicated and contradictory about belonging entangled among the fear and anxiety; as Lena says: 'I don't like it in the flats, but I wouldn't feel right in a new house.'

Space is powerfully constitutive of children's understandings of the world and their *place* within it. Growing up on a sink council estate means having to continually negotiate the feelings of shame that permeate. It is important not to underestimate this dialectic of self and place: 'Just as there is no place without body – without the physical or psychical traces of body – so there is no body without place ... For the lived body is not only locatory ... it is always already implaced' (Casey, 1993, pp. 103–4). However, the working-class children have their own tactics for fighting free of negative emplacement. They are creating their own dis-identifications, constructing divisions between themselves and pathological others. Working-class children too have their projections even if they lack a middle-class capacity for distance. I suggest all this contributes powerfully to the children's resistance to being labelled as 'working class'. Rather, the working classes are those others on the estate: those who are not coping, who are too evidently struggling both financially and psychologically.

Ironically, since this chapter is about working-class children, very few of them wanted to see themselves, or be seen, as working class, and only Darren and Lucy volunteered that they and their families were poor. Instead, most of the working-class children claimed to be middle class in a reconstruction of reality concerned to avoid the stigma of poverty rather than any positive embracing of what middle-classness constitutes. For them to be middle class is primarily about what middle-classness excludes (poverty) rather than what it includes. They grapple with a conceptualization of 'the poor' which seems infinitely reducible to a constituency which stops short of their own experience. For example, Carly in an unemployed single-mother household on a 'sink' council estate still defines herself as middle class because 'being middle class is like not being like rich, rich, rich ... like, you've got things that you can afford and you can live, but some people don't even have proper clothes'. It is connotations of poverty that working-class children are desperate to guard against. Instead, in the working-class children's discourses being 'posh' has replaced middle-classness as the signifier of an unacceptable 'class' difference. It is a term they use over and over again to delineate between 'people like themselves' and others. The tensions are evident in Marisa's description of the pre-dominantly middle-class area she has moved into: 'It's nice, it's quite pretty and posh. I mean I don't really like it being posh. I'm not used to it.'

'Envy flows upwards and very often, unfortunately, derision flows downward' (Bell, 1994, p. 75). Just as in Bell's rural village, there are manifestations of working-class envy – an envy so potent that a ten-year-old working-class boy can name it:

DARREN: I think there are lots of jealous people in this area. You know full of envy.

DIANE: Why do you think they are full of envy?

DARREN: Cos they ain't got much and they want more.

The derision Bell refers to is less evident among the peer group. The few middle-class children in the class come, as their teacher points out to me, 'from enlightened middle-class families'. Yet there is a degree of middle-class condescension and distance which the working-class children are patently aware of, and which they often respond to with an antagonism. Simon is one of two middle-class children in a focus group which also includes three working-class children:

DIANE: What do you like about the local area, Simon?

SIMON: Not much, not much at all.

ANDREW: There's the theatre in the Strand, you like that.

SIMON: But that's not local is it . . . The local area is congested. It makes it very crowded in the morning and noisy and things.

MIA: No it isn't, your house is quiet. Your street is very quiet.

SIMON: Once you get down my street it's quiet . . . When you get on the main road it's very polluted.

LENNOX: But you don't live on a main road. Your road isn't polluted. It's all quiet and posh.

This short piece of interaction is infused with class symbolism and a degree of class antagonism. Andrew's first comment is a veiled reference to Simon's social positioning and his possession of a very different variant of cultural capital to that which the working-class children possess. For example, none of the three working-class children in the group had ever been to the theatre with their families. The working-class children go on to dispute Simon's reading of the local area not because it does not reflect their experiences of the locality – it does. Rather, he is not articulating his own more privileged relationship to local spaces and places, and they all interject to modify his version so that it reveals rather than elides his privilege.

Working-class histories

Carolyn Steedman has written of the possibility of linking the words of eight- and nine-year-old girls in the late twentieth century with the words of working-class girls of the same age from the mid-nineteenth century (Steedman, 1986). I have no need to tease out any links because Lucy does it for me: she tells the group that if she'd been living in Victorian times she would have been a little watercress girl with no shoes to wear. When I asked why, she replied: 'Because I would have been poor then as well.' Apart from the work of Kuhn (1995), Steedman (1986), Walkerdine (1990) and Skeggs (1997), there has been little recognition in academic writing of the messy confusion of envy, acceptance, longing and class antagonism that constitutes working-class selfhood in either the past or the present. However, there is a largely untold complex, psychological history of working-class subjectivities which spans Lucy and the little watercress girl and within which I am also ensnared.

In her eloquent study of growing up and moving away from 'an almost

totally working-class council estate', Valerie Hey asks: 'Why do I continually adhere to this girl I once was before the longing and the wanting?'
(Hey, 1997, p. 142). My habitus too (Reay, 1997) is still a confusing,
contradictory concoction of working-class past and middle-class present.
This clinging to an increasingly elusive 'working-classness' is one of the
reasons that I give in to the constant hazard I face in conducting qualitative
fieldwork. As I have done in earlier research (Reay, 1996), I begin to
identify with my working-class respondents. In particular, I identify with
Lucy, start to see myself in her. I fantasize about adopting her, dream
about her at night, and then one day I come into the classroom and she is
no longer there. The classteacher whispers about a domestic incident of
such magnitude that Lucy, her mother and siblings have had to be whisked
away by social services. She tells me brightly that the family is being
relocated 'in the suburbs, in a much more middle-class area where it will be
a lot better for them'. I still think about clever, plucky Lucy and how she's
coping out there in alien territory, subject to the 'redemptive, civilizing'
influences of the middle-class suburbs. Although this is a very different
process to my exit from working-class places, it reminds me of my experience at eighteen of going to a traditional university because both moves are
about suddenly having to negotiate middle-class spaces (Reay, 1998a).
There exists a conundrum for these children. In the inner city they are
surviving in hostile territories, but at least they are still places, however
bleak, that they can in a limited way call their own. Middle-class places, the
suburbs, no less than the traditional university, may be reassuring and
inviting for the middle classes, but they are simultaneously relatively
hostile places for working-class children and young people (Reay,
1998a).

Yet, for many working-class individuals, part of the ambivalence
surrounding being working class grows out of the desire to enter these
more privileged middle-class spaces (see Skeggs, 1997). As dominant
discourses around class are being reworked to position all those with
'enterprise, initiative and intelligence' as middle class (Pakulski and
Waters, 1996; Saunders, 1995), those who remain working class are often
seen, and find it increasingly difficult to avoid seeing themselves, as a
residuum – an inferior, poor 'under' class, rather than a decent 'working'
class (Morris, 1994). As I have discussed earlier, the resulting resistances
to being seen as inferior make these identifications, at least in relation to
class, problematic. In a classroom exercise all the working-class children
included winning the lottery as one of their three wishes for the future. As

Steedman asserts, working-class desires for what is lacked are wholly understandable, not pathological. While the desire for and benefits of material security are self-evident, what is less well understood are the psychological effects of these border crossings between working- and middle-class terrains.

For a number of the working-class children, such as Andrew and Marisa, processes of border crossing, particularly in the form of maintaining a distance between themselves and others living on the local estates, were already in play. Andrew tells me his estate is safe 'as long as you don't hang around, as long as you don't mix. You have to keep to yourself.' There are complex issues here concerning 'keeping your distance' as an initial stage in aspirant working-class families' trajectories out of the working classes and into desirable middle-class spaces. Andrew's parents are very ambitious for their son. They want him to do well in 'middle-class terms' and I suggest that the family's inclination to 'keep their distance' is part of the genesis of class mobility – a generational process of moving up and away which is already under way. Stephen Pile argues that the places we grow up in become maps 'of visible and invisible relations of meaning, identity and power into which the subject is placed and has to find their way around – and possibly, one day, to escape' (Pile, 1996, p. 245). 'Keeping your distance', then, can be seen as part of the training for middle-classness – a preparation for escape, in which practices of 'keeping to ourselves' can be seen to express the aspirational desires of some sections of the working classes.

This is not just an attempt to make sense of Andrew's experience but also my own. My mother, despite being surrounded by her own immediate family of parents and sister, reinvented our estate as a hostile terrain for her eight children; somewhere we should cross as rapidly as possible to places more inviting, more 'nice' (with all the loaded class connotations 'nice' has). Andrew also tells me 'my estate isn't very nice'. He too always runs from his flat to get to somewhere more inviting, in his case the football pitch. And yet in seeing my experiences in Andrew's, am I risking intellectual projections of a very different time and place? There is very little literature which discusses the methodological hazards of emotive identifications of class, and the small amount that does exist is written by 'working-class' researchers (Walkerdine and Lucey, 1989; Reay, 1996). The academic consequences are that middle-class empathies in the field are seldom revealed as problematic, despite the affectivity of all class identifications and dis-identifications between researcher and researched.

What is clear is that both Andrew and I, at very different times and places, have become caught up in parental desires and aspirations. For Andrew these shape the possibilities of the present as much as the future. The whole of the estate he lives on has been constructed by him and his parents as a danger zone, full of threat and menace – a place he has to pass through as quickly as possible because it may imprison him and prevent him from ever reaching those desired middle-class spaces. To mention continuities of class is to risk reprobation when academic orthodoxies tell us everything is changing so rapidly in the postmodern city. However, I would contend that contemporary discourses of both widespread social mobility and classlessness are myths which operate to ensure dominant class hegemony and perpetuate class inequalities (Reay, 1998b). Most of the working-class children had invested in such myths – they were going to be vets, lawyers, air hostesses and teachers. Yet, for the majority, their movements across social space are destined to be as constrained as their current movements across geographical space (Blackburn and Jarman, 1993; Egerton and Halsey, 1993).

Conclusion

In *The Tidy House* Carolyn Steedman contrasts the easy centrality of bourgeois accounts of childhood with the relative invisibility of tales told by working-class children (Steedman, 1982). When working-class children do get the space to tell their stories, we have access to very different versions of working-class and, as the example of Simon illustrates, middle-class lives from those inscribed in dominant discourses. The ways in which children's lives are differentially regulated within 'geographies of risk and uncertainty and other geographies of trust, hope and security' (Kenway, 1998) need to be set alongside tendencies to either homogenize childhood (Qvortrup *et al.*, 1994) or operate with notions of working-class childhood as a falling from grace – a failure to meet the middle-class ideal (Walkerdine and Lucey, 1989). This chapter only glimpses beneath the surface of working-class experiences of growing up in contemporary urban society. What it does do is indicate the need for far more working-class versions to challenge the hegemonic middle-class ones which have dominated our understandings of working-class lives for far too long.

Notes

1. The research was carried out in collaboration with Helen Lucey, who conducted similar research in a primary school in the same borough. Her ideas and insights have contributed substantially to this chapter.
2. In total I interviewed 20 children individually, and conducted 24 focus group interviews. Three class teachers and 8 parents were also interviewed.

Bibliography

Bell, M. (1994) *Childerley: Nature and Morality in a Country Village*. Chicago: University of Chicago Press.

Blackburn, R. M. and Jarman, J. (1993) 'Changing inequalities in access to British universities'. *Oxford Review of Education* 19(2), pp. 197–215.

Casey, E. (1993) *Getting Back into Place*. Bloomington: Indiana University Press.

Egerton, M. and Halsey, A. H. (1993) 'Trends by social class and gender in access to higher education in Britain'. *Oxford Review of Education* 19(2), pp. 183–96.

Entrikin, J. N. (1991) *The Betweenness of Place: Towards a Geography of Modernity*. London: Macmillan.

Hey, V. (1997) 'Northern accent and southern comfort: subjectivity and social class'. In P. Mahony and C. Zmroczek (eds), *Class Matters: 'Working-Class' Women's Perspectives on Social Class*. London: Taylor & Francis.

Holland, P. (1992) *What Is a Child? Popular Images of Childhood*. London: Virago.

Kenway, J. (1998) 'Local/global labour markets and the restructuring of gender, schooling and work'. Paper presented at the American Association for Research in Education Conference, San Diego, April.

Kuhn, A. (1995) *Family Secrets: Acts of Memory and Imagination*. London: Verso.

Massey, D. (1993) 'Power geometry and a progressive sense of place'. In J. Bird *et al.* (eds), *Mapping the Futures: Local Cultures, Global Change*. London: Routledge.

Massey, D. (1994) *Space, Place and Gender*. Cambridge: Polity Press.

Massey, D. (1995) 'Making spaces, or, geography is political too'. *Soundings* 1, pp. 193–208.

McDowell, L. (1996) 'Spatialising feminism: geographical perspectives'. In N. Duncan (ed.), *Body Space*. London: Routledge.

Morris, L. (1994) *Dangerous Classes: The Underclass and Social Citizenship*. London: Routledge.

Pakulski, J. and Waters, M. (1996) 'The reshaping and dissolution of social class in advanced society'. *Theory and Society* 25, pp. 667–91.

Pile, S. (1996) *The Body in the City: Psychoanalysis, Space and Subjectivity*. London: Routledge.

Qvortrup, J. *et al.* (1994) *Childhood Matters: Social Theory, Practice and Politics*. London: Avebury Press.

Reay, D. (1996) 'Insider perspectives or stealing the words out of women's mouths: interpretation in the research process'. *Feminist Review* 53, pp. 55–71.

Reay, D. (1997) 'Feminist theory, habitus and social class: disrupting notions of classlessness'. *Women's Studies International Forum* 20(2), pp. 225–33.

Reay, D. (1998a) 'Surviving in dangerous places: working-class women, Women's Studies and higher education'. *Women's Studies International Forum* 20(1), pp. 11–19.

Reay, D. (1998b) 'Rethinking social class: qualitative perspectives on gender and social class'. *Sociology* 32(2), pp. 259–76.

Rose, G. (1993) *Feminism and Geography*. London: Routledge.

Saunders, P. (1995) 'Might Britain be a meritocracy?' *Sociology* 29(1), pp. 23–42.

Sennett, R. (1990) *The Conscience of the Eye: The Design and Social Life of Cities*. London: Faber & Faber.

Sibley, D. (1995), 'Families and domestic routines: constructing the boundaries of childhood'. In S. Pile and N. Thrift (eds), *Mapping the Subject: Geographies of Cultural Transformation*. London: Routledge.

Skeggs, B. (1997) *Formations of Class and Gender: Becoming Respectable*. London: Sage.

Steedman, C. (1982) *The Tidy House*. London: Virago.

Steedman, C. (1986) *Landscape for a Good Woman: A Story of Two Lives*. London: Virago.

Thrift, N. (1997) ' "Us" and "Them": re-imagining places, re-imagining identities'. In H. Mackay (ed.), *Consumption and Everyday Life*. Buckingham: Open University Press.

Walkerdine, V. (1990) *Schoolgirl Fictions*. London: Verso.

Walkerdine, V. and Lucey, H. (1989) *Democracy in the Kitchen*. London: Virago.

Williams, R. (1977) *Marxism and Literature*. Oxford: Oxford University Press.

Part 3

Gender, Fictions and Working-Class Subjectivities

10

'Who Do You Say I Am?' Jesus, Gender and the (Working-Class) Family Romance

Sandy Brewer

The story of Jesus told to children has always meant to be instructional. But the lessons it offers are not always regulative, for the narrative has several features derived from the utopian impulse which drives many folk and fairy tales. According to Zipes, folk and fairy tales 'ferret out deep-rooted wishes' and 'tell us that we want to become kings and queens, ontologically speaking to be masters of our own realms . . . to stand upright as the makers of history' (Zipes, 1979, p. ix). Central to these tales is the hope of self-transformation and of a better world viewed as a communal project. Through the Jesus story told at primary school I learned how to follow rules and be a good girl, but the Jesus narrative refracted through the stories told at home also taught me that the world was a dangerous and unfair place and that sometimes rules had to be broken. As an irreligious woman born into a working-class family, I remain fascinated by the potential of that story to yield emancipatory, as well as regulatory, readings. Therefore, this chapter explores how the Jesus story has provided children with the means to address and resolve some of the conflicts generated by working-class familial and socio-economic positioning.

The Jesus story underpins the narrative of the film *Whistle Down the Wind* (1961; directed by Bryan Forbes), which tells of how three children discover a dishevelled man, played by Alan Bates, in their father's barn whom they believe to be Christ (see Figure 10.1). The narrative focuses on the actions of the older girl, Kathy (Hayley Mills), who organizes the other children in deciding how to save their 'Jesus' from discovery by the adults.

Figure 10.1 Still from *Whistle Down the Wind* (1961), courtesy of Carlton International Media Ltd and BFI Stills, Posters and Designs.

I was eleven years old when I first saw the film, with a residual belief in Jesus as our invisible guardian, the silent listener to childhood prayers. I identified with Kathy because of the courage she displayed in trying to keep the man hidden from the adult authority which threatened his safety. While it was apparent to the children in the film – and to me – that although the adults thought it was a good thing to tell children stories of Jesus and his return to Earth, they themselves did not believe them. I identified with Kathy's efforts to protect 'her Jesus' from discovery by the adults and ensure that this time around he would be saved from harm. Through my identification with the narrative, Kathy and I became as one in the hope that we would be strong and clever enough to save him from the destructive actions of the corrupt adult world, for my generation's emotional engagement with Jesus ran deep. But this was no chance result. It was directly related to the schooling practices of Britain in the 1950s in which the Jesus story was central to the primary curriculum.

The Protestant story of Jesus presented to children in Britain in the twentieth century has never been a closed narrative. It has been told in a thousand different ways through books, pictures, hymns, prayers and school plays. Even in the New Testament the narrative is told four times over by different authors in the gospels of Matthew, Mark, Luke and John, each providing their own account of Christ's life. It seems that Jesus will always be mediated through the eyes and emotions of others, for while within the myth of Jesus he is described as telling many stories, he cannot tell the one concerning his own life. This is left for others to attempt, and even in the late twentieth century, film directors and novelists continue to try to depict the man blessed/cursed with a divine destiny. Thus Jesus' question to his disciples two millennia ago, 'Who do you say I am?'[1] remains open to many different responses, some of which are explored in this chapter.

The life of Jesus is the most widely circulated of all Western narratives and through the Church of England's influence on the school curriculum, it has been an important tool in the inculcation of civic and moral values. It is surprising, therefore, that this 'myth' which has been so central to the British national educational project[2] should have been given so little academic attention.[3] As the target audience for the Jesus story has invariably been working-class children, it becomes even more puzzling that this popular narrative has never fallen within the remit of Cultural Studies with its original aims of investigating 'the most basic and pervasive of social processes, practices and meanings' (Turner, 1990, p. 2). The lack of academic engagement with the narrative could be explained away if we could accept that the Jesus story has only ever been a crude ideological weapon in the regulation of children, and thus of the working class. But the dominant ideology thesis has long since given way to more complex theoretical explanations of the ways popular narratives might function in the formation of identity. If we now acknowledge that audiences are actively engaged in ferreting out their own meanings from media texts (Hall, 1981; Morley, 1980; Radway, 1987), we might also need to draw upon such theoretical insights in trying to understand what appeal the story of Jesus might have had for working-class children, particularly those attending primary school in Britain in the 1950s.

Cultural Studies and working-class religiosity

Stuart Hall has highlighted the problems raised by theorizing popular culture by reference to an agenda which has tended to 'oscillate wildly between the twin poles of containment/resistance'. He emphatically denies the simple equation of popular culture being only an expression of resistance, stating that although 'we understand resistance nowadays rather better than we do reform' we might need to take a closer look at those areas of cultural production and consumption previously omitted from the popular culture agenda because of their surface ideological content of reform. Hall's argument clearly asserts that what he calls the evangelical police should be accorded closer scrutiny in the study of popular culture:

> The magistrate and the evangelical police have, or ought to have, a more 'honoured' place in the history of popular culture than they have usually been accorded. Even more important than ban and proscription is that subtle and slippery customer – 'reform' (with all the positive and ambiguous overtones it carries today). One way or another the people are frequently the object of 'reform'; often for their own good, of course – 'in their own interests'. (Samuel, 1981, p. 229)

While Hall does not make clear which specific groups are to be classified as the evangelical police, I understand him to mean that panoply of philanthropic Christian-inspired organizations which functioned in the latter half of the nineteenth and the first half of the twentieth century. This would comprise Sunday Schools, the various youth organizations such as the Boys' (and Girls') Brigade and campaigning groups such as the temperance-inspired Band of Hope. To date, that call for closer scrutiny of the activities of these groups has been largely ignored within Cultural Studies. Since the late 1970s (Willis, 1977) there has been little work in *British* Cultural Studies dealing with schooling and we need to ask why this is the case. Caughie (McCabe, 1986) has observed that while Cultural Studies in the USA appears to 'work through the disciplines of the academy', British academics, being

> not yet free of the *tradition of shame* which is associated in the British left with academic study, seem always to seek for a very immediate engagement with a politics which cannot be found in the academy. (McCabe, 1986, pp. 158–9; my emphasis)

It could be argued that the desire for a very immediate engagement with politics has been made irrelevant by the shift to postmodernist theory in Cultural Studies; a shift in emphasis among the British intellectual left which Sivanandan has described as a move 'from changing the world to changing the word' (Sivanandan, 1990, p. 49). Nevertheless, as Caughie claims, the study of popular culture was originally shaped by an intellectual altruism.[4] This makes it all the more surprising that religious narratives have been accorded so little attention within Cultural Studies when there is ample evidence that the Jesus story clearly lends itself to interpretations which find resonance with the conflicts which accompany the familial and socio-economic location of the working class. But *location* in class terms also involves social positioning which is *in relationship* to another group – thus the acquisition of working-class consciousness is predicated at a basic level on the acceptance of a 'them and us' view of the world. According to E. P. Thompson:

> class happens when some men, as a result of common experiences . . . feel and articulate the identity of their interests as between themselves, and as against other men whose interests are different from (and usually opposed to) theirs . . . Class-consciousness is the way in which these experiences are handled in cultural terms: embodied in traditions, value-systems, ideas and cultural forms. (Thompson, 1968, pp. 8–9)

One of the ways in which class consciousness has been 'handled in cultural terms' is through the activities of trade unions. The symbolic language of late-twentieth-century labour movements provides evidence of the continuing influence of nineteenth-century radical Protestant nonconformism. In Britain in the 1990s, members at most union branch meetings will still use 'brother' and 'sister' as the appropriate mode of address, and the print and newspaper unions (GPMU and NUJ) are still organized as 'chapels'. The New Testament themes of persecution, sacrifice and redemption have long been a feature of the rhetoric used by the groups described as a 'defensively organised collective' (Clarke, 1976). Therefore it is not surprising to find a reworking of the Crucifixion on the cover of an insider's account of the 1980s British miners' strike[5] (see Figure 10.2). Here a striking miner is depicted bound with barbed wire to a wooden cross, his head crowned with a safety helmet adorned with a miner's lamp. Slag heaps substitute here for the hills of Calvary, and in the distance is the scaffold-like pithead winding gear. Emerging from the pithead is a line of miners on their way to congregate with others at the foot of the cross. The story of Jesus is used as an allegory of the miners' fight to save their jobs and communities, of their collective sacrifices and the remembrance of their comrades who died in that struggle. To some Christians the picture may

Figure 10.2 Painting of a crucified miner. Frontispiece to Ken Ambler, *A Coalfield in Chaos*. Reproduced by kind permission of the artist, John Storey.

appear sacrilegious in its use of religious imagery as political propaganda, but to those familiar with trade union activism, it is simply an effective means of conveying deeply felt beliefs about solidarity in struggle and the need to put the interests of the collective before those of individuals.

Richard Hoggart focuses on the neighbourhood rather than the workplace in *The Uses of Literacy* (1957) to explore what he termed 'Primary Religion'. In this section of the book, Hoggart employs colloquialisms to illustrate the way that the people of Hunslett in Yorkshire use a pragmatic version of Christianity geared to the concerns of working-class communal life and observes that:

> Insofar as they think of Christianity, they think of it as a system of ethics; their main concern is with morals, not meta-physics ... they hold firmly to the view that *Christianity is the best form of ethics* ... that we ought all to try to 'live according to Christ's teaching' ... That a sense of moral duties is what they chiefly understand ... Christianity is morals ... 'Christ's teaching' is the one most commonly heard when the talk is in favour of religion. *Christ was a person, giving the best example of how to live*; one could not expect to live like that today, still the example is there. They like to speak of 'practical Christianity'. The emphasis is always on what is right for them to do, as far as they can, as people; *people who do not see the point of 'all this dogma', but who must constantly get along with others, in groups; people who must learn how to*

co-operate, how to live on an exchange basis, how to give and take. The assumption behind the treatment of others is not so much that we are all children of God ... as that we are all 'in the same boat together' *... the sense of religion as a guide to our duty towards others, as the repository of good rules for communal life* ... (Hoggart, 1957, pp. 93–4; my emphasis)

But class consciousness is not the exclusive preserve of adults. Children also inhabit and experience the social world in which the phrases above relentlessly circulate, teaching them about their position in the social and economic hierarchies which govern the world outside the family. In the discussion which follows I will show how the polysemic story of Jesus can be seen to 'handle' those experiences in cultural terms. For example, it can be read as a manifesto for the need to take political action to fight injustice and oppression, as when the angry Jesus (the rebel with a cause who knows right from wrong) overturns the tables of the traders in the temple while brandishing a scourge against the moneylenders. For girls charged with the social obligations of caring, the narrative accords status to so-called feminine activities[6] because it can be interpreted as the story of Jesus the maternal male, whose qualities are intuitively recognized by children, the sick, the poor and emotionally distressed. It is also the story of a man who challenged heterosexual social norms and forsook family ties and cultural obligations to marry, choosing instead to live among men and to use his short life in the pursuit of wisdom and the practice of teaching. One of the most disturbing and compelling interpretations is that of the good and gentle Jesus betrayed by his followers and cruelly murdered for his beliefs. This is a version of the story which can convey a political message about power which is accessible even to the developing consciousness of a child.[7] It is also the story of how, even as a baby, Jesus was so much more important than his parents that three wise men travelled thousands of miles to visit him. It can be read as the story of the self-willed Jesus who gave short shrift to his mother – and his 'legal' father – when having gone missing in Jerusalem at the age of twelve, he upbraided her for not realizing that he was obviously to be found in the house of 'His Father'. For those working-class children hailed by the educational discourse of the meritocracy in the 1950s and 1960s, it can be seen as the story of the man who left behind his family and his community to follow another 'higher' path – a choice which was respected because it was acknowledged that he was born to be other to his good but commonplace parents.[8]

Narrative, social class and the family romance

It might appear that psychoanalysis has relatively little to offer in the analysis of issues around socio-economic location (Steedman, 1986, p. 111), but Freud's 1909 essay, 'Family Romance', acknowledges that society is hierarchical and, further, that it is the fate of every ordinary child to have to give up their early fantasies of their parents' omnipotence through acquiring knowledge of the world outside the family. According to Freud, the child's acquisition of this knowledge, through becoming aware of parental socio-economic status, is an important stage in the development of the personality:

> The liberation of an individual ... from the authority of his parents is one of the most necessary though one of the most painful results brought about by the course of his development. (Freud, 1977, p. 221)

This shift in the child's perception of the parents happens because:

> as intellectual growth increases, the child cannot help discovering by degrees the category to which his parents belong ... Small events in the child's life which make him feel dissatisfied afford him provocation for beginning to criticize his parents, and for using, in order to support his critical attitude, the knowledge which he has acquired that other parents are in some respects preferable to them. (Freud, 1977, p. 221)

and thus the:

> child's imagination becomes engaged in the task of getting free from the parents of whom he now has a low opinion and of replacing them by others, who, as a rule, are of higher social standing. (Freud, 1977, pp. 222–3)

Freud's essay provides the means to understand how the story of Jesus might be incorporated into such imaginative fantasies when he writes that there are all too many experiences when a child feels slighted by his/her parents and that:

> His sense that his own affection is not being fully reciprocated then finds a vent in the idea ... of being a step-child or an adopted child. People ... very frequently remember such occasions, on which –

usually as a result of something they have read – they interpreted and
responded to their parent's hostile behaviour in this fashion. (Freud,
1977, p. 222; my emphasis)

As noted earlier, the Jesus story told to children has much in common with
fairy tales and, according to Bettelheim (1978), it is through their engagement with fairy tales in particular that children are able to explore – albeit
symbolically – their bad as well as good feelings towards others and to be
able to resolve their existential dilemmas and their Oedipal conflicts.
Bettelheim sees the motif of the death of a mother or father as providing the
child with the means to come to terms with her/his fears of losing a loved
parent, but he does not consider that a child might also fantasize about
killing or eliminating that same loved parent *not* because of Oedipal desires
but because they are perceived as an obstacle to a better material quality of
life. Freud's 'Family Romance' thus provides us with one way of reapprais-
ing the children's story of Jesus so that other subject positions of
identification emerge, in addition to that of Christ as the super-ego role
model of passive perfection and sacrifice. If children know that they are not
always good and they are also encouraged to see the life of Jesus as a model
for their own, it is possible to 'read' that story from a perspective which
presents Jesus as self-possessed, single-minded and certainly not humble,
but nevertheless the central focus of his parents' love and attention.[9]

By applying Freud's notion of the family romance to the story of Jesus
we can begin to see that it might, like the fairy tales it often resembles, offer
the child the opportunity to fantasize about being the child of some higher-
born person. For the Jesus in the stories told to young children is second
only to the most powerful being – God. Jesus is referred to in familial terms,
but in addition to being our father, brother and friend, he is also referred to
as our Lord, the Prince of Peace and the King of the Jews. Within all
hierarchies, both familial and regal, Jesus is positioned as a powerful and
influential being. But identification with the story can also be seen as
sending out other messages about the sacrifices that parents make for their
children. In addition, it places the wisdom of the 'doctors' (teachers) over
parents; knowledge and destiny are prioritized over familial bonds.

History and the myth-making of the working class

Reading the children's story of Jesus as a family romance provides a way of
exploring how imaginative fantasies might be reflective of the material

reality of children's experiences and explain why the narrative has had a particular relevance for some working-class children. In British society since the Industrial Revolution, the progress of this social group has been measured in terms of the dissemination of the bourgeois values of individual advancement. Each successive generation of working-class children is seen as being both a threat to and a hope for what society might be. Progress for the children has been framed in terms of disjunction and movement from – rather than a continuum or reproduction of – the culture and values of their parents. Through the myth of the meritocracy, access to education for the working class has been equated with access to self-improvement, producing a discourse of individual progress which has tended to erase the desire for progress as a collective enterprise.

There is a particular genre of writing influenced by Cultural Studies which documents the movement of individuals from their working-class origins. It is often presented as a one-way journey told by the 'escapee', making invisible the positive aspects of the culture 'left behind'. In their autobiographical writings Raymond Williams and Richard Hoggart have both challenged this mythology by stressing the enduring value of their working-class origins and of the many 'return' journeys they have made. Hoggart and Williams have written accounts which, rather than rejecting their origins, seek to understand their influence. Similarly, Freud ends his essay by emphasizing that the child's fantasizing of the higher-born person as the 'real' parent is not a rejection but a reconstitution of the parent(s), for:

> we find that these new and aristocratic parents are equipped with attributes that are derived entirely from real recollections of the actual and humble ones; so that in fact the child is not getting rid of his father but exalting him. Indeed the whole effort at replacing the real father by a superior one is only an expression of the child's longing for the happy, vanished days when his father seemed to him the noblest and strongest of men and his mother the dearest and loveliest of women. (Freud, 1977, pp. 224–5)

This fantasizing thus involves a reconstitution of the parents to take account of the accruing knowledge of their social positioning. This reconstitution mediated through the Jesus story can facilitate a reparation of the disrupted psychological relationship between a child and its parents. But such an analysis must also take into account the specificities of historical location because, as Steedman has observed, 'we live in time and politics, and exclusion is the promoter of envy, the social and subjective sense of the impossible unfairness of things' (Steedman, 1986, p. 111).

Through the 1944 Education Act, religious education was established in the curriculum of all state schools, institutionalizing the Christian ethic of emancipatory altruism expressed in the view of children as the hope of the world. In the 1950s the impact of this legislation was seen in primary school timetables, making religious activities a central feature of the teaching day. The pedagogies developed through Sunday School teaching were adapted in state primary schools where, for many girls like me, the story of Jesus was used to inculcate a sense of altruistic citizenship. But conversely it also communicated a sense of the self as a powerful – and sometimes angry – agent in a changing world. From a child's perspective, going to infant school was experienced as entering a world of colour and warmth which was in sharp contrast to the drabness of most homes in the austerity of postwar Britain. But most especially it was the place where we gathered together sitting quietly on the floor and listened to stories told by our teacher.

The teacher who told the story of Jesus in my 1950s infant school in the mining town of Barnsley, South Yorkshire, struck an emotional chord in me which has persisted through the years. Although I cannot remember the actual words she used, I can recall that she told the Good Friday story, and that in describing Jesus' capture, imprisonment and death, she said that she was sure that if we had been there 'we would have saved him, wouldn't we?' I learned that day that Jesus had been killed *even though* he had always gone about doing good to people, especially children, and was the most perfect of men. Still no one had gone to his aid, or if they had they had not been able to save him.[10] The story upset me deeply, because it appeared to tell me something very frightening, which was that goodness was no protection from the dangers of the world. But the story of Jesus as told to children also emphasized the debt which they, in particular, owe him. That only through their efforts to continue his work can the horror of his death be overcome. For many of my generation, the wartime sacrifices our parents spoke about and the story of Jesus, the children's friend, coalesced around our perception of ourselves as the chosen ones, the hope of a better world. In my case the story of Jesus was connected with a working-class 'them and us' sensibility for it came after other stories told me by my paternal grandfather. The man who sang sentimental Edwardian songs to me from the moment I could sit on his lap was also the man who taught me that Winston Churchill, the wartime leader, was hated in the Yorkshire coalfields for having ordered the troops to attack local striking miners. Thus the Good Friday story was for me refracted through the lens of an emerging class-consciousness which positioned working-class men as being particularly at risk from a vaguely discernible and distant 'them'. I believe that this interpretation of the story of Jesus, combined with the effectiveness of the promotion of him as a role model for children, provided me with a class-based model of society and a subjectivity in which duty was framed by reference to class and familial loyalties, rather than patriotism.

My own engagement with the myth-making story of Jesus in all its many forms has had an undoubted influence on my desire to be seen as a 'good' girl. But 'being good' has not been seen exclusively in terms of conforming self-discipline. Rather the wider knowledge of Jesus' life, together with the stories told by my family, has produced a notion of 'being good' based on the ability to be strong and willing to stand up against injustice in the world. If 'class entails the notion of historical relationship' and is a relationship which 'must always be embodied in real people and in a real context' (Thompson, 1968), then the historical specificities of the 1944 Education Act which promoted a Christian ethic, the setting up of the socialist-inspired Welfare State and the postwar consensus all contributed to my seeing education as providing opportunities (and duties) to redeem the losses and indignities suffered by others in a capitalist society. As a working-class girl, my engagement with the story of Jesus was, in the end, an emancipatory reading which undoubtedly contributed to my continuing adult involvement in class-based politics and which led others of my generation to similar activities in collective struggles for other causes.

Notes

1. Matthew 16:15.
2. The 1944 Education Act viewed the teaching of Christian ethics as the vehicle for inculcating citizenship through schooling.
3. In contrast, the study of popular piety is well established in the USA, South America and mainland Europe.
4. Thompson's oft-quoted aim of rescuing the working class 'from the enormous condescension of history' is emblematic of such academic altruism.
5. See Ken Ambler, *A Coalfield in Chaos* [1987].
6. See Skeggs (1997) for a discussion of caring as cultural capital among working-class women.
7. See Brewer (1996) for a more detailed exploration of these issues.

8. This reading is based on Protestant retellings of the story. Catholicism's emphasis on Mariolatry would not be consonant with this interpretation.

9. This in contrast to many views which see Jesus only ever functioning as a role model for masochistic passivity. See Daly (1973).

10. Ken Ambler writes: 'I'm not very religious myself, but I have always believed that Jesus must have been a socialist. He cared for the sick and weak, would hurt no one and hated corruption . . . And we all know how he was repaid, don't we?' (1987, p.110).

Bibliography

Ambler, K. (1987) *A Coalfield in Chaos*. Bridlington: Ken Ambler.

Bettelheim, B. (1982) *The Uses of Enchantment*. Harmondsworth: Peregrine.

Brewer, S. (1996) 'The political is personal: father–daughter relationships and the formation of class consciousness'. *Feminism and Psychology* 6(3), pp. 401–10.

Clarke, J. (1976). In S. Hall and T. Jefferson (eds), *Resistance through Rituals: Youth Subcultures in Post-War Britain*. London: Hutchinson.

Daly, M. (1973) *Beyond God the Father*. New York: Beacon Press.

Freud, S. (1977) *On Sexuality*. Harmondsworth: Pelican.

Hall, S. (1981) 'Notes on deconstructing "the popular"'. In R. Samuel (ed.), *People's History and Socialist Theory*. London: Routledge & Kegan Paul.

Hoggart, R. (1957) *The Uses of Literacy*. London: Chatto & Windus.

McCabe, C. (ed.) (1986) *High Theory/Low Culture: Analysing Popular Television*. Manchester: Manchester University Press.

Morley, D. (1980) 'Texts, readers, subjects'. In S. Hall, D. Hobson, A. Lowe and P. Willis (eds), *Culture, Media, Language*. Birmingham: CCCS.

Radway, J. (1987) *Reading the Romance: Patriarchy and Popular Literature*. London: Verso.

Samuel, R. (ed.) (1981) *People's History and Socialist Theory*. London: Routledge & Kegan Paul.

Sivanandan, A. (1990) *Communities of Resistance: Writings on Black Struggles for Socialism*. London: Verso.

Skeggs, B. (1997) *Formations of Class and Gender: Becoming Respectable*. London: Sage.

Steedman, C. (1986) *Landscape for a Good Woman*. London: Virago.

Thompson, E. P. (1968) *The Making of the English Working Class*. Harmondsworth: Pelican.

Turner, G. (1990) *British Cultural Studies: An Introduction*. London: Unwin Hyman.

Willis, P. (1977) *Learning to Labour: How Working Class Kids Get Working Class Jobs*. Farnborough: Saxon House.

Zipes, J. (1979) *Breaking the Magic Spell*. London: Routledge.

11

Death in the Good Old Days: True Crime Tales and Social History

Anita Biressi

The true crime magazine has been a specialist 'leisure interest' genre in Britain since the 1950s when it achieved considerable commercial success. Its status as a popular form has been acknowledged and simultaneously denigrated by left cultural critics (see Orwell, 1970 and Hoggart, 1957). The acknowledgement of the political value of studying literature aimed at a predominantly working-class readership has often been hedged with anxiety, and shot through with reservations about the influence of commercial mass culture upon the undereducated reader. Since the late 1970s true crime magazines and books (together with television programmes) have once again captured a significant niche in the popular literary market place, targeting a working-class readership which is also predominantly female.[1] This chapter addresses the popularity of recent true crime magazines, its representation of working-class people and its address to readers.

As Stuart Hall has noted, both 'popular' and 'people' are always highly problematic terms: 'Just as there is no fixed content to the category of "popular culture", so there is no fixed subject to attach to it' (Hall, 1981, p. 239). On the other hand, these two terms can be deployed strategically when the cultural field within which discourses of class, gender and criminality are formed, negotiated, co-opted or contested is to be examined. The conflation between the 'people' as readers and the 'subordinate' or working classes is to some extent inevitable where mass readerships are concerned, for 'mass' must contain within it 'subordinated' social groupings. True crime magazines certainly address such a readership, but this is not to say that readers would recognize themselves in the mirrors of class or socio-economic categorization. For 'working-class' as a category was formed through 'middle-class' conceptualizations, consolidated in the nineteenth century through mechanisms of surveillance, moral ordinance and the organization of capital. It is a political designation which is not necessarily recognized by readers themselves. But as Beverley Skeggs's (1997) work demonstrates, any scholarly attempt to bypass the historical establishment of class also forecloses any engagement with its long-term material and psychological consequences. This chapter examines 'classic' true crime stories which depict the lives and deaths of people in the nineteenth and early twentieth centuries, people who, thanks to a variety of cultural and ideological markers, would be commonly recognized by readers as 'working class'. Bearing in mind the caveats just raised, the strategic deployment of concepts of 'class', of 'people' and of 'popular culture' will be used to forge analytic connections between true crime, its narratives and its readers.

The case of Kitty Breaks and Frederick Holt

> Abstracted and redeployed, history seems to be purged of political tension; it becomes a unifying spectacle, the settling of all disputes.
> (Wright, 1985, p. 69)

Many true crime monthly magazines include a selection of 'classic cases' which are set in earlier eras and interspersed with contemporary stories. These stories, like most true crime, typically focus upon the messy business of murder. Usually set in the nineteenth or early twentieth century, they feature a range of locations and protagonists from a variety of social backgrounds. The Blackpool Double Bill featured in *True Crime Summer Special* (1996) begins with a full-page illustration of Central Beach in the 1920s.[2] Superimposed over the picture is the statement: 'They came to the famous seaside town with their lovers . . . and left them as corpses' (*TC SS*, 1996, p. 43). A story entitled 'Corpse on the beach was worth a fortune' (*TC SS*, 1996, pp. 48–51) provides a flavour of the material on offer to readers, revealing how readers are positioned and the ways in which relations of class and gender are negotiated. Set in the 1920s it tells the true story of how 'ex-mill girl' Kitty Breaks fell in love with a demobbed lieutenant called Frederick Holt, the man who was eventually to murder her on Blackpool beach. The account relates their affair from his perspective, underlining her naivety, emphasizing his greed and vicious manipulation of Kitty and his attempts to insure her life for a considerable sum of money. This account, like most true crime stories, presents a unified and apparently incontrovertible reading of past events consolidated through the use of stock characterization, common-sense interpretation and popular generic conventions. The story begins *in medias res*, harnessing the discourses of stage melodrama to set the scene:

> Six foot tall, good-looking Frederick Holt smoothed his moustache and sidled up to the pretty little wide-eyed girl standing alone on the edge of the dance hall floor. 'May I have the pleasure?' he murmured in a clipped, cultured accent. Kitty Breaks fluttered her eyelashes. With a weak, slightly awed smile she gave her consent. (p. 48)

Here Holt is clearly coded as a predatory cad within a narrative which the reader already knows can only end in murder. From the outset Kitty is marked out as an unlucky victim of circumstance – wide-eyed little girl. The account stresses the vulnerability of a woman of Kitty's social class and limited experience compared to Holt who, in her eyes, was the model of refinement and security with an 'income twice the national wages'. Kitty sends Holt a long, 'illiterate' love letter in which she confesses to a divorce (described here as her 'sordid affair').

> The epistle was both drooling, disjointed, and something of a literary shambles, and when Freddie read it, with one eyebrow slightly lifted, he metaphorically shrugged his shoulders. (pp. 48–9)

The letter itself is not reproduced. Yet the reader is invited to peep over Holt's shoulder as he reads it, to vicariously share his contempt. In this context Kitty's illiteracy is not so much a mark of her class as the sign of her natural victimhood and her inability to save herself from a threat which seems (in retrospect of course) so obvious to current readers. That the letter is 'drooling and disjointed' seems explanation enough for Kitty's inability to avoid death. Here the appearance of death in the figure of Holt is the most exciting thing in Kitty's life. He transforms her life, introducing her to the thrill of motor cars, dining out and holidays. Kitty's joy in travelling from Bradford to Blackpool is noted, 'for holidays at seaside hotels had not figured much in her drab life' (p. 49). It is here that she meets her apparently inevitable end, battered and shot by Freddy. Freddy, with equal inevitability in a story whose end is made clear at the outset, is executed for murder.

In this story and in many others, class and gender relations underpin the narrative even as they seem to elude scrutiny. They slip between the competing and sometimes conflicting discourses which true crime habitually deploys: melodrama, police procedural, reportage, whodunnit. The historical advantages and disadvantages of class and gender which might still resonate with contemporary readers 'are purged of political tension', recast into those of character and individual agency (Wright, 1985, p. 69).

Richard Hoggart provides some insight into the appeal of what he refers to as 'working-class art'. He notes, for example, the popularity of radio soaps, newspapers and magazines all of which pay close attention to the 'human condition':

> working-class art is essentially a 'showing' (rather than an 'exploration'), a presentation of what is known already. It starts from the assumption that human life is fascinating in itself. It . . . has to begin with the photographic, however fantastic it may become; it has to be underpinned by . . . moral rules. (Hoggart, 1957, p. 94)

Hoggart argues that while the 'ooh—aah' sensationalism of sex or crime is appealing, the fundamental success of such stories is based upon the assumption that 'ordinary life is intrinsically interesting'. This is borne out by advertisements for the True Crime Library which link crime (murder, rape and gangsterism) to picaresque biography in the manner of Daniel Defoe: 'The lives, loves and extraordinary adventures of a host of amazing people will fascinate and excite all who read them' (*MMF*, Issue 22 (undated), p. 32).

True crime is by definition an entertainment based on 'what is known already'. 'Classic' stories are heavily illustrated, as if to substantiate their version of events, but the perceived accessibility of photographs and news clippings also affirms a continuity between the text and everyday life. Photographs in this sense enable readers to 'know' the protagonists. Representative figures such as the 'jealous husband', 'greedy wife', 'master criminal' or 'beast' are personalized through the liberal use of family photographs, line drawings and so on, pointing to links with earlier popular adult literatures such as chapbooks, executions sheets and serialized stories. Even when photographs are printed without context, their very form as indexical representations link the present tenuously with the past, bearing a stamp of authenticity and providing readers with points of identification for victims such as Kitty Breaks. They invite readers to 'apply to them the perceptual schemes of their own ethos' which produces 'a bracketing of form in favour of "human" content' (Bourdieu, 1989, p. 44). Moreover, with photographs, the 'narratives nearly always fall within the competence of women ... the custodians of human feelings' (Seabrook, 1991).

From another perspective, photographs also have the stamp of mortality upon them. Photographs used to illustrate the still-notorious murder of Fanny Adams in the 1830s are exemplary here (*TC SS*, 1996, pp. 2–8). A full-page sepia-tinted photograph of a little girl and her family hop-picking in Hampshire is superscribed with gothic lettering which advertises the horrible story to follow: 'THE HORRIBLE DEATH OF SWEET FANNY ADAMS. She was eight years old and playing with friends in a meadow when a man picked her up and carried her into a wood. What followed was the nightmare every mother dreads ... ' (see Figure 11.1). Its presentation is reminiscent of a Victorian theatre poster. The partial obliteration of the image by the text anticipates the destruction of the family through the assault, murder and dismemberment of the little girl. In a double-movement it both anticipates and fixes the fatal event within the photographic moment: 'Photography is a kind of primitive theatre, a kind of *Tableau Vivant*, a figuration of the motionless and made-up face beneath which we see the dead' (Barthes, 1984, p. 32).

Roland Barthes contends that the photograph precariously links together three points in time: the moment when the photograph is taken, the point at which the subjects of the photographs die and the point at which the viewer looks at the image. The poignancy of the photograph is due to its imbrication with mortality, we look at the subject and know both that 'he is dead and he is going to die' (p. 95). Even a photograph of a stranger from another century speaks to the viewer of their own inevitable mortality. Examining an 1865 photographic portrait of a young murderer awaiting execution, Barthes comments grimly, 'I observe with horror an anterior future of which the stake is death' (p. 96).

The Kitty Breaks story is replete with contemporary monochrome illustrations of the period: Blackpool beach, the Big Wheel and the helter-skelter, and a Bradford Mill, as well as with photographic portraits of Kitty, Freddie, the trial judge, defence lawyer and headlines from contemporary newspapers. The photograph's status as evidence and truth underwrites the sensationalized story. Randomly placed and only loosely anchored to the story, these photographs and scraps of documentation taken together

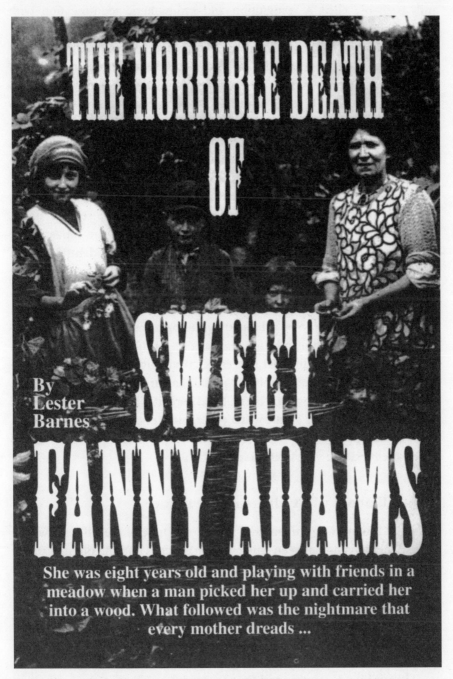

THE HORRIBLE DEATH OF SWEET FANNY ADAMS

By Lester Barnes

She was eight years old and playing with friends in a meadow when a man picked her up and carried her into a wood. What followed was the nightmare that every mother dreads ...

Figure 11.1 Reproduced from *True Crime Summer Special*, 1996, p. 3. By kind permission of Magazine Design and Publishing, London.

loosely suggest the place and time occupied by Kitty and her murderer and, perhaps, elicit a recognition and sympathetic identification with Kitty, which the text itself fails (or does not choose) to invoke. In addition, 'Blackpool' is a topos which in itself mobilizes discourses of class, of Englishness and of pleasure into an evocative and even nostalgic configuration. Just as the protagonists are rendered 'familiars' via family photos, so too locations such as Blackpool are also 'known already' even by those who have never visited the resort.

A sense of place then, as epitomized by the liberal use of photographs, is fundamental to magazine true crime. Urban, rural and seaside settings are far from idyllic. These stories do not represent the picturesque but the picaresque, parochial and the popular: high streets, markets, music halls, servants' quarters and so on. Region, village, suburb, seaside hotel, respectable household or slum dwelling is presented as the topos of the English/Scottish/Welsh people, the source of their national identity and the location of danger, threat and criminality. Often there are scenes of degraded public life: 'white slavery', taverns, mobs, prostitution and execution crowds, but they are without the currency or acute social observation of a Gilray or a Hogarth. Photographs born of nineteenth-century fascination with and surveillance of the unruly poor are redeployed as the backdrop to individual stories of criminality. The subjects which nineteenth-century photography helped to construct appear now to have always been there. If nostalgia is exhibited here, it is not for a golden age of low-level crime, but for a time when experiences of crime and punishment were, to all appearances, less complex and conflicted, when the unruly poor were rendered visible and identifiable.

'Read all about it!' Addressing the reader

The grim humour, voyeurism and sensational tone of the titles signal the generic relationship between true crime magazines and the popular press. Incongruous titles such as 'Devon love bungalow killing' or 'Last tango in Sussex' problematize any notion of earnest reading. The use of vernacular in particular recalls the pungent address of the *News of the World*. This is especially apparent in editorials such as this one which echo a sales pitch famously deployed by the *Sun*:

There's blood and gore and so much more! . . . What can be better than lazing around, reading a Summer Special? Give yourself a pat on the back for thinking of such a thrilling way of cooling off – by reading these blood-chilling stories! (*TD SS*, 1995, p. 4)

Vernacular, pun and internal rhyming all point to a generic relationship with an oral tradition of popular entertainment, as well as with the press. The provision of narrative coherence through enplotment rather than through 'referential information and logic' links true crime to fictional modes of storytelling more closely than to journalism (Dalgren, cited in Storey, 1996). Vestiges of spoken storytelling are invoked through a number of tropes, some of which are particular to 'classic' true crime narratives. For example, some stories are introduced in a manner which suggests that the writer is not simply reporting a story but is actually recollecting the events related to the reader: 'John Cupples recalls ... BIRMINGHAM'S MOON MURDERER' (*TC DM*, December 1993, pp. 24–5). This strategy presents the tale as occurring within living memory even though this is often clearly impossible, and manufactures an intimacy between writer and reader. These 'recollections' seek to establish an experiential and cognitive connection between readers' contemporary experience and perception of crime and criminality and the everyday experiences of crime within earlier eras. Here crime and the popular memory of crime are presented unproblematically as a constant and perceptible connection between the present and the 'past'. The cursory social commentary provided to contextualize stories poaches 'human interest' social history. One editor makes the ambitious claim that 'stories ... hail from a diversity of times and places, allowing the serious reader to plot a chart in social history, from the criminologist's point of view' (*MD SS*, 1995, p. 4). Yet oddly, basic information such as the date of the event, which is needed to orientate the reader in time, is often withheld for pages. Like fairy tales, these narratives seem to have occurred 'once upon a time'.

Geoffrey Pearson (1983) has argued that popular memory plays a significant role in our perception of the contemporary state of law and order. The experience and the perception of crime are measured against a notional golden age which occurred some two decades earlier and against which crime today is inevitably judged to be more virulent, less controlled and less punished. Narratives of past crimes therefore occupy a paradoxical position within the parameters of true crime magazines. For while the editorial, letters page and articles on recent shocking crimes construct our own period as the most dangerous in the history of crime, 'classic' cases usually present crime as eternally ubiquitous and horrid. For example, in true crime, nineteenth-century working-class experiences of crime are not cast in a golden hue, nor are they contrasted with the more 'civilized' conditions of today. Rather as Hoggart noted above, crime is the dramatic motor for a variety of stories whose apparently timeless 'human interest' speaks to the current reader.

The case of George Vass and Margaret Docherty

Most classic true crime stories do little to explore the political and economic context of crime and punishment. At most they present a cursory and haphazard social history of the few issues which directly relate to the events in question: prostitution, penology, temperance, the Elizabethan 'underworld' and so on. Stories of 'classic' crime bear headlines which lend social history the spurious currency of today's news. For example, events which occurred in Newcastle in 1862 are flagged 'Woman stripped, raped and murdered in street' (*TD SS*, 1996, pp. 38–9) (see Figure 11.2). This refers to the case of George Vass and Margaret Docherty:

> A sex-crazed brute with rape on his mind, a drunken housewife, and New Year's Eve in Newcastle is a lethal cocktail. It ended with the violent death of housewife Margaret Docherty and the hanging of killer George Vass. (*ibid.*)

The story, part of a 'Tyneside Double Bill', suggests that George Vass followed a trajectory of violent criminal behaviour which ended with the rape and murder of Margaret Docherty. At 21 years old, Vass, who was illiterate, was a well-known figure in Newcastle. He had a history of violent criminality, including sexual assault, rape and pub fights. As a reprobate 'he would drive the most patient reformist to drink' (p. 38). Margaret Docherty was a 'housewife' who usually didn't drink much, but who was out drunk on New Year's Eve. Docherty had an altercation with her husband who tried to take her home. The altercation was only stopped when passers-by intervened in the belief that he was molesting her. She was staggering away when she was spotted by Vass: 'Watching her from the shadows, George Vass's cruel lips tightened. "She'll do," he said to himself' (p. 41). Again, as in the murder of Kitty Breaks discussed above, Docherty is styled as the natural victim of a man destined to kill. In other words 'she'll do', but so would the next available woman – 'available' signifying the victim's own 'complicity' in her demise. In both accounts,

Figure 11.2 Reproduced from *True Detective Summer Special*, 1996, pp. 38–9. By kind permission of Magazine Design and Publishing, London.

class and gender are not the explicit determinants of events, but their given, naturalized and unspoken backdrop. Docherty, drunk and refusing to return home with her husband, was a working-class woman who had temporarily eluded the regulation of moral behaviour, which was being instituted during the period (Skeggs, 1997, p. 42); she had evaded the domestic 'ideal' which putatively guaranteed her safety. Away from the alleged safety of the domestic realm, she is dragged to the West Wall which has its own history of violence, rendered more ironic by her earlier fight with her husband:

> With some kind of superhuman effort she still managed to cry 'Murder!' But the West Wall was badly lit . . . It was a place where husbands frequently beat their wives, and the wives frequently cried 'Murder!' and no one took any notice. (*TD SS*, 1996, p. 41)

What does such a story offer to the reader, who is often working-class and frequently female? In this account there is no heroine to outwit and outlive the murderer. If there is a 'hero', it is Vass, cheered on in court and afterwards by Newcastle's 'biggest villains', temporarily allocated the role of anti-authoritarian rebel. In both the Breaks and Docherty narratives, readers are textually aligned with the male predators right up until their executions.

> Vass listened intensely to the chaplain reading the Bible to him . . . he was visited before his execution for the last time by his tearful family; his mother . . . had to be torn away from him. (*ibid.*)

Only at the end is the reader torn away also, joining the crowd who watched Vass hang. 'As his body shuddered for a few minutes on the end of the rope a woman shouted: "God forgive him all his sins!" ' Only at the final moment is the female reader textually aligned with the female witness to Vass's punishment. The reader's only apparent consolation is that she is *still* here even if Mary Docherty is not. In a culture where randomized male-on-female violence is perceived by women to constitute a real threat, and familial male-on-female violence an actuality, true crime narratives (and other crime narratives, such as TV reconstructions) can at least affirm readers' present security and contain the sense of threat (while also of course reinforcing their perception of ubiquitous danger). In addition, the construction of women, especially working-class women, as culpable of their own victimization, is already naturalized within crime reportage.

Overall, true crime fits in neatly with the network of dominant discourses which aligns women with vulnerability and victimhood.

The idea that there has always been violent crime among the working class from working-class men onto working-class women, and that this is the inevitable corollary of class formation (rather than of sedimented gender relations), is embedded in everyday historical consciousness. Its entrenchment is effected in part through stories such as these which, unencumbered as they are with political interpretation or collective memory, normalize socially conservative explanations of criminal behaviour. Most stories portray a crime-ridden working class in which psychological complexity and even the 'elemental simplicity of class-consciousness is refused' (Steedman, 1986, p. 13). In Benjamin's terms they have a 'chaste compactness which precludes psychological analysis' (Benjamin, 1992a, p. 90). As a consequence, these tales are historical set pieces which are made meaningful through their address to late-twentieth-century anxieties and prejudices about crime and criminality, gender and class relations. In the Docherty case the ill-fitting metaphor of the city as a lethal cocktail, the figuring of Geordie violence, inebriation, moral dissolution and male violence speak to the reader's preconceptions and fear of personal attack and the crumbling of the social bond. The case of Kitty Breaks articulates still-evident suspicions about social mobility and educated, middle-class masculinity. The case of little Fanny Adams becomes the 'nightmare every mother dreads', adding its sad story to the plethora of recent crime reportage and public opinion which has focused upon the child as an object of sexual and physical vulnerability. In these ways the past is ascribed relevance retrospectively, 'charged with the time of the now' (Benjamin, 1992b, p. 253).

Notes

1. Established magazines such as *Master Detective*, *True Crime Monthly* and *True Detective* have a combined readership of 195,000 plus and claim to target all ages and socio-economic groups (BRAD). The newer magazines, such as the collect-and-keep partwork *Real Life Crimes ... and how they were solved* (anticipated circulation 300,000), explicitly target a readership which is 68 per cent female, aged between 16 and 34 and occupying the C1, C2 bracket (BRAD). See also Deborah Cameron (1990).

2. Full magazine titles:
   MD SS Master Detective Summer Special
   MMF Murder Most Foul

TC DM	*True Crime Detective Monthly*
TC SS	*True Crime Summer Special*
TD SS	*True Detective Summer Special*

Bibliography

Barthes, R. (1984) *Camera Lucida* (trans. R. Howard). London: Flamingo.

Benjamin, W. (1992a) 'The storyteller'. In *Illuminations* (ed. H. Arendt, trans. H. Zohn). London: Fontana.

Benjamin, W. (1992b) 'Theses on the philosophy of history'. In *Illuminations* (ed. H. Arendt, trans. H. Zohn). London: Fontana.

Bennett, T. (1986) 'Introduction: popular culture and the turn to Gramsci'. In T. Bennett, C. Mercer and J. Woollacott (eds), *Popular Culture and Social Relations*. Buckingham: Open University Press.

Bourdieu, P. (1989) *Distinctions: A Social Critique of the Judgement of Taste*. London: Routledge.

Cameron, D. (1990) 'Pleasure and danger, sex and death'. In G. Day (ed.), *Readings in Popular Culture*. London: Macmillan.

Hall, S. (1981) 'Notes on deconstructing "the popular" '. In R. Samuel (ed.), *People's History and Socialist Thought*. London: Routledge & Kegan Paul.

Hoggart, R. (1957) *The Uses of Literacy*. Harmondsworth: Penguin.

Orwell, G. (1970) 'Boys' weeklies'. In *The Collected Essays, Journalism and Letters of George Orwell: An Age Like This, 1920–1940*. Harmondsworth: Penguin.

Pearson, G. (1983) *Hooligan: A History of Respectable Fears*. London: Macmillan.

Seabrook, J. (1991) 'My life in that box'. In J. Spence and P. Holland (eds), *Family Snaps: The Meaning of Domestic Photography*. London: Virago.

Skeggs, B. (1997) *Formations of Class and Gender: Becoming Respectable*. London: Sage.

Steedman, C. (1986) *Landscape for a Good Woman: A Story of Two Lives*. London: Virago.

Storey, J. (1996) *Cultural Studies and the Study of Popular Culture*. Edinburgh: Edinburgh University Press.

Wright, P. (1985) *On Living in an Old Country: The National Past in Contemporary Britain*. London: Verso.

Acknowledgement

I would like to thank Heather Nunn and Sally Munt for their advice during the writing of this chapter.

12

'Can't Help Lovin' Dat Man': Social Class and the Female Voice in *Nil by Mouth*

Glen Creeber

Released in Europe in 1997, *Nil by Mouth* was written and directed by British actor Gary Oldman, who is best known for his leading roles in films such as *Sid and Nancy*, *Bram Stoker's Dracula* and blockbusters like *The Fifth Element* and *Lost in Space*. Oldman's directorial debut, however, draws its influence more from relatively low-budget British film and television drama than the Hollywood movies where he made his name. Dedicated to the memory of his alcoholic father and apparently biographical in inspiration, the film is a harrowing portrait of working-class life in contemporary Britain. Set in Deptford, south London, where Oldman grew up, the film graphically depicts a severely dysfunctional family and community whose spiralling despair is fuelled by drink, drugs and an unforgiving and relentless violence. In this chapter I aim to chart the historical influences of Oldman's film, drawing both similarities and differences between the sort of working-class life it depicts with that of earlier British films and television which have clearly had an influence on both Oldman's subject matter and style of film-making. In particular, I will show how the portrayal of working-class women in Oldman's film reveals a development of themes and techniques which distinguish it from some of its generic predecessors, perhaps heralding a new purpose and significance to the presence of the 'female voice' in contemporary British drama.

Despite being set and made over thirty years after Ken Loach's *Up the Junction* (1965), the beginning of *Nil by Mouth* is strangely reminiscent of the opening of that earlier television drama. Despite the technical restraints of the former (heavy electronic television cameras as opposed to new lightweight film equipment), both are typified by their intimate use of the camera as it frames their working-class characters in close-up, observing them as they talk, drink, smoke, laugh and exchange mumbled vernaculars. Both re-create a crowded, confined and claustrophobic social club which focuses on an array of overlapping dialogue and centres briefly on one of its characters telling a personal and scatological anecdote. In *Up the Junction*, the film's scriptwriter Nell Dunn has Terry (Michael Standing) recount a tale of being discovered taking a bath by the landlady of a house he is meant to be refurbishing (an event later dramatized in Loach's *Riff Raff* (1993)). 'Now the fellows,' he explains to his female companion, 'instead of telling her I'm having a toilet or something ... they lets her walk *right in*, and she sees me standing there in the nude ... My life you should've heard her scream.' Similarly, Oldman has Mark (Jamie Forman) tell a story about his accidental arrival at an orgy. 'Right?,' he tells his mates, 'I'm looking at her, thinkin' ... fuckin' 'ell, I'd like to get hold of that. I look around, she's gettin' it from behind ... She is getting a severe portion, right up the fuckin' Gary.'

Despite the sexually explicit nature of Oldman's narrative compared to the now innocent-sounding story provided by Dunn's screenplay, the function of both is clear: to immediately reveal to the audience something fundamental about the people and culture each narrative is attempting to portray. This is a world where sex is often the most frequently discussed topic, yet where communication between the sexes is severely impoverished. Such a contradiction is reinforced in *Up the Junction* by the contrast between this open and casual talk of sex and the later harrowing abortion scenes, while in *Nil by Mouth* the characters' sexually explicit language and dialogue are juxtaposed with the brutal and shocking violence perpetuated by men on women.

This wider connection with an older tradition of British film-making is subtly implied in the very aesthetics of Oldman's film. According to the film's production designer Hugo Luczyc-Wyhowsk, Oldman 'wanted it to look halfway between a documentary and a drama in that he didn't want it to feel that it was art directed. What we tried to do was create realism with a lot of detail, so that the camera felt it was in the room with the people' (cited by James, 1997, p. 9). Such techniques are not exactly unique in today's British film and television, but there is something in the *mise-en-scène* of Oldman's film which suggests that earlier British film-makers have influenced its very look and design. In particular, Oldman has paid tribute to the British director Alan Clarke, whom he first met when starring in Clarke's *The Firm* (1989), a violent and explosive portrayal of football hooliganism in Thatcher's Britain. Clarke's uncompromising endeavour to expose and explore the often brutal and harsh realities of working-class life in films such as *Scum* (1977), *Made in Britain* (1983) and *Rita, Sue and Bob Too* (1986) was clearly an inspiration. According to Oldman, '*Nil by Mouth* is something of a tribute to a man whose work was really loved and respected' (cited by Kelly, 1998, p. 8). In terms of technique, Clarke's pioneering use of the continuous take (lighting his sets for 360 degrees' movement) and his (and cameraman John Ward's) pioneering use of hand-held camera and the Steadicam (a lightweight camera strapped to the body which enables a greater fluidity, movement and intimacy with actors, sets and location) are clearly reflected in *Nil by Mouth*. Oldman's fidgety camera work, its dimly lit interiors and its naturalistic style of acting are certainly reminiscent of Clarke's film-making. Style and performances are also similar to the work of British director Mike Leigh, whose naturalistic working-class narratives are created out of intense and carefully researched improvisation. Indeed, Oldman's second film role came in Leigh's *Meantime* (1983), where he played a racist skinhead alongside other Clarke devotees Phil Daniels and Tim Roth. Resembling Clarke and Leigh, even Oldman's choice of lesser-known actors (Ray Winstone, Kathy Burke and Oldman's sister, Laila Morse) deliberately seems to add to the film's overall sense of realism. With Oldman investing two million dollars of his own money into the film, such crucial decisions could be made independent of large studio pressures which, he has argued, would have certainly demanded a cast with a higher national and international profile.

Like Clarke and Leigh, Oldman's film-making clearly comes out of a tradition of British cinema which has its roots in the 'Social Realism' or 'New Wave' films of the 1960s. Such a heritage is not only reflected in the film's concern for a realist style and aesthetics, but can also be detected in many of its central themes and overriding concerns. A notoriously slippery and complex term, Social Realism has frequently been defined and redefined, but perhaps Marion Jordan's work on *Coronation Street* still gives us one of its clearest accounts and definitions. Drawing on the work of Raymond Williams (1977), Jordan suggests that in Social Realism 'life should be presented in the form of a narrative of personal events'; that 'these events are ostensibly about *social* problems'; that the 'characters should be either working-class or of the classes immediately visible to the working classes'; that 'the locale should be urban and provincial'; that 'the settings should be commonplace and recognisable'; that 'the time should be "the present" '; and 'that the style should be as to suggest an unmediated, unprejudiced and complete view of reality' (Jordan, 1981, p. 28).[1] Arguably, Oldman's film satisfies all these categories, reflecting and borrowing from a form of British Social Realism stretching back at least to the work of directors like Karel Reisz, Lindsay Anderson, Tony Richardson and Ken Loach.[2]

However, one aspect of the work not accounted for in Jordan's and earlier definitions is the tendency of British Social Realism to offer a gender bias in terms of narrative organization. As the film critic John Hill has explained in *Sex, Class and Realism: British Cinema, 1956–1963* (1986), one of the founding characteristics of British Social Realism in the past has been its tendency to construct a narrative primarily from the perspective of a 'male norm':

> Just as many of the original novels (*Room at the Top, Loneliness of the Long Distance Runner, A Kind of Loving, This Sporting Life*) were written in a male first person narration, most of the subsequent films assume a 'male norm', in their narrative organisation, employment of subjective techniques and patterns of identification. As Ken Worpole suggests of 'masculine style' in the working class novel, the strengths are those of working class virility and aggression, 'the celebration of individual resistance to arbitrary authority, its quick-witted repartee in response to authoritarianism', the weaknesses, 'the avoidance of engaging with the reality of personal and sexual relationships', the denial of their 'mutuality and reciprocity'. (Hill, 1986, p. 163)[3]

Likewise, the opening of *Nil by Mouth* clearly immerses the spectator in an intensely 'masculine' world, one which the audience is actively invited to observe and possibly enter. Ray's (Ray Winstone) air of simmering and explosive violence suggests a hostile and dominant male culture (reminiscent of John Osborne's Jimmy Porter or Karel Reisz's Arthur Seaton) where love, tenderness and respect between the sexes is clearly in short supply. At its beginning Ray is the dynamic focus of the film's narrative and the camera is forever positioning him at the centre of the action. As if to emphasize such a tradition, the film's opening (heightened by Eric Clapton's bluesy guitar) is strangely reminiscent of an older time, place and even tradition. The social club portrayed almost seems trapped in a cultural 'time-warp' with its third-rate comedians, its enforced communal participation and its segregation of men and women. 'You wanna drink that or fuckin' wear it?' are Ray's first words to his mother-in-law, when she taunts him about taking his time at the bar. When his downtrodden wife Val (Kathy Burke) asks him where he's going with the rest of the drinks, he curtly replies, 'Talk to a pal', before quickly disappearing into the darkness of the crowd. This is clearly a working *men*'s club and, if women are allowed in at all, it is not to socialize with the men. Such an opening seems to suggest that little has changed in working-class culture in twenty or thirty years, perhaps heightened and reinforced by the film's apparent borrowing from an older tradition of Social Realism.

Such a portrayal of men and women would not appear outdated in Richard Hoggart's *The Uses of Literacy* (first published in 1957), his quasi-sociological book on British culture which for almost a whole generation helped to define the portrayal of working-class life in British literature, drama, television and film.[4] Forty years before Oldman, Hoggart implicitly defined the working-class social club as a masculine-dominated space, where wives were only allowed to attend at weekends, 'usually as guests'. Indeed, Hoggart's portrayal of working-class mothers and wives tended to portray a dour and defeated population. 'It is evident,' he explains, 'that a working class mother will age early, that at thirty, after having two or three children, she will have lost most of her sexual attraction; that between thirty-five and forty she rapidly becomes the shapeless figure the family know as "our mam"' (Hoggart, 1990, p. 46). It is not difficult to imagine such a future for the plain, pregnant and disillusioned Val, seemingly unhappy in an oppressive marriage and a male-dominated culture which appears to deny her any self-respect or even identity. In her own home she is again physically excluded from the men's social exchange, this time by her role and positioning in the kitchen which is cut off from the living room (and the men) by a glass partition. On the few occasions she does make (or is allowed to make) a comment she is the object of ridicule, indifference and abuse. 'What am I, a spade?' Ray grunts when, looking after her guests, she forgets to offer her husband a cup of tea. As Ray and Mark recount their past escapades and sexual exploits for the captivated Billy (Charlie Creed-Miles), a twenty-second head-and-shoulders shot of Val silently drinking tea alone in the kitchen (but still within earshot) heightens her physical and emotional isolation.

The same sort of treatment is also inflicted on Janet (Laila Morse), Ray's mother-in-law. He addresses her as she comes out of the toilet. 'I just timed you,' he shouts. 'You been in there twenty fuckin' minutes.' Her embarrassment is heightened when he and Mark take infantile delight in constantly blowing raspberries at her. Even Kath (Edna Doré), Val's grandmother, is not exempt from the brunt of such behaviour and later has to contend with Ray's drunken harassment. When she threatens to kick him in the genitals, he replies, 'I'm surprised you know what a pair of bollocks are! I mean, the last time someone was hanging out of you they must have been on horseback!' Such an exchange suggests that Ray's disrespect for women is boundless and crosses all generations. Later Ray is criticized by Val for never directly addressing his own daughter. 'She has got a name you know,' she tells him, 'she *was* christened. Not that you'd fuckin' remember.' When Mark and Val exchange a brief and affectionate exchange in the domestic space of the kitchen, Ray's jealous and suspicious look suggests the full extent of this oppressive male culture which simultaneously excludes and imprisons its female members.

The first section of Oldman's film, then, would seem to suggest that both technically and thematically it looks back to a past world and tradition. While British films about the working class made during the 1980s tended to increasingly foreground the presence and role of women (one thinks of *Letter to Brezhnev* (1985) or even *Educating Rita* (1983)), Oldman's masculine-dominated narrative appears to reconstruct, if not re-validate male 'working-class virility and aggression', re-marginalizing its women for a contemporary era. Indeed, Oldman goes so far as to attempt to make such a male-dominated culture appear almost 'attractive'. His black but witty script, supported by Ray Winston's brutal yet charismatic performance, deliberately encourages the audience to laugh and empathize along with the men (despite even their sexist and racist jibes). Obviously not all viewers will respond in the same way, but the first section of the film attempts nonetheless to draw the audience into (reluctantly or not) this white, male working-class camaraderie. Oldman uses close-ups of the two men to enhance the viewer's feeling of involvement as they exchange stories, jokes and cigarettes. Like Billy, the spectator is invited to simply sit and watch enthralled, ambiguously seduced into enjoying the spectacle of two old friends who know and instinctively understand the nuances of their shared lives, culture and the intimate rhythm and speed of each other's speech, language and delivery. All it takes is a word or a phrase for one of them to know exactly which anecdote will be delivered next, as quick reaction shots of Billy's excited face reaffirm the pleasure of the spectacle. 'Do you remember my heart attack?' Mark asks Ray. 'Oh fucking hell!' cries Ray, sitting back in anticipation. 'Listen to this, Bill . . . ?'

Signalled by Tony Christie's *Las Vegas* and the lurid and

semi-pornographic neon lights of Soho, the men's trip to London's West End (which includes their absurd game of camel racing in the amusement arcade and their rowdy behaviour in the strip club) reveals a boisterous but relatively harmless group of men out on the town and in the mood for some gratuitous entertainment: albeit fuelled by drink, marijuana and cocaine. But the deliberate seduction into this male working-class machismo is quickly undermined when the evening ends on an ominous note, an indication of what can lie at the bottom of such a culture. Again the spectator is encouraged to see through Billy's eyes when Ray violently assaults an unsuspecting man over a drug dispute, watched by Mark and Billy from a nearby car. As Billy is told by Mark to 'watch and learn ... watch and learn', the camera stays in the parked vehicle so as to match the audience's point of view with Billy's, connecting his shocked and frightened expression with the reaction of the audience to our first real sight of Ray's brutal violence. 'Sweet as,' applauds Mark, 'nice one, mate – nice one.' It is at this moment that the film's focus and direction begin to shift. In the cold light of the morning after, the male camaraderie of the night before is completely shattered by Ray's discovery that Billy has stolen his drugs. Ray's violence now erupts, culminating with him 'savagely' biting into Billy's nose. With no Mark to humour or appease him, Ray's real character (and the essence of the male culture portrayed up to this point) is blatantly and shockingly revealed. 'Get him out,' Ray cries at Val, 'or I'll kill him! Then I'll fucking kill you, and your slag shit cunt family' (Oldman, 1997, p. 44).

Having initiated the viewer into the ambiguous attractions of this male culture, Oldman's film now allows a different narrative to slowly and gradually take charge. The attraction inherent in the masculine discourse is increasingly untenable, the momentum of the male discourse is broken down (as above) and the voices of the women (who, up to this point, have remained virtually silenced) begin to emerge. In contrast to the quick overlapping dialogue and fast editing techniques which tended to typify the male space, the female space the film portrays tends to be shot in longer takes, punctuated with lengthier speeches and occasional silences. There is no dialogue, for example, for 35 seconds when Billy first wakes up at his mother's home, offering a stark contrast to the lively and chaotic world of Soho and the strip joint.

Indeed, Billy is central to the gradual emergence of the female voice as a whole.[5] Ray and Mark's junior by a good ten or fifteen years, he is a heroin addict of no fixed abode. But in contrast to Ray, Billy is no Jimmy

Porter or even Mike Leigh's Johnny in *Naked* (1993), for he seems to be one of the few characters able to move easily between the mutually exclusive worlds of the men and women. When he first arrives at Ray and Val's house, he openly greets Val with a kiss in the domestic space of the kitchen and even plays with their child before Ray coldly interrupts. Indeed, his addiction to heroin has kept Billy in a 'childlike' state himself, still dependant on his mother for money and shelter when he needs it. Despite their constant rows over the money to pay his £60-a-day habit, her first words to him are 'hello darlin'', suggesting a tenderness and respect she displays for no other man. When she watches him inject heroin from a deal she has just paid for, her face is a mixture of fear, sadness, bewilderment and compassion, in contrast with the hatred and contempt she so openly feels for Ray.

In many ways, Billy represents both a newly emerging form of masculinity and a newly emerging underclass – partly signalled by the abandonment of Clapton's bluesy guitar for the more contemporary multicultural sound of Francis Ashman's *Peculiar Groove*. Pushed to the edge of this working-class community and family, Billy has learnt the art of addiction and thieving from his elders, but in choosing heroin he is unable to keep up even the charade of old-fashioned working-class respectability. Billy's choice of drug is also in contrast with Ray's drinking, the heroin initially results not in violence inflicted outwards, but in an introversion and a self-destruction inflicted *inwards*. Ultimately interested in only one thing (scoring the next hit), he blatantly steals from Ray, his need for the drug apparently transcending even his desire for acceptance into his own family or even the masculinized brotherhood of the older men. While Ray's 'robust' and 'imposing' body represents power, brutality and violence, Billy's 'strong but not muscular build', his arms 'a battle-ground of scars and puncture marks', is, in contrast, a site of constant self-mutilation and abuse. Seen in this light, Billy is Ray turned inward, a subject of introverted violence, inflicting damage on himself rather than others. When Billy inadvertently steals a photograph of Ray's mother, he suddenly becomes a 'hero' for the female community, who find Ray's frantic concern for the loss of the picture highly amusing. In this way, Billy helps to break down the working-class masculine culture of an older generation. In not following and adhering to important social codes of behaviour – such as respecting the image of the mother and in stealing from one's own family – he unconsciously undermines the very culture Ray represents. Yet, in doing so, Billy temporarily gains acceptance from the women who are themselves imprisoned and contained by that very world. 'Mum, you still upset with me?' Billy asks. 'No I love ya', is Janet's affectionate reply.

Similarly, Billy's friend Danny's (Steve Sweeney) whole body and face are covered in cheap tattoos, biro and body piercing, a striking symbol of a masculinity in crisis which has unconsciously subverted and rejected the 'suited and booted' world personified by Mark and Ray's conventional attire and appearance. Even more on the margins of society than Billy, Danny seems to have learnt his own notion of identity and masculinity from contemporary Hollywood movies such as *Apocalypse Now* (1979), parts of which (notably Dennis Hopper's psychotic photographer) he has learnt by heart. So far is he from Ray and Mark's acceptance that despite his presence there is never any communication between him and them. Like a character from Coppola's Vietnam epic, he also befriends a small puppy, showing a caring and even 'maternal' nature not imaginable in the older men. Interestingly, the sight of the dog reminds Billy of the German Shepherd he adored as a child which his father had killed while he was away on holiday, suggesting a violence and even a jealously in Billy's own father akin to Ray's. This reading is further enforced by Ray's revealing speech about his father which suggests little has changed between his generation and the one before it:

> She took his dinner into him one night. Me mum, in the pub, and plonked it on the bar in front of him . . . on a tray. Knife and fork, salt and pepper. He said, 'What's this?' She said, 'It's your dinner. I thought you might be hungry. You ain't eaten for three fuckin' days. You live here, you might as well fuckin' eat in here.' Well, he didn't like that, did he? Mugged him off in front of his mates. Thought more of 'em cunts than he did us. She got a clump over that. (Oldman, 1997, p. 103)

It is not, however, until Ray's horrific and brutal beating of his own wife that the masculine world, so carefully and painstakingly constructed in the first half of the film, finally collapses beyond repair. Dressed only in his underpants, Ray viciously assaults Val in the middle of the night for having an innocent game of pool with a male friend, head butting her to the ground and (out of sight of the camera) kicking her senseless. Later, her face 'the size of a water melon', she begins a miscarriage on the stairs and is rushed to hospital. It is only now that the female presence in the film is really foregrounded, forced as the women are to stand firm against the now out-of-control Ray. In one scene, all four generations of women (not one of them connected any longer with a male partner) stand together in their night clothes, united as Ray begs and shouts through the letterbox of Janet's flat. In another, Val and Kath dance quietly and gently together, separate generations safely removed from the dangers of the men they know or have known. Silenced for most of the film, Val finally has her chance to vocalize her own situation when Ray calmly approaches her on the steps of her mum's flat on her thirtieth birthday. As her moving and heart-felt speech reaches momentum, so she moves up the steps to address him on the same level, her back facing her mother's flat and the safety of the female space. Reduced to an uncharacteristic silence, Ray stands powerless and dumb as she firmly and finally takes control of the narrative. 'I mean, when you go out, you go out with your mates,' she tells him. 'And then when you are indoors, you're pissed out of your fuckin' brain asleep in front of the television! ... Either that or you're knocking me about!' Whether this finally forces Ray to connect his own dysfunctional behaviour with his father's is not clear, but Val's speech, the longest and by far the most powerful she has in the film, repositions the place of all the women, an individual but pivotal refusal to accept her role as a passive victim of an oppressive and violent male culture.[6]

The film's final return to the social club would seem to support such a reading. In contrast to before, the women now appear to form a large majority of the audience, further emphasized by the absence of Ray and Mark. After a rendition, ironically enough, of *My Heart Belongs to Daddy*, Val's grandmother is persuaded to take the stage to sing 'Can't Help Lovin' Dat Man' (lip-synched by the actress Edna Doré, but actually sung by Oldman's own mother). The song's romantic and fatalistic lyrics about putting up with years of masculine neglect and abuse offer a stark contrast to Val's determination to *stop* loving her man unless he changes his ways. Here women's past role in working-class culture is strikingly spelled out by the lyrics of the song as the women look on with love and admiration, momentarily caught up in a sentiment which none of them is willing to accept any longer, but with which they still strongly identify. This reading is supported by the final scene where the women have seemingly repositioned and reinvented the family dynamics of the past. All drinking tea in Ray and Val's newly furnished kitchen, it is the women who are doing the majority of the talking in what was previously the women's space, while Ray bounces his daughter on his lap and Mark stands hemmed in with his back to the sink. The women, already in their coats to visit Billy in prison, talk quickly and animatedly about the lad's complex situation inside, while the men remain strangely silent. Now the women seem to possess the dominant voice, with Val even making a joke at the expense of the 'nonces and rapists' which everyone enjoys, including the men. When they all leave, it is literally Ray who is left holding the baby.

Such an ending deliberately offers itself up to a number of possible readings. In some respects the audience is given a completely reconstructed family unit: Ray is apparently 'off the booze', we see him cuddle and kiss his daughter (with a genuine gentleness and an intimacy) for the first time in the film. Val seems to have moved back in, and even her mother-in-law and grandmother do not appear unhappy about the arrangement; indeed, Janet even compliments Ray on the work he has done on the house. In this respect Oldman offers a conventional 'happy ending'. There is even talk of Billy being off the drugs in prison. But despite these positive signs of hope, the film refuses to make any firm guarantees. Firstly, the view offered of this new life is far too brief and inconclusive for the audience to come to any definite conclusions. Indeed, one female viewer I spoke to found it impossible to believe that Val had returned to Ray, preferring to interpret the ending as Val simply visiting her ex-husband. From what the audience already knows of Ray it would certainly be naive to think that he is a completely reformed character, abandoning his violent and alcoholic past to become a reconstructed 'new man'. When a women's name is mentioned, the brief but shady look exchanged between Mark and Ray suggests that secrets *are* still being kept from Val, who looks at them both suspiciously. Even Billy's apparent new health is undermined by Ray's observation about drugs being as available inside prison as they are outside. The film's ending, then, attempts to construct a balance between hope and despair, suggesting that change *is* possible but that multi-generational dysfunction and the material conditions of these people's lives cannot be swept away or resolved overnight.

But if Ray hasn't changed, then all the indications suggest that Val has. No longer willing to accept the neglect and abuse handed out to her in the past, there is a real sense that she will only stay with Ray (and will continue to be supported by her own family) while he continues to give her the love and respect she needs and deserves. She is clearly not the independent middle-class career woman epitomized by DCI Jane Tennison (Helen Mirren) in Lynda La Plante's *Prime Suspect* (1991), but in her own way she does finally deconstruct a dominant and oppressive male culture, helping to reinvent herself, her family and perhaps even her community in the process. The triumph of Oldman's film lies in its ability to examine not just working-class masculinity in a contemporary setting, but to do so by setting up and reconstructing the very dynamics by which such a culture has been portrayed and represented in the past. Rather than prioritizing female concerns and voices from the beginning, the masculine viewpoint is shockingly prioritized and then gradually and carefully dismantled. In doing so, it uses the mechanics of a past filmic tradition to initially enhance and then interrogate what Ken Worpole refers to as a 'masculine style', one which has tended to result in the dramatic and thematic subordination of its female characters through a dominant 'male norm'. The film should be measured by its ability to reinvent such a tradition, to produce a realism which no longer marginalizes its female characters, but allows them the space and the power to overturn and reinvestigate the narrative through which they would have previously been constructed and contained. This is not exactly a new enterprise, but the effectiveness of Oldman's script and direction lies in the subtlety of an operation which invites you to participate, re-examine and finally reinvent the means by which class and masculinity have been culturally constructed.

Notes

1. For a fuller discussion of Jordan and Williams's work on realism see John Fiske (1987), pp. 21–47. See also Raymond Williams (1976), pp. 257–62, and (1977).
2. For a historical account of British Social Realism and its evolution from the British documentary tradition see Andrew Higson (1986).
3. Here Hill is quoting from Ken Worpole (1983), p. 94.
4. For example, *Coronation Street* was originally nicknamed 'Hoggart Street' after its warm and nostalgic portrayal of northern working-class life.
5. It is interesting to note that, as Oldman told Melvyn Bragg, Billy was the first character he wrote and through which he discovered the women. 'God, these women's voices,' he suddenly realized, 'these women are interesting' (Bragg, 1998).
6. When asked what originally attracted her to the screenplay, Kathy Burke replied: 'I really enjoyed the way the women were written. He's [Oldman] definitely got a different outlook on women. And I do think this has got to do with him being brought up by them' (Bragg, 1998).

Bibliography

Bragg, M. (1998) *South Bank Show: Gary Oldman*. Carlton Television, 15 March.

Fiske, J. (1987) *Television Culture*. London: Routledge.

Higson, A. (1986) ' "Britain's outstanding contribution to film": the documentary-realist tradition'. In C. Barr (ed.), *All Our Yesterdays: 90 Years of British Cinema*. London: BFI.

Hill, J. (1986) *Sex, Class and Realism: British Cinema, 1956–1963*. London: BFI.

Hoggart, R. (1990, first published 1957) *The Uses of Literacy*. London: Penguin.

James, N. (1997) 'Being there'. *Sight and Sound* 7(10), pp. 6–9.

Jordan, M. (1981) 'Realism and convention'. In R. Dyer, C. Geraghty, M. Jordan, T. Lovell, R. Paterson and J. Stewart (eds), *Television Monograph: Coronation Street*. London: BFI.

Kelly, R. (ed.) (1998a) *Alan Clarke*. London: Faber & Faber.

Kelly, R. (1998b) 'A firm favourite'. *Observer Review*, 2 August, p. 8.

Macnab, G. (1997) 'Review of *Nil by Mouth*'. *Sight and Sound* 7(10), p. 55.

Oldman, G. (1997) *Nil by Mouth: The Screenplay*. Eye, Suffolk: Screen Press Books.

Williams, R. (1976) *Keywords: A Vocabulary of Culture and Society*. London: Flamingo.

Williams, R. (1977) 'A lecture on realism'. *Screen* 18(1), pp. 61–74.

Worpole, K. (1983) 'The American connection: the masculine style in popular fiction'. *New Left Review* 139, pp. 92–103.

Acknowledgement

My thanks to Susan Burnett, Jonathon Burrows, Kevin Donnelly, Andrew Higson, Jacob Leigh, Catrin Prys, Jamie Sexton and Sue Spowart.

13

Homophobic Violence: The Hidden Injuries of Class

Leslie J. Moran

> LUCIE: What about it made you feel more unsafe?
>
> JOAN: Loads of rough scally lads ...
>
> DAMIEN: ... I think drunk straight lads are the biggest threat and there are lots of them around and it seems that every night is a night to get drunk ...

These extracts are taken from focus group discussions conducted with lesbians and gay men as part of ongoing research into homophobic violence in Britain (Lancaster, 1997). The use of the term 'lads', references to the 'pub' and associations between public drunkenness and violence give the fear of homophobic violence that is being discussed a specific class dimension. The working class are here presented as key perpetrators of violence. There is also another class dimension here. The speakers, as victims and potential victims, are classed over and against the perpetrators. By way of gender and sexuality they are made remote from the gender, sexuality and class that is violence personified: masculine, heterosexual, working-class men. In their resort to 'working class' to make sense of violence, they are rendered by default middle class or respectable working class.

The associations found in these extracts echo a longstanding theme within the discipline of criminology: of violence and the working/lower classes. While there are different positions within criminology on the correlation between male violence and the working/lower classes, all have attempted to document and explain the association between male violence, the working class and various manifestations of an underclass (Levi, 1997).

When set in the context of the existing work on violence and class, the silence about the importance and influence of class in homophobic violence and its influence upon activism and scholarship concerned with that violence are conspicuous. In order to examine this silence the following analysis will examine the place of class in a body of work on violence that is closely aligned with homophobic violence: feminist scholarship on sexual violence. My focus will then reflect upon the significance of class for current initiatives relating to homophobic violence and safety. It is to the fate of class in feminist work on violence that I now want to turn.

The challenge of feminist scholarship and the decline of class?

Feminist work on sexual violence has challenged much existing scholarship within criminology which uses class to explain violence. Most work on violence and class has been on violence by men (and violence between men), yet the sexed and gendered nature of that violence has had no significance in traditional analysis. Gender has remained pervasive but unmarked and invisible, either as a category that might explain patterns of violence, or as a category that might have significance in developing understandings of the cause of violence (Morris, 1987; Naffine, 1997; Smart, 1990; Young, 1996).[1] Feminist scholarship has drawn attention to various consequences that flow from this invisibility. Violence by men against women, a major form of violence whose effects impact upon the day-to-day lives of a majority of the population, has received little attention by scholars and criminal justice practitioners, being defined out of existence (as a private rather than a public matter) or treated in a derisory way. In general, feminisms have challenged the gender-blind analysis that has been, and continues to be, a pervasive characteristic of much work on violence and demanded that it be taken into account. What has been the fate of class in the context of this challenge?

Gender, violence and class

Within feminist work on sexual violence, class analysis has been used to challenge work that reproduced, in an uncritical manner, the association between violence and the working/underclasses. Lees (1996) notes that rape is a category of violence frequently associated with men from the lower class(es) and from racial minorities. In contrast to this she refers to

Diana Russell's survey (1984) in the USA of 930 women. Russell's research suggests that the higher the class the greater the likelihood of rape. Nearly 50 per cent of the women surveyed whose fathers had upper-middle-class occupations had been victims of rape/attempted rape in contrast to 33 per cent of women whose fathers had middle-class/lower-class occupations. Other feminist work suggests that class is significant in the generation of the wider definitions of rape and in the analysis of the criminal justice responses that are informed by those definitions. For example, correlations between the lower classes and rape are most prevalent where rape is thought of in terms of a random act of violence by a stranger in a public place. Lees (1996, p. 41) notes another example of this association in the context of gang rape. She challenges this class correlation by reference to research carried out in the USA on fraternity gang rapes, which suggests that the lower-class/violence connection in this context is far from established. The correlation is further problematized when rape is thought of as an act of violence by someone known to the victim occurring in the context of an established relationship carried out in the home. Stanko and Radford (1996, p. 41) suggest that the police and the criminal justice system focus on random acts of stranger violence in public, which generates and sustains a class bias in the criminal justice system.

Class also appears to be significant in other aspects of the criminal justice process. For example, it appears to be significant in the way crimes of sexual violence are reported. The prevalent assumption is that lower-class women report rape less frequently (Lees, 1996, p. 216). While this might be explained on the basis that the lower classes have a higher level of tolerance towards violence, the lives of these classes being characterized by violence, feminist work suggests that there is a need to extrapolate cautiously. The assumptions at work here should, by now, be familiar: for the economically disadvantaged violence is normalized. In contrast to this Mooney's research (1993) suggests that under-reporting might also be found in other class contexts. Her research suggests that a woman who defines herself by reference to a higher class is less likely to report conjugal violence to an outside agency. Here a class/sexual violence analysis offers a conclusion contrary to that found in traditional class analysis: the higher the class the lower the rate of reporting rape. This suggests that the upper classes, and not the lower classes, might take intra-class sexual violence either as a norm to be lived with or as a practice that is to be dealt with by means other than the public process of criminalization.

Middle-class men are not culturally associated with violence as there is an assumption that violence (as pathology) is a characteristic of the criminal 'Other', the working and underclass. The higher the social status of the perpetrator of violence the less likely the belief in that person's capacity to commit acts of violence. Evidence in support of these observations is to be found in Godenzi's work (1994), which suggests that middle-class men explain their acts of sexual violence by reference to their own sexual needs, not as a manifestation of dysfunctional gender or sexual behaviour. Other consequences follow: thinking sexual violence by reference to sexual needs in contrast to pathology reinforces perceptions of the perpetrator's 'innocence' and victimization. These class factors might also both inform the impact of reputation in the criminal trial which may work in favour of middle- and upper-class 'respectable' rapists and assumptions about the reliability of middle-class witnesses.

In turn, class may also have significance upon the victim's experience. Middle-class women may be seen to have more traumatic responses to sexual violence. Again there is some need for caution here as this may perpetuate myths about the prevalence and normality of violence within working-class communities and the willingness of lower-class women to accept violence (Lees, 1996, p. 193).

In surveying many of the class assumptions reproduced in work on sexual violence, Lees (1996, p. 210) concluded that no connection could be upheld between class and sexual violence (1996, p. 210).[2] Her conclusion draws attention to the way in which feminist research has challenged some of the class assumptions in existing work on sexual violence. Feminists have used class analysis to draw a different picture of violence. Here class has been used to suggest that gender and sexual violence are not so much the problem of a particular class-based masculinity, but more a problem about masculinity. In crude terms, in the move to draw attention to the pervasive significance of masculinity, class has disappeared from the analytical and explanatory framework.

A focus on gender to the exclusion of other factors at work in the generation of the social order might be understood in terms of a de Certean strategy (de Certeau, 1984, pp. 34–9); as a manipulation of those power relations implicated in the generation of a feminist subject with will and power to produce self-knowledge, sustained and determined by the power to provide oneself with one's own place. This might suggest that the rise of gender and the attendant disappearance of class analysis ought to be understood in terms of the contingent delimitation of emerging subject positions. The danger here is that the strategic move that displaces class from the analytical framework may become institutionalized as a new silence about class. The silence around class may produce masculinity (gender) and sexuality (heterosexuality) as a singular, unified totality. At best, a more nuanced class-sensitive analysis might return in the deployment of distinctions between hegemonic masculinity and subordinate masculinities. Here the pervasiveness of coercive male sexual behaviour is associated with hegemonic masculinity.[3] The exclusion or marginalization of class in an analysis of male sexual violence threatens to leave the hegemonic/subordinate distinction at best untheorized and at worst untheorizable.

The fate of class within feminist work on sexual violence is particularly significant for work on homophobic violence. Class analysis might be used to challenge some of the class assumptions that inform the experience of homophobic violence, such as those evidenced in the extracts from the lesbian and gay focus group discussions. This may be used to particular effect – to draw attention to the prevalence of violence within the heterocentric social order. But as feminist work suggests, there is a need for caution here, a consequence of the resort to class in this way might undermine an analysis of the classed nature of heterosexed violence and our class-based experience of it. Before reflecting further on the significance of class for homophobic violence research and activism, I want to turn to the fate of class analysis in the context of homophobic violence.

Homophobic violence

The largest, and one of the most recent, surveys undertaken on homophobic violence and harassment was conducted in Britain by Stonewall, a lesbian and gay rights lobbying organization. The national survey was disseminated via the lesbian and gay media and via Stonewall's own contacts lists, generating 4000 responses. Its main objective appears to have been to document levels of violence and harassment against lesbians and gay men in the previous five years. While the questionnaire included questions pertinent to class analysis (economic and employment status), these variables had little significance in the final report (Mason and Palmer, 1996). The data generated about economic and employment status appears to suggest that most people who experience homophobic violence and harassment are employed and on lower incomes. However, there is a need for caution in the interpretation of this data. It might tell us more about the dissemination of the questionnaire, the economic and employment status of the readers of the gay and lesbian press, and the class membership of Stonewall, than provide data about correlations between violence, harassment and economic/employment status.

Most critical reflections by community activists and scholars concerned with homophobic violence have been silent on the significance of class. This is not to suggest that activists and scholars have been slow to analyse some of the problematic assumptions and silences informing work on homophobic violence. For example, Mason (1997) and Stanko and Curry (1997), influenced by feminist scholarship on sexual violence, have drawn attention to the gender assumptions that have informed political initiatives and research around policing and homophobic violence. They have drawn attention to the way in which the concerns of gay men have dominated policing and criminal justice initiatives relating to homophobic violence. In part this reflects the gendered structure of the criminal law and criminal justice system which continues to criminalize most sexual activity between men and the formal absence of criminal sanctions against sexual relations between women. Gender is also prevalent in the police obsession with the enforcement of laws to regulate public sex between men and the tendency to think of sexual relations between men in terms of intergenerational encounters. Likewise, a focus on stranger violence in contrast to violence by friends and family and an emphasis on violence in public rather than violence in the home have tended to silence the issues that are of primary concern to lesbians. In turn, Mason (1997), Jennes (1995), Jennes and Broad (1994) and Mary Eaton (1995) have begun to draw attention to the absence of and insensitivity to questions of race and ethnicity in political activism and scholarship around homophobia.

In part the silence around issues of class reflects the fate of class analysis in lesbian, in gay and, more recently, in queer scholarship. The Gay Left movement and in particular its intellectual faction, the Gay Left Collective, put sexuality on a class agenda informed by Marxism (Weeks, 1980; Gluckman and Reed, 1997, p. xx), challenging the liberationist, biologist, essentialist and heterocentric view of that class analysis (Gay Left Collective, 1980; Watney, 1981). In the wake of putting sexuality into the frame, class seems to have suffered a particular fate. This may be illustrated by way of comments found in the Introduction to the collection of essays, *Modern Homosexualities*:

At the core of understanding the changes of the past two decades must be a heightened awareness of the role of the new social movements . . .

Part of the new political landscape has been the decline of traditional exclusively class-based politics and the rise of new social movements, often based around Utopian images of the future, which create identities, rights, and an awareness of difference ... (Plummer, 1992, p. 22)

While it suggests that class has gone into decline as a category of political and analytical interest and significance, class still has some significance. However, the place of class in the essays that follow does not support such a reading of this observation. The introductory essay contains the only reference to class in the whole collection. What follows is a recognition of a plurality of homosexualities where that plurality is defined by reference to sex, gender, ethnicity and health status. This suggests that in the wake of putting sexuality onto the agenda, class analysis has disappeared from the frame.

However, such a conclusion about the fate of class would be premature. First, it would be wrong to conclude that either the work of the early gay liberation intellectuals in the Gay Left Collective or work that followed inevitably generated the marginalization of class analysis in the context of sexuality. Cohen and Dyer's essay, 'The politics of gay culture', in the seminal Gay Left collection, *Homosexuality: Power and Politics* (1980), is of particular interest here. Dyer's analysis provides a subtle and nuanced reading of the constitution of sexualized class positions (a particular middle-classed homosexuality). Cohen imagines gay sexuality as a distinctive and discrete class with revolutionary potential. In doing so, his analysis is insensitive to the class specific (middle-class, bohemian, countercultural and artistic) practices he associates with the revolutionary practices of gay sexuality. Dyer's analysis suggests that the Gay Left did produce work on class and sexuality that keeps both in the frame. More recently, the work that seeks to sustain a sensitivity to the significance of class in the analysis of sexuality is to be found in the work of scholars associated with the cultural materialist tradition of literary and cultural analysis such as Dollimore (1985), Dollimore and Sinfield (1991) and Sinfield (1989, 1992). In addition, there has been a revival of interest in class as evidenced in the historical studies of Chauncey (1994) and Kennedy and Davies (1994) and in more general work collected together in Gluckman and Reed's *Homo Economics* (1997) and Susan Raffo's *Queerly Classed* (1997).

Class and homophobic violence

In the context of work on homophobic violence, recent writing has drawn attention to the importance of class politics in the generation of activism focusing upon homophobic violence in Britain (Whittle, 1994; Quilley, 1997). For example, the homophobic violence initiative established in Manchester, the first of its kind in Britain, has its roots in the left-wing lesbian and gay municipal labour activism of the late 1970s (Cooper, 1994).[4] At best, this political activism at the state and local level sought to develop rainbow alliances, bringing together identity politics/activism and more traditional class-based activism. However, it is perhaps ironic that the Mancunian homophobic violence initiative arose out of what at worst might be described as the failure of that class-based politics or at best its adaptation to a political agenda set by successive Thatcher governments.

Gary Comstock's study, *Violence against Lesbians and Gay Men* (1991), seeks to document homophobic violence according to a range of criteria, including class. To date, in his resort to class as an analytical category, Comstock's study is exceptional. Based in part upon his own survey and in part on the basis of a review of other research and newspaper reports of incidents of homophobic violence, Comstock's data suggests that class is significant for an understanding of homophobic violence in interesting (and unexpected) ways. It is to this pioneering work that I now want to turn.

Comstock's analysis suggests that class is of significance in the analysis of characteristics of perpetrators and victims of violence. His survey found that perpetrators of homophobic murder (all men) were predominantly middle class. Where perpetrators acted in groups, they were either middle class or working class. When analysed by reference to income, those defined as middle income were the most likely to report anti-gay/lesbian violence, whereas when analysed by reference to class the upper class were the most likely to report violence and the middle class least likely to report it. When gender is added to the frame, Comstock found that middle-income men were almost twice as likely to report violence than the women. The upper-class men were twice as likely to report violence than the women. Class also seems to have some significance in the levels of reporting different types of violence. A crude summary suggests that acts of physical violence were more frequently reported by the lower class, in contrast to more emphasis on reports of property crimes by the upper class. Class also seemed to play a role in the defences offered by the perpetrators.

Middle-class defendants relied upon character witnesses, anecdotal evidence of such things as family background, exemplary school behaviour, participation in organized athletics. This had an impact on conviction rates and sentencing rates, the more severe sentences being handed down to perpetrators from lower classes.

While Comstock's work is significant, drawing attention to the need to take class seriously in the context of homophobic violence, it is important to recognize its limits. Largely based on secondary sources, its scope is problematic and it suffers from significant methodological limits. Its resort to class and income draws attention to the continuing problems of defining (economic) class. It works within a particular focus on victims. Its primary focus is violence by straights against lesbians and gay men.

Conclusion

Traditional criminology and feminist scholarship on violence suggest that class is an important analytical and heuristic category in any attempt to understand violence and in the development of responses to it. There is (albeit tentative) evidence of some of the ways in which class is produced within and informs all experiences and initiatives concerned with homophobic violence. For example, the extracts from the lesbian and gay focus groups at the beginning of this chapter draw attention to the way it may inform and invest the experience of the fear of homophobic violence and the generation of definitions of homophobic violence. An emphasis upon homophobic violence as random acts of strangers in public not only produces a certain gender-blind analysis and practice, but also threatens to (re)produce problematic correlations between violence and the working or underclass and to create new silences about the violence produced in other class contexts. Class is produced by and informs our understanding of the distribution of violence. Furthermore, there is a need to be sensitive to the ways in which a victim politics might reproduce problematic correlations between the lower classes and violence in the context of a new underclass, in this instance disaffected underclass hetero-masculinity in the constitution of the (middle, respectable working) classed position of the victim. Resort to criminal justice may re-valorize many of the problematic class-based practices for a new victim politics. To conceptualize homophobic violence by reference to crime and criminal justice might be always already implicated in a particular class perspective.

Another consequence of the influence of victim politics on homophobic violence is that it may also limit our understanding of violence associated with lesbians and gays and the violence of lesbians and gay men. Pioneering work has documented some of these difficulties in the context of violence between lesbians (Taylor and Chandler, 1995; Lobel, 1986). Other pioneering work is to be found in Hart's study, *Fatal Women* (1994), which examines criminal violence and female sexuality. It explores the ways in which violent women have been represented as lesbian. Murray Healy's work on gay skinheads, *Gay Skins* (1996), is another key study. Its major contribution is as a study of working-class masculinity and gay sexuality. It not only challenges the pervasive yet unmarked assumptions about working-class sub (gang) cultures, but also takes some tentative steps that begin to examine gay sexuality and masculine violence.

Any attempt to engage with work on class and violence will have to be sensitive to the problems revealed during the course of the development of scholarship on class and violence. Class is hard to define. It might relate to structure, identity, consciousness and/or forms of action. In addition, there are problems associated with its measurement. Some of this work suggests that class analysis at worst has to be rejected as a social characteristic peculiar to the modernist epoch now past, or at best has to be dramatically transformed by and in the postmodern/post-Fordist world (Skeggs, 1997). Many of these points have arisen within debates on class. Other criticisms of work on class and violence have come from outside that genre of scholarship, for example from feminist scholarship. Any resort to class in the context of homophobic violence will have to be sensitive to the reasons offered by others for the abandonment of class as an explanatory and analytical category. In turn, class analysis will have to be subject to the insights that have been generated by lesbian and gay scholarship and by the insights into the forces at work in the (re)production of social order by queer theory. In order to avoid the tendency to unified and totalizing categories, of gay, lesbian or heterosexual, any resort to class as a factor in homophobic violence will have to struggle with ways of making sense of classed sexualities. While Messerschmidt's work (1997) on the interface between race, gender and class and Krenshaw's work (1995) on the intersection of race and gender in the context of violence raise questions about the intersection between different social categories, this aspect of scholarship on violence is in its infancy. Work on homophobic violence that promotes an analysis by way of the multiple factors that are made and make social action will have to re-imagine social analysis.

Notes

1. There are a number of exceptions to this within contemporary criminology (see Collier, 1998).
2. Lees suggests that attempts to pursue work on the characteristics of rapists are fraught with problems. The legal system does not provide an accurate picture of who commits acts of rape. There are problems of under-reporting. There is an unwillingness to go to court. There is the threat of intimidation.
3. Much of the work by men informed by feminist work on violence and the men's studies movement deploys the distinction between hegemonic masculinity and subordinate masculinity (see Collier, 1998).
4. However, it would be wrong to conclude that the left wing necessarily took up and developed a class perspective or examined the intersection of class and sexuality in any detail. The Labour/Left interest in issues around sexuality and race might be a reflection of the decline of class as an organizing category of Left political party activism (cf. Walkerdine, 1995).

Bibliography

Chauncey G. (1994) *Gay New York: Gender Urban Culture and the Making of the Gay Male World, 1890–1940*. New York: Basic Books.

Collier, R. (1998) *Masculinities and Criminology*. London: Sage.

Comstock, G. D. (1991) *Violence against Lesbians and Gay Men*. New York: Columbia University Press.

Cooper, D. (1994) *Sexing the City: Lesbian and Gay Political within the Activist State*. London: Rivers Oram Press.

de Certeau, M. (1984) *The Practice of Everyday Life* (trans. S. Rendall). Berkeley: University of California Press.

Dollimore, J. G. (1991) *Sexual Dissidence: Augustine to Wilde, Freud to Foucault*. Oxford: Clarendon Press.

Dollimore, J. G. and Sinfield, A. (1985) *Political Shakespeare*. Manchester: Manchester University Press.

Eaton, M. (1995) 'Homosexual unmodified? Speculations on law's discourse, race, and the construction of sexual identity'. In D. Herman and C. Stychin (eds), *Legal Inversions: Lesbians, Gay Men and the Politics of Law*. Philadelphia: Temple University Press.

Gay Left Collective (eds) (1980) *Homosexuality: Power and Politics*. London: Allison & Busby.

Gluckman, A. and Reed, B. (1997) *Homo Economics: Capitalism, Community, and Lesbian and Gay Life*. London: Routledge.

Godenzi, A. (1994) 'What's the big deal? We are men and they are women'. In T. Newburn and E. Stanko (eds), *Just Boys Doing Business*. London: Routledge.

Hart, L. (1994) *Fatal Women: Lesbian Sexuality and the Mark of Aggression.* Princeton: Princeton University Press.

Healy, M. (1996) *Gay Skins: Class, Masculinity and Queer Appropriation.* London: Cassell.

Jennes, V. (1995) 'Social movement growth, domain expansion, and framing processes: the gay/lesbian movement and violence against gays and lesbians as a social problem'. *Social Problems* 42(1), pp. 145–70.

Jennes, V. and Broad, K. (1994) 'Antiviolence activism and the (in)visibility of gender in the gay, lesbian and women's movements'. *Gender and Society* 8(3), pp. 402–23.

Kennedy, E. L. and Davies, M. D. (1994) *Boots of Leather, Slippers of Gold: The History of a Lesbian Community.* New York and London: Penguin.

Krenshaw, K. W. (1995) 'Mapping the margins: intersectionality, identity politics and violence'. In K. W. Krenshaw *et al.*, *Critical Race Theory: The Key Writings That Formed a Movement.* New York: New Press.

Lancaster (1997) Transcripts of Manchester lesbian and Lancaster gay men's seedcorn focus groups.

Lees, S. (1996) *Carnal Knowledge: Rape on Trial.* London: Penguin.

Levi, M. (1997) 'Violent crime'. In M. Maguire, R. Morgan and R. Reiner (eds), *The Oxford Handbook of Criminology*, 2nd edn. Oxford: Clarendon Press.

Lobel, K. (ed.) (1986) *Naming the Violence: Speaking about Lesbian Battering.* London: Seal Press.

Mason, G. (1997) 'Sexuality and violence: questions of difference'. In C. Cunneen, D. Fraser and S. Tomsen (eds), *Faces of Hate: Hate Crime in Australia.* Sydney: Hawkins Press.

Mason, A. and Palmer, A. (1996) *Queer Bashing: A National Survey of Hate Crimes against Lesbians and Gay Men.* London: Stonewall.

Messerschmidt, J. W. (1997) *Crime as Structured Action.* Newbury Park, CA: Sage.

Mooney, J. (1993) *The Hidden Figure: Domestic Violence in N. London.* London: Islington Council.

Morris, A. (1987) *Women, Crime and Criminal Justice.* Oxford: Basil Blackwell.

Naffine, N. (1997) *Feminism and Criminology.* Cambridge: Polity Press.

Plummer, K. (1992) 'Speaking its name: inventing a lesbian and gay studies'. In K. Plummer, *Modern Homosexualities: Fragments of Lesbian and Gay Experience.* London: Routledge.

Quilley, S. (1997) 'Constructing Manchester's "new urban village": gay space in the entrepreneurial city'. In G. Brent Ingram, A. Bouthillette and Y. Retter (eds), *Queers in Space: Communities, Public Places, Sites of Resistance.* Seattle: Bay Press.

Raffo, S. (ed.) (1997) *Queerly Classed: Gay Men and Lesbians Write about Class.* Boston: South End Press.

Russell, D. (1984) *Sexual Exploitation*. Beverly Hills, CA: Sage.

Sinfield, A. (1989) *Literature, Politics and Culture in Postwar Britain*. Oxford: Basil Blackwell.

Sinfield, A. (1992) *Fault Lines: Cultural Materialism and the Politics of Dissident Reading*. Oxford: Clarendon Press.

Skeggs, B. (1997) *Formations of Class and Gender: Becoming Respectable*. London: Sage.

Smart, C. (1990) 'Feminist approaches to criminology or postmodern women meets atavistic man'. In L. Gelsthorne and A. Morris (eds), *Feminist Perspectives in Criminology*. Milton Keynes: Open University Press.

Stanko, E. A. and Curry, P. (1997) 'Homophobic violence and the self "at risk": interrogating the boundaries'. *Social and Legal Studies* 6(4), pp. 513–32.

Stanko, E. A. and Radford, J. (1996) 'Violence against women and children'. In M. Hester, L. Kelly and J. Radford (eds), *Women, Violence and Male Power: Feminist Activism, Research and Practice*. Buckingham: Open University Press.

Taylor, J. and Chandler, T. (1995) *Lesbians Talk Violence Relationships*. London: Scarlet Press.

Walkerdine, V. (1995) 'Subject to change without notice'. In S. Pile and N. Thrift (eds), *Mapping the Subject: Geographies of Cultural Transformation*. London: Routledge.

Watney, S. (1981) 'On gay liberation: a response to David Fernbach'. In D. Adlam (ed.), *Politics and Power*, Vol. 3. London: Routledge.

Weeks, J. (1980) 'Capitalism and the organisation of sex'. In Gay Left Collective (eds), *Homosexuality: Power and Politics*. London: Allison & Busby.

Whittle, S. (1994) 'Consuming differences: the collaboration of the gay body with the cultural state'. In S. Whittle (ed.), *The Margins of the City: Gay Men's Urban Lives*. Aldershot: Arena.

Young, A. (1996) *Imagining Crime*. London: Sage.

Acknowledgement

Thanks to Beverley Skeggs, Anjie Rosgae and the participants at the American Law and Society Association Conference seminar for their comments. Special thanks to Julie Wallbank for her eleventh-hour assistance. This research is part of an ongoing project on homophobic violence, 'Violence, Sexuality and Space', being undertaken with ESRC funding as part of its Violence Research Programme.

14

Millwall Football Club: Masculinity, Race and Belonging

Garry Robson

> That competitive edge got me into fights at school, even at primary
> school. There's always that myth when you're kids that the best foot-
> baller is always supposed to be the best fighter. It's stupid, but I know it's
> the same all over the country because I've talked to other players who
> found themselves in the same situation. (Wright, 1996, p. 40)

The field of what might be called 'football studies' has, despite its exponen-
tial growth throughout the 1990s, yet to convincingly come of age. Though
there is much talk of taking football seriously as a terrain of cultural activity
– frequently accompanied by the old adage about it being a matter of 'life
and death' – there is still a dearth of sufficiently detailed British work
connecting the meanings of the game to its customary social sources.
While it is recognized that football must somehow have a part to play, for
many fans, in their experiences of social 'identity', it is still the case that the
generic and ontologically lightweight conceptual figure of the 'fan' dominates analysis. But fans are people, in so far as they are (or were),
predominantly, working-class men and boys, grounded at the deepest
experiential levels in specific regional and cultural formations. The depth
of identity characteristic of some of these contexts cannot be conveyed by
approaching their links with particular clubs as though the latter are simply
external symbols or sites of emotionally saturated consumption.
  Millwall football club, home of England's most notorious fans and an
informal cultural arena in which the maintenance of particular modes of
regional masculine identity has been paramount, might be considered as
an exemplary instance of the significance of these matters. Situated in

inner south-east London, the overwhelming bulk of Millwall's support has historically come from the boroughs of Southwark and Lewisham. It grew, to be more precise, out of the long-established, white working-class populations formerly located in some of the city's 'roughest' and most mythologized areas. The central position of Millwall fans in the development of 'football hooliganism' since the 1960s – in terms of both actual events and media/sociological narratives of the phenomenon – is therefore connected to a much older narrative history of lawlessness, local patriotism and territorial urban masculinity.[1]

Recent decades have, however, seen the spatial displacement of these cultural formations. Rapid social and demographic change in this area of inner London has been characterized by two broad processes: the dispersal of a significant proportion of the white working-class population into the suburbs of Kent, and increasing ethnic heterogeneity – mainly Afro-Caribbean, African and Chinese/Vietnamese – in the locales they have left behind. The identities of these areas are shifting dramatically, and in this context Millwall has become an important source of continuity for many fans living many miles away but still connected to the cultural specificities of working-class, south-east London regionalism. It is, in this sense, less an arena in which people 'create' identities for themselves than one in which individuals engage in a public, collective and ritualized pageant of identity. This pageant is not, however, merely played out explicitly, but practically, through adaptive practices which express a science of the concrete (Lévi-Strauss, 1966); the continual, situated and ritualized affirmation and celebration of the Millwall identity at and around games. Millwall fans, their mythic status notwithstanding, are in this sense little different from those of many other clubs of similar size or regional-patriotic cast. Before looking at these questions of identity in more detail, we must briefly consider just why football has been as important as it has in British working-class culture.

Masculinity, cultural continuity and football

It is difficult to overestimate the significance of the role played by Association Football in the lives of millions of working-class men and boys over the last hundred years or so. The intensity of emotional investment in the game, since its professionalization in the late nineteenth century, is explicable if connected to the general direction of the cultural politics of that era. The gradual tightening of bourgeois cultural hegemony and the civilizing process throughout the latter half of the nineteenth century ensured – in its tendency to constrict the range of arena in which more customary and volatile male subjectivities could find public expression – that, for many men, football would become a highly charged focus for these historical undercurrents in the development of modern social relations. Its unique central role in these processes has made football, to this day, perhaps the most highly charged sphere in public culture: as a vehicle for the (usually implicit) celebration and reproduction of specific and enduring class-based moral forms it has no parallel.

Arguing for football as an historical vehicle of embodied cultural reproduction necessitates a marginalizing of contemporary debates around the nature and causes of hooliganism, the focus of so much of the formative football literature. I proceed from the view that 'football hooliganism' and matchday disorder in general have at their core no inner truths or obscure causes awaiting revelation. The nature of the game, together with the social sources from which it draws, adds itself quite naturally to 'periodic excess and the carnivalesque' (Armstrong and Giulianotti, 1997, p. 8), and has done for centuries. Robert Malcolmson's account (1973) of popular recreational forms demonstrates that the close identification of football with drunken rowdiness and violent local conflict was well established by 1700, and that attempts to suppress and control the game in the interests of the growing requirements of labour, discipline and the consolidation of puritan ideology were also well under way by this time.

The struggle over permissible forms of bodily practice, emotionality and morality for which football has provided a focus has been a long and bitter one. The hunger amongst working-class men for playing the game around the time of its professionalization in 1863 appears to have been of a depth inexplicable in terms of mere leisure. How else could such men express their apparently insatiable need for physicality, competition, visceral collectivity and ludic expression? The culture of the modern professional game soon came to reflect these things in heightened public form. Football, having been re-appropriated from the gentleman-amateurs of the public schools, entered the twentieth century as, first and foremost, a celebration of intensely male working-class values 'where skill and cunning were valued, but hardness, stamina, courage, and loyalty were even more important. Fairness and good manners were not held in high regard' (Holt, 1989, p. 173).

The social definition of sport has itself been a central terrain of class struggle, 'part of the larger field of struggles over the definition of the legitimate body and the legitimate use of the body' (Bourdieu, 1991, p. 360). The overwhelmingly apolitical nature of the subculture surrounding football attests to its status as a primarily practical-cultural sphere. The fact that football culture had to wait until the fanzine explosion of the late 1980s for any meaningful, internally generated textual elucidation exemplifies this status. 'Football' is a set of practices within which implicitly counter-hegemonic masculine identities may be lived, and articulated in embodied demonstrations of social competence, grace and excellence. Absolutely central to the frequently obscure social cosmologies of young working-class men, football – as the black south-east Londoner and England striker, Ian Wright, observes – is thus impacted with meanings and experiences which, embedded as they are in extended social backgrounds, may elude discursive articulation. The game can, in this sense, be understood metaphorically as a symbolically condensed set of practices which express a more general mode of consciousness and sense of reality – the feel for the game of football connects to the feel for the game of practical-collective life:

> The habitus as the feel for the game is the social game embodied and turned into a second nature. Nothing is simultaneously freer and more constrained than the action of the good player. He quite naturally materialises at just the place the ball is about to fall, as if the ball were in command of him – but, by that very fact, he is in command of the ball. The habitus, as society written into the body, into the biological individual, enables the infinite number of acts of the game – written into the game as possibilities and objective demands – to be produced; the constraints and demands of the game, although they are not restricted to a code of rules, *impose themselves* on those people – and those people alone – who, because they have a feel for the game, a feel, that is, for the immanent necessity of the game, are prepared to perceive them and carry them out. (Bourdieu, 1990, p. 63)

The meanings which inhere in participation in the game may therefore be seen as transposable to the other spheres of activity in which practical mastery defines the bases of social participation. Thus should the best footballer, with his innate charisma and aura of improvisatory excellence,[2] also be the best fighter. In this interpretative universe a single movement may mimetically summon up, beneath the level of explicit awareness, an entire aesthetics of masculine presence. These crucial and characteristic elements in working-class male culture, played out daily in parks, football stadia and elsewhere, circulate in a space significantly beyond the word. Beneath its contemporary veneer of rule-bound and high-performance modernity, the game remains a *practical* medium par excellence, encouraging all participants to 'reflect on the limits of "rationality", provoking the heart that aches and memories that linger' (Archetti, 1992, p. 233).

'Millwall through and through': identity, boundary and a blood tradition

The attempt to apply the kinds of marketing principles which have been so successful in the higher echelons of the professional game to Millwall has consistently floundered because of the club's customary meanings and identity. The fear that Millwall will 'lose its identity' (or at least have it radically transformed) in the manner of Arsenal, Manchester United or Newcastle United has been countered by the intransigence of these associations and a widespread refusal of the new consumerist practices such as buying tickets in advance of match days and sitting in allocated seats. In these kinds of ways, fans assert a conception of Millwall which is essentially metaphorical, a category which cannot be reduced to a material institution, the control of specific administrative personnel or novel sets of business practices. Millwall, in this sense, defines a volatile, unpacified and passionate interpretative community unevenly pushing against the new footballing times and continuing to make the brand name virtually unsaleable in the new markets. It is first and foremost, as in the impassioned argument of Bob McCree in the fanzine *The Lion Roars*,[3] a matter of belonging:

> Little did the non-Millwall rooted directors understand that supporting Millwall is a blood tradition, you are either born into a Millwall circumstance, or you are not. There are no neutrals where Millwall is concerned, and I know of very few real converts to the faith. Other people have always been put off joining us. So to talk of producing another 5,000 out of the oven was always pure fantasy. (*TLR* 64, p. 29)

This broad concept of a 'blood tradition' works here, it is important to note, as an extended metaphor for long-standing patterns of both familial lineage *and* affiliation through place. This is important in two main respects; first, because though it is true that 'converts' are few, they *do* exist; and second, because elective association with the club often proceeds on local, rather than familial ties. That is, *some* boys and young men find their way to the club in the absence of patrilineal precedent. This is most obviously the case with Millwall's small minority of black fans, who tend to forge attachments with the club on the basis of affective localism; the very existence of such fans – tenuous as their position often appears to be – indicates a degree of negotiability around the boundaries of inclusion in Millwallism. I would suggest that the notion of 'blood' is intended to reference the important sphere of *authenticity*. There is no doubt that the cultural significance of being born into, or otherwise emerging from, a 'Millwall situation' is considerable for many fans, and underpins an apparent and widespread preoccupation with a 'metaphysics of belonging' (Gilroy, 1993, p. 23). This desire to maintain the integrity of Millwallism is manifested in discussions of authenticity ('Millwall through and through') and a generalized secondary preoccupation with the boundaries of inclusion and exclusion. This latter, which is a clearly situated example of the kinds of masculine boundary-drawing processes characteristic of working-class culture, centres on three broad themes: first, there is the widely diffused, and for the most part unchallenged, understanding of Millwall as coterminous with hegemonic masculinity; second, there is an overwhelmingly implicit association of Millwall with particular embodi-ments and communicative aesthetics of *class*, understood and acknowledged as an experiential rather than economistic category; and third, the connection of these central elements of Millwallism to a sense of broader, situated social identities in ways that are frequently, though unevenly, racialized.

The ways in which this informally maintained boundary around authenticity may be articulated in racialized terms is arguably more com-plex, and certainly more ambiguous, than it is at its intersection with class (which can, at Millwall, be considered a given). As with everything else at Millwall, the approach to the issue of race is complicated by the existence of a pre-constituted and widely diffused attributive schema circulated in the popular media and public consciousness. The primary image here, linked to a geographically inaccurate but convenient association of the club with the ostensibly Far Right-inclined Millwall electoral ward in the London borough of Tower Hamlets, is of the club's home – the Den – as a hotbed of organized racist and neo-fascist activity with firm roots in the late 1970s. Though the links between concerted Far Right activity and con-temporary football culture have been revealed – at Millwall as elsewhere –

as opportunistic rather than organic, this imagery remains deeply rooted and widely accepted. But it misrepresents the nature of the problem in ways which obscure the complex realities of relationships between Millwallism, identity and race. These are complexities which the extension to Millwall of the currently prevailing moralizing discourses, aimed at combating racism in the culture of the game, does little to either apprehend or account for.[4] The easy demonizing of Millwall fans, in this sphere as elsewhere, serves to obscure the sometimes paradoxical role played by race in constructions of Millwallism. Something of the depth of these paradoxes can be glimpsed in the recent comments of Ian Wright, who, as an Arsenal player, experienced an eventful and frequently bitter public relationship with Millwall fans, and who has been raucously vilified in a succession of closely contested games throughout the 1990s. In an interview in *Total Sport* (Febuary 1997), Wright spoke of his jealousy of former colleague Mark Bright's short spell at Millwall:

> When you put that shirt on, you are living Ian Wright's dream of pulling on a Millwall shirt. If you look at how Millwall fans expect their forwards to play and how I love to play, then I'm a Millwall player. I've had so much stick. They would love me. I give my all and I score goals. It's the team I first watched and no matter what we've had in the past, no-one can take away my love for Millwall.

A south-east Londoner himself, Wright the black footballing icon thus expresses a love for Millwall which seems capable of somehow transcending or displacing his experience of often racially framed abuse. His blackness, in short, seems not to constitute an impediment to his view of himself as a potentially emblematic Millwall player. His avowed understanding of the core values of Millwallism feed directly into his self-definition as being Millwall 'through-and-through'. This indicates a potential space of belonging for black men at the club predicated on the adherence to and expression of these central orientations, and discussions of race at Millwall therefore highlight in their turn the ways in which that belonging, as well as the complexities of racist expression, is understood.

Racist expression and the carnivalesque

The 1977 *Panorama* BBC television documentary on Millwall fans which did much to seal their infamy presented a compelling and spectacular portrait of a violent, hyper-masculine and *racist* subculture (Robson, forthcoming). The public furore generated by the programme did much to make Millwall the specific and, in the long term, fixed exemplar of a general moment of heightened Far Right political activity. It is important to note, in this connection, the ease with which these links are routinely imputed (via the 'racist/hooligan' couplet)[5] on the basis of often scant empirical evidence. This ease indicates widespread anxieties, notably from liberal and leftist as well as populist-right viewpoints, around manifestations of politically unfocused working-class physicality: the white male body and its characteristic forms of expressive vigour are framed and understood as incipiently fascistic.[6] It is this very distancing of vulgar corporeality and physical expressivity from liberal culture and imagination which tends to drive the initiative in these matters rightward into a space where working-class masculine vitality can, at least notionally, be fascistically celebrated. The attempt of the Far Right to periodically associate itself with football culture expresses an implicit grasp of these processes, and proceeds from an understanding of such spaces as somehow historically conceded to them. The extremely limited and still waning impact of their interventions underlines the historical folly of conceding the field, and the widely accepted, if relatively belated, arrival of concerted anti-racist counter-argumentation within the culture of the game confirms this.

But these counter-arguments, in their circulation at Millwall, set up a tension between explicit anti-racist perspectives and a still widely diffused though diminishing tendency towards a vernacular of casual racist expression. The sheer intensity of the emotions invested in Millwall as a symbol of identity has probably arrested the development of arguments aimed at altering – and, it is feared, attenuating – the expressive order of the stadium in which that identity is collectively expressed; if campaigns aimed at eliminating racist songs, chants and individual commentaries have been somewhat less effective at Millwall than elsewhere, this close and highly charged conflation of 'Millwall' with very particular working-class identities and traditions is largely responsible.

Thus a long-lasting conspiracy of silence and passive collusion with racist expression within the stadium, motivated perhaps by fear or perhaps by this tendency to adhere to specific notions of local authenticity and Millwallism, has been mirrored in the pages of *The Lion Roars* and the other Millwall fanzines. Letters, and a coherent anti-racist editorial stance, did not appear until a series of exchanges little short of the fiftieth issue in

1993. In a letter which anticipated animated exchanges on the subject of race in subsequent editions, M. Coyne expresses his disgust at the racist chanting of 'some fans', and asks:

> What about the black supporters we have, imagine how they must feel when a crowd around them are shouting racist abuse at a player. Despite all this, they still come back because they love Millwall, just like any of us. (*TLR* 46, p. 29)

'Jamie' is equally alarmed:

> Judging by the amount of racist abuse that goes on around me in the South Stand upper tier, something drastic has to be done ... I realise that taking a firm anti-fascist stance is about as popular as a West Ham fan in a boozer down the Old Kent Road, but it has to be done. The majority of Millwall fans are not BNP dickheads, as the gutter press would have everyone believe, and it's about time we proved it. (*TLR* 51, p. 30)

Jamie's analysis provides an important clue to the resistance to the development of a 'firm anti-fascist stance' at Millwall. The central perspectives of Millwallism are implacably opposed to liberal culture. Anti-fascist 'stances' are associated with leftist local authorities and liberal progressivism in general. If, as I have argued, Millwallism is best understood as an expression of defensive but culturally entrenched opposition to bourgeois cultural hegemony, then a certain reluctance to embrace 'politically correct' moral perspectives is one of its central characteristics. Some correspondents to *The Lion Roars* are unambiguous on this point. Time and again racism is related to the Millwall sense of humour, centred as this is upon the customary medium of the 'piss take'.

An adherence to the cardinal values and practices of Millwallism – in this case expressed by physical and personal inviolability, contempt for pretension, volatile emotionality and ruthless gallows humour – is considered by participants to encompass a depth and complexity of experience inaccessible to the stereotyping crudities of media portrayals. One of the central pleasures of this depth lies in participating in the generation of the intimidatory Millwall match-day atmosphere. For many participants, racist expression is intimately bound up with the prevailing dynamics of hostile partisan fervour and vulgar orality which underpin intimidation, and arguments about racism tend to be completely subsumed under these categories.

This perspective, obviously, articulates the widely held view that racist expression is not racism *per se*, but an aspect of expressive practice aimed at intimidating and humiliating opposition players. The blackness of the player is seen as a target towards which to direct abuse. This is frequently justified by the claim that certain white players making good targets are equally vehemently abused on the basis of personal or physical character-istics. Such abusive expression, whether in collective song or in individual tirade, is intended as hostile rather than politely humorous. It is designed to be offensive to individual dignity and liberal sensibilities alike, and Millwall fans are famous for it. It is one of the defining practices of Millwallism, and many fans react with horror at its apparent decline. Typical is a refusal to accept connections between ritualized racist expres-sion and the wider social dynamics which structure racism in general, locating the primary significance of these practices in a sense of carniva-lesque mischief. The deliberate affront to polite sensibility represented by this rather menacing sense of carnival at Millwall is an important theme which runs parallel, in matters of race, to the informal monitoring of and preoccupation with cultural authenticity already noted.

At Millwall, the symbolic and gestural possibilities of 'grotesque real-ism' – the essential principle of which is 'degradation' (Bakhtin, 1965, p. 19) – tend to be channelled in a negative direction which is not always especially playful but which is clear in its contempt for 'polite forms of conduct' or, in what is understood as a contemporary variant, political correctness. But this suspicion of the latter has not emerged out of a vacuum. Back, Crabbe and Solomos (1996) note the effective – and indeed epistemological – limitations of moral anti-racism in situations of com-plexly racialized expression. But there are signs that the tendencies towards ideological oversimplification, therapeutic individualism (Gilroy, 1987, Chapter 4) and political miscalculation set in motion in this area over the last twenty years by municipal anti-racism have actively helped lead to problematic and unintended consequences. The excoriation of insuffi-ciently 'progressive' working-class groups in London by cadres of correct-thinking middle-class activists (Morgan, 1993) has triggered alarm bells in the folk memories of many of those whose predecessors knew well enough the firm smack of nineteenth-century missionary authority. Cohen (1996, p. 194) notes, as an outcome of this frequently misguided zealotry, the 'pariah status experienced by some white working-class groups excluded from due political processes'. If Cohen's view of some of the aggrieved responses to these developments is on the sceptical side, Hewitt (1996) is clear that the widespread undermining and driving underground of white claims to pride in cultural identity *per se* has been a disaster, and instrumental to the emergence and consolidation of new forms of distorted and aggressive white nativism. Though the extent of the latter at Millwall is difficult to quantify – and easy, probably, to overestimate – it is without doubt characteristic of the orientations of a significant minority of fans.

The rather attenuated version of carnival which often obtains at Millwall may, in addition, be used to convey a wilfully unpleasant offensiveness and an all-out attack on any form of hubris or pretension. This potential for viciousness has, over the years, been frequently unleashed upon black players. Three interconnected but perhaps analytically distinguishable strains of racist expression may therefore run concurrently at Millwall: we will abuse you out of contempt for your blackness; we will abuse you because it is fun, it upsets you and it puts you off your game; we will abuse you because it offends liberal sensibilities. Those choosing to participate in this sphere may locate their priorities within each or all of these aspects, ritually connecting with those wider repertoires of racist sentiment and expression – complex and otherwise – which continue to characterize much of white working-class life in the region.

This, on the whole, is not the romanticized carnival of literary theory and Cultural Studies, overturning prevailing social classifications with playful zest. There is not the merest hint of any utopian impulse. What is involved, rather, is a manifestation of 'traditional' working-class physical culture and sensibility. The impulse is, ultimately, towards the confirmation of boundaries as opposed to their dissolution, and the symbolic affront to bourgeois-expressive orthodoxy is accompanied by a specific and normalizing rationale: ideal-type Millwallism is (with few exceptions) white and male and (with no exceptions) hegemonic-masculine and working class.

Conclusion

Those dispositions towards boundedness and conservatism characteristic of much of working-class culture express themselves, in the Millwall context, as fundamental symbolic imperatives in the attempt to keep the shared sense of what the club means integral. As a cultural institution in which questions of identity could scarcely be more central, the boundaries of inclusion are marked by the kind of localist working-class 'insiderism' which is understood as the only guarantor of appropriate knowledge and commitment. This sets cultural limits to the club's support which no community initiatives or moral crusades will be able to convincingly transcend. But it does not, as is mistakenly and widely believed, mean that Millwallism revolves around race hatred. It means that the passion on which the culture has historically drawn has its sources in white working-class experience. This is why there is a small space at Millwall for black – that is, *black cockney* – fans exhibiting the same expressive dispositions and steeped in the requisite lore and experience, but not for those without mastery of the appropriate embodied forms. It is, however, important to recognize the racialized limits informally placed upon black participation by the implicit but non-negotiable requirement that Millwall 'Blackskins' must be, if anything, more Catholic than the Pope: a steepening in specifically south London forms of disposition and expression must be demonstrably fused, at all times, with an absolutely unequivocal commitment to the club which announces, despite the blackness of his skin, that he is 'Millwall through and through'. The participatory responsibilities of the small minority of black fans at Millwall are therefore such that the *cockney* half of the equation must, in ritual-performative terms at least, occlude the *black*; there is, ultimately, only one way to *be* Millwall in the archetypal moment of its ritual, match-day actualization. This informal racialization of the passport to participatory inclusion places, given the prevailing cultural politics and characteristic modes of affiliation at work in the region, a clear numerical limitation upon the proportion of likely candidates.

This highlights the complex way in which Millwall is kept Millwall less out of white nativism pure and simple than a demand for the right to the kind of cultural particularism which is perceived as acceptable when practised by other groups than the white working class, and positively encouraged among them by the liberal/leftist culture of municipal antiracism in inner London. Any syncretic or interpersonal overlap between cultural forms and identities must be achieved, according to the principles of the practical logic which operate on both sides of the race divide, through *real* relationships and connections and not ungrounded ideological gestures or edicts. Millwall should therefore be understood not as a uniquely vengeful and hermetic institution, but one which revolves around stable and collective forms of identification, and to which those from beyond the customary pale may be tentatively admitted on the basis of genuine connection, real commitment or detailed knowledge. These characteristics, though it *is* especially demanding in this respect, do not make Millwall unique among the informal institutions of multicultural southeast London. If such practical settlements are social phenomena with which the liberal imagination must continue to struggle, they are, on the ground, already well understood and unlikely to change to any significant degree. The abstractions of progressivist ideology must contend, as ever on this kind of cultural terrain, with the science of the concrete. Sociological analyses of working-class life must face up to the task of looking hard at the way in which such cultural institutions as Millwall *actually* function, rather than burdening them with the kinds of normative and prejudiced speculation which makes clear sight impossible.

Notes

1. McMullan (1984) contains an account of the central role played by Southwark in the long evolution of London's various criminal and (semi-criminal) entrepreneurial subcultures. Pearson's seminal (1983) work on the nineteenth-century 'hooligans', the postwar 'Teddy Boys' and the moral panics around them frequently reads like a social history of south-east London. It is also worth noting the way in which King, in the most compelling example yet of the hooligan-memoir genre, cannot help but locate Millwall fans in an historical *tradition*, 'raised on docker history spanning the century. A hundred years of kicking the fuck out of anyone who strays too far down the Old Kent Road' (King, 1996, p. 225).

2. 'Only a virtuoso with a perfect mastery of his "art of living" can play on all the resources inherent in the ambiguities and indeterminacies of behaviours and situations so as to produce the actions appropriate in each case, to do at the right moment that of which people will say "There was nothing else to be done" and to do it in the right way' (Bourdieu, 1992, p. 107).

3. This is by far the most widely read and best established of the Millwall fanzines (abbreviated in references to *TLR*). Though I argue here, as elsewhere (Robson, forthcoming), for a view of Millwallism as characterisically non-discursive at its core, there is insufficient space here for the extended analysis required to fully support the assertion.

4. The authors of the Commission for Racial Equality's *Alive and Still Kicking* report point out that moralizing approaches are doomed to limited success because they rely on a 'moralism that does little to understand the social configurations of racism ... Limiting our understanding of racism to the racist "folk demon" may help to sustain moral support for the campaign but will do little to identify and tackle the forms of banal racism which still haunt our

national game both within its institutions and amongst its loyal fans' (Back, Crabbe and Solomos, 1996, p. 58). Such folk demonizing has an invariable tendency to settle itself around Millwall, so often the symbolic focus of moralizing liberal anxieties.

5. Back, Crabbe and Solomos (1996) note that the reluctance of football institutions to meaningfully engage with widely diffused, complexly articulated racism at games helps retain a focus on an oversimplified and empirically dubious racist/hooligan stereotype.

6. Hoberman's account of the consequences of the leftist-intellectualist 'renunciation of the body' (Hoberman, 1984, p. 119) is relevant in this connection.

Bibliography

Archetti, E. (1992) 'Argentinian football: a ritual of violence?' *International Journal of the History of Sport* 9(2), pp. 209–35.

Armstrong, G. and Giulianotti, R. (1997) *Entering the Field: New Perspectives on World Football*. Oxford: Berg.

Back, L., Crabbe, T. and Solomos, J. (1996) *Alive and Still Kicking: An Overview Evaluation of Anti-Racist Campaigns in Football, Advisory Group against Racism and Intimidation*. London: Commission for Racial Equality.

Bakhtin, M. (1965) *Rabelais and His World*. Bloomington: Indiana University Press.

Bourdieu, P. (1990) *In Other Words: Essays towards a Reflexive Sociology*. London: Polity Press.

Bourdieu, P. (1991) *Language and Symbolic Power*. Cambridge, MA: Harvard University Press.

Bourdieu, P. (1992) *The Logic of Practice*. Cambridge: Polity Press.

Cohen, P. (1996) 'All white on the night? Narratives of nativism on the Isle of Dogs'. In T. Butler and M. Rustin (eds), *Rising in the East*. London: Lawrence & Wishart.

Gilroy, P. (1987) *There Ain't No Black in the Union Jack*. London: Hutchinson.

Gilroy, P. (1993) *The Black Atlantic: Modernity and Double Consciousness*. London: Verso.

Hewitt, R. (1996) *Routes of Racism: The Social Basis of Racist Action*. Stoke-on-Trent: Trentham Books.

Hoberman, J. (1984) *Sport and Political Ideology*. London: Heinemann.

Holt, R. (1989) *Sport and the British*. Oxford: Oxford University Press.

King, J. (1996) *The Football Factory*. London: Jonathan Cape.

Lévi-Strauss, C. (1966) *The Savage Mind*. Chicago: University of Chicago Press.

Malcolmson, R. (1973) *Popular Recreations in English Society, 1700–1850*. Cambridge: Cambridge University Press.

McMullan, J. (1984) *The Canting Crew: London's Criminal Underworld, 1550–1700*. New Brunswick, NJ: Rutgers University Press.

Morgan, G. (1993) 'Frustrated respectability: local culture and politics in London's Docklands'. *Environment and Planning: Society and Space* 11, pp. 523–41.

Pearson, G. (1983) *Hooligan: A History of Respectable Fears*. London: Macmillan.

Robson, G. (forthcoming) *No One Likes Us, We Don't Care: Millwall Football Club, Community and Identity*. Oxford: Berg.

Wright, I. (1996) *Mr Wright: The Explosive Autobiography of Ian Wright*. London: HarperCollins.

Index

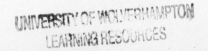